Under the Camelthorn Tree

Under the Camelthorn Tree

Raising a Family Among Lions

KATE NICHOLLS

First published in Great Britain in 2019
by Weidenfeld & Nicolson

1 3 5 7 9 10 8 6 4 2

© Kate Nicholls 2019

All rights reserved. No part of this publication may be
reproduced, stored in a retrieval system, or transmitted, in
any form or by any means, electronic, mechanical,
photocopying, recording or otherwise, without the prior
permission of both the copyright owner and the above publisher.

The right of Kate Nicholls to be identified as the author of
this work has been asserted in accordance with the
Copyright, Designs and Patents Act 1988.

The author and publisher are grateful to Benjamin Walter, David Lovett, Edward
James, Milton Dwane, Marcus Oliver, Johnstone Mumford, Winston Aubrey and
Aladar Marshall for permission to reproduce lyrics from 'Little Lion Man' on p.61
Publisher: Universal Music Publishing Group

A CIP catalogue record for this book
is available from the British Library.

HB ISBN 978 1 4746 0 995 1
TPB ISBN 978 1 4746 0 996 8

Typeset at The Spartan Press Ltd,
Lymington, Hants

Printed and bound by CPI Group (UK) Ltd,
Croydon, CR0 4YY

Weidenfeld & Nicolson

The Orion Publishing Group Ltd
Carmelite House
50 Victoria Embankment
London, EC4Y 0DZ
An Hachette UK Company
www.orionbooks.co.uk

For my family

Author's note

This is not an 'and I was born' memoir: it is a story told in snapshots of some events between 1994 and 2016. For clarity and brevity there are omissions. Thus, regretfully, many valued friends and collaborators do not appear in the story.

1

Gomoti Camp, Botswana 2001

The distant chugging of a car struggling through deep sand aroused a certain nonchalant curiosity, most likely it would continue on towards the Gomoti River – nevertheless all ears in camp casually attuned to the engine.

I was concentrating on the barefoot boys high above me in the spreading branches of the camelthorn acacia tree. During the night, a funnel of wind had blown down the radio mast, and Pieter and the boys were reattaching the antenna. Relaxed and focused on their task, they were moving easily among the thick branches, while I imagined them lying in crumpled, lifeless heaps at my feet.

'It's not fair,' grizzled seven-year-old Oakley, 'I'm the best climber. Why aren't I allowed to do that?'

'Because you are my favourite child, and thus indispensable.'

'I heard that, Mum,' Angus laughed, wrapping his arm around a gnarled branch for support, before leaning out precariously to hand the rope up to Pieter who was reaching down from the branch above.

'You concentrate on what you're doing,' I snapped. Watching my tousled blond boy dangling forty feet above me made my bones ache.

The tree was coming into flower, a smattering of soft, mimosa-yellow blossoms releasing an earthy sweetness. She was an old tree: she must have been producing seeds for many decades, for the elephants had learned her ways, and came from far and wide to feast on her grey-velvet seedpods. Usually, I shooed the huge animals out of our unfenced camp by shouting and banging a wooden spoon on a saucepan, but when the seeds ripened the beasts would gather under the wide umbrella of our tree and browse undeterred by my Betsey Trotwood vehemence. Four years ago Oakley had renamed the irresistible pods 'elephant Smarties', and annually we declared a pachyderm truce until the last crescent had been hoovered up.

Maisie was sitting cross-legged on the roof rack of the Land Rover, observing her older brothers and drawing the action in a notebook. It was a late-winter morning, and she had a blanket wrapped lightly around her thin shoulders, but the sun was moving up in a clear sky and soon she would be as warm as her sweaty siblings. Her animated, delicate face was already smeared with grey Kalahari sand, and when her dusty, unbrushed hair fell over her eyes she carelessly tied it back in an untidy knot in the nape of her neck. Briefly she tipped her head in response to a new sound – the gears of the distant car had shifted down a tone.

'They've turned into the palm scrub,' she remarked, 'are we expecting anyone, Mum?'

'Nope. It's probably the wildlife department,' I replied, looking up and briefly catching Pieter's eye. Maybe there would be some news. Our life was precariously rooted – a thin slip of paper could puff us away. I had grown used to pinpricks of anxiety spiking my bloodstream – fear keeps you alive in the wild. But the fear of losing home sat in a deeper place – its movement through my body was whittling and wearing.

'Whoever it is can't drive,' Travers commented wryly, lying outstretched along a branch with the radio antenna dangling from a wire in his hand, 'did you hear those gears grinding, Pete?' I hadn't got used to my sixteen-year-old son's man voice, it still had the lilt of youth but the androgyny had gone.

'Will all of you stop drivelling, and get that bloody antenna up? I can't stand the tension,' I barked, marching to the kitchen tent to put the kettle on. If my progeny were going to fall to their deaths I didn't want to witness it, and whoever was coming to see us would need some sustenance. Bush etiquette was simple in the Okavango: help those in trouble, and offer food and drink to new arrivals.

Maybe the wildlife department was coming to tell us about a problem lion killing cattle on the other side of the buffalo fence, or maybe they'd found another poisoned lion. I looked at Sauvignon's skull, bleached salt-white by the sun, lying on the sand beside the campfire. A month ago Pieter had found the female's desiccated body beside a pool of water – her cubs' carcasses scattered nearby – and all around lay dead vultures that had nibbled on the lions' toxic flesh.

The kitchen tent was open on three sides, covered by a ten-metre-long canvas flysheet stretched across a frame, and supported on metal legs that splayed out onto the sand. We had constructed reed walls to make the space cosy, and keep out the wind. The termites had been at work, and some of the reeds were no more than dust held together by filaments of cellulose. It was time for repairs. I liked project days. Simple days. Days that bound us. Our stalwart second-hand gas cooker stood beside a long wooden counter, on which sat an excellent set of cast-iron gas burners. Lighting up a burner, I watched a weak blue flame emit a few polite puffs before going out with a mild pop-pop. The car was ambling closer – about six minutes away – plenty of time to change the gas cylinders over and boil the kettle.

'Probably another problem lion killing cattle,' I mumbled to myself, detaching the regulator from the empty cylinder, 'they'd never deliver news about our research permit in person.'

I remembered the first time the children and I had fitted the stove to a gas bottle six years ago, and how afraid I had been that I would blow us up. What a pale little English family we had been.

How many times had we moved in our first years in Botswana, four or was it five? We were settled now.

'The government wouldn't just throw us out,' I drivelled on, heaving the full cylinder into place, 'not after all this time, all our new data on poisoning and tumbling numbers are helping them get a clearer picture.'

Giving the regulator one last twist, I flipped the lever and a faint waft of rotten cabbages rose up, swiftly dissipating into the dusty air.

Filling the scorched enamel kettle from the tap at the sink, I smiled. After several years of hauling water containers across the bush, I relished the luxury of running water pumped from a borehole near the river. In the dry season the elephants dug up the pipes – sucking on them like straws. I collected rusks and biscuits from the metal trunks in the pantry. Food was always locked away from acacia rats and marauding hyena – nevertheless the fridge door had puncture marks left by large canines.

A squeal and a short bark from the edge of the palm scrub drew my attention to a troupe of baboons mooching about lazily picking ticks off each other. A few females pottered to and fro displaying tumescent bottoms – not yet ripe enough to cause much excitement. The baboons had learned the invisible boundary between their world and ours, and rarely tested my tolerance – when they did, all I had to do was to bang on a pot and they moved off. For the most part, sharing the wilderness with my children and wild animals was a subtle game of give-and-take with sporadic spats for dominance.

I set out tin mugs, sugar, Ultra Mel long-life milk and plates of Ouma Buttermilk rusks and Chocolate Romany Cream biscuits on our huge kitchen table. It had been modestly constructed by tying four metal tables together and covering them with my mother's white damask tablecloths: the table was the heart of family life.

'Maisie,' Travers yelled down to his sister, 'check the radio will you? Call us from the car now – now.'

I rolled my eyes – had those children learned nothing?

'So not actually,' I shouted, 'you come down and *then* she can test if it's working.'

'Aw mum... Pieter said it would be fine just for a moment.'

'Yes, well you're not related. No genetic investment. Seriously guys, if you're that close to the antenna, RF waves are dangerous. Down *now*.'

Pieter was already sitting at the office desk in the adjoining mess tent fiddling with the camp radio – I wandered over to kiss the back of his neck. His silver hair smelled of apple shampoo, and burying my nose in his skin I felt the familiar rush of oxytocin triggered by a complex trail of testosterone, sweat, tobacco, a hint of CK One, and something I couldn't define, an echo of him: an olfactory message deep in his skin that lingered from his past.

'So... you left my children up there by themselves. Nice with the step-parenting.'

'I thought you wouldn't miss one or two,' he said, kissing me perfunctorily, 'it was just Trav being anal... it doesn't need testing. It's fine.'

His unimpeachable confidence was well deserved. He could mend anything. He tinkered, welded, glued, thumped into life, wired, creatively duct-taped, nailed, hammered, fine-tuned, sawed, screwed, and, if in doubt, simply disassembled and re-assembled any broken object in camp.

'Do you think it's news?' I asked.

'No idea,' he sighed wearily, 'they've had all our documents for months... in duplicate. It'll be fine.'

The Department of Wildlife and National Parks issued precious research permits, and in return required regular reports and updates from field researchers. Our quarterly reports, and triennial permit renewal applications, were delivered promptly, but bureaucracy in Botswana moved as nimbly as a vertiginous sloth on a tightrope. It caused me deep anxiety. Our lives were bound to the lions, we lived to the rhythm of their days and our home was in their wild space. It seemed a romantic idyll, but the reality was more brutal: we lived day by day in a dangerous place, exposed to the whims of the elements, with very little funding, and routinely stressed by documentation.

In the early days I had been less concerned, but during the last few years the politics of lion conservation had become increasingly bitter: the battle between hard data and hyperbole was in full swing, and my family was in the heart of the fray.

The car slowed down as it passed the generator, and, spewing a flurry of sand behind it, came to a halt in front of the kitchen tent. I felt an unsettled relief, it was a government vehicle but it wasn't the DWNP. No one had been sent to break bad news, so we were safe for the time being. The children gathered like a brume around the two exhausted uniformed individuals emerging from the Toyota Land Cruiser, blinking the sand from their eyes.

'Dumelang, le kae?' I said, greeting them with a warm handshake.

'Dumela Mma-re teng,' replied the shorter and stouter of the pair, his eyes darting nervously around our camp. It was immediately obvious the officers were not used to the bush – most probably they had desk jobs in Maun: a two-hour drive away.

Oakley ran to pour them welcoming glasses of water, while Pieter led them into the shade of the kitchen, where the men quenched their thirst in gasping gulps.

'What is this place?' the taller man asked, looking around at the hodgepodge of tents, a trampoline and a full-size volleyball court. His finely chiselled cheekbones were too prominent, and his uniform hung too loosely over his shrunken frame: a familiar sorrowful sight.

'Lion camp,' replied Maisie.

'Ah that is good.'

The men were clearly relieved they had reached their destination, yet somewhat bewildered by what they had encountered. Obviously, they were neither in a glamorous Safari camp nor in a temporary fly camp.

Under the shade of the camelthorn, a spacious ex-army mess tent acted as the sitting room and project office. Supported by central poles, the sagging canvas roof protected a welcoming clutter of old sofas, splattered with colourful blankets and dusty soft toys; a comprehensive library; and the office desk. Our electrical equipment was connected to an acid-stained car battery by a bewildering web of wires, which slipped under the canvas wall and snaked along the sand to a bank of solar panels set out in the middle of camp to optimize every vestige of sunlight. Metal cupboards in the back of the mess tent housed project equipment: radio telemetry receivers, veterinary drugs, biopsy darts, an air-powered rifle used for immobilizations and biopsies, a foot pump, new and old lion collars, test tubes and sample pots of all sizes, desiccant, formalin, a centrifuge, tape measures, a gauge to measure lion canines, data books and liquid nitrogen canisters.

Our campfire was nestled between the mess tent and the kitchen. Usually we sat on the fire-warmed sand but there was also a comfy metal daybed and an elephant skull to rest on. Leading from the fireplace, towards our bedroom tents and the shower, was a path we had made from dried elephant dung, demarcated by giraffe femurs (collected from abandoned lion kills) now filigreed by bone beetles.

We had built the camp over the years from nothing.

'We are taking the census,' announced the slender officer, 'we are here for your details. This is your home?'

'Yes,' I replied, 'this is our home.' I could have kissed him I was so happy: we were to be part of a captured moment in Botswana's story.

'Does anyone else live here?' he asked.

'Yes,' replied Pieter, pointing to a smaller, fenced, camp a few hundred yards away, 'Lettie, Rhoda and Stephen are in camp.' The team helped us to keep our busy life running efficiently, and we loved each person dearly. I had laid down strict rules, and the children's tents were only cleaned if the kids had left them tidy. Lettie and Rhoda did the washing by hand, and their immaculate ironing was achieved using a hand iron heated by warm cinders from the fire. Woe betide the child who 'hung' clean clothes on the floor or dropped damp towels in the sand.

Aged twenty, Stephen was younger than the women: he was six foot five, ravishing, promiscuous, and in regular need of penicillin.

'Eesh Mma, my dick is so bad – do you want to see?' he had asked me last month.

'No, my angel, rather not – I'll take you at your word. This is the third time Stevie – when are you going to take this seriously?'

'Ah Mma, it is my culture!' he had roared with laughter, 'I must have plenty of girlfriends.'

'Yes, well that's all very well, but wear a condom, indeed several. I give you packets and packets each month. What do you do with them?' I laughed.

'Ah Mma, you are the best.'

'Stevie have you been tested yet? You promised me faithfully.' I was deadly serious, but he cared not a jot.

'I am beautiful – I am too strong,' he had laughed. He was a merry Adonis relishing his youth: unthreatened by a pernicious virus.

Now the shorter officer stood up, collected his papers and wandered across camp to find the others, while his companion stayed with us.

Before starting, he smoothed out the form on his clipboard and tested the flow of his pen on a scrap of paper.

Our answers to the following questions were painstakingly recorded in black biro:

What are the names of the persons who spent last night here?

Have you included babies?

Have you included elderly persons?

Have you included people living with disabilities?

Have you included the sick?

Have you included visitors, and those who normally spend the night here but were away on night duty, at prayer meeting etc.?

Does any member of this household own any of the following: cattle, goats, sheep, pigs, poultry, donkeys/mules, horses, ostrich, game or none?

An hour later, a small rectangle of tin embossed with our census number was hammered with precision into the trunk of the camelthorn.

It was official: home was a tree in the Okavango Delta.

2

Comeragh Road, London 2010

'If you don't stop this I'll leave. I mean it. Mum, you must believe me. You threw me out in the middle of the night. I had no home, Mum. How do you do that? I don't understand you any more.'

Oakley was sixteen. He wasn't shouting. He had been stripped of his rage.

I was still toxic from the night before. Whisky in my cells leaked through my epidermis. I forced myself to climb the stairs to his room to view the carnage. I remember attacking him. I remember ripping up the passports he treasured. His brothers' and sisters' digital faces were strewn across the bedroom floor. My children's lives in fragments. I picked up a page. A faded date on an official Zambian stamp. What trip was that? There had been so many? The pages felt heavy. I forced myself to look at their eyes. Clear. So much trust. So young. Botswana 15 May 1995. The day our new life began. Don't look back. I could taste the smell of his baby hair – sweet hay with a dash of pheromone. I could feel the squish of absorbent gel in a wet nappy. Don't look back.

3

On the Road, Botswana 1994

The ten-hour flight from England had been uneventful, and on arriving in Gaborone, Botswana's capital, I hired a 4×4 truck at the airport and set off north towards Maun: a small town eight hundred and twenty kilometres away on the outskirts of the Okavango Delta.

Tremulous heat spirals flurried across the tarmac, sucking sand into vortices. Displaced air gushed through the open window whipping my long red hair into dreadlocks, and bleaching sun burned my right arm. Strapped into his car seat beside me, Oakley entertained himself wisely by pouring water over his head from a beaker, his eleven-month-old skin protected by a bizarre floor-length cheesecloth garment made by my mother.

Botswana is flat and dusty grey. The Kalahari is not a sweeping Lawrence of Arabia desert. It is pragmatic, arid scrub with wisps of silver grass, stunted bushes and low-growing trees, flattened by the effort of surviving on dregs of ancient water sucked up through long taproots. Thin land strains uninterrupted across the earth's crust until it falls over a clean horizon. Trundling along I became enveloped in big space, and my claustrophobic soul released a sigh that had been locked inside me for as long as I can remember. I knew nothing about this land, and that was fundamentally liberating.

I was on reccy for a new life. Why a new life? Because the life

I was leading in England was neither preparing me nor enabling me to participate in a world that was changing more rapidly than at any time in human history. My life was safe and comfortable, and thus not challenging. Without challenge there is no growth.

I wanted my children to adventure. Adventures are not luxuries, nor are they frivolous escapades. They are the fundamental building blocks on which our species stands. Our Pleistocene ancestors took risks, met unusual experiences and resolved problems daily. Our ancestors were all successful adventurers.

Looking at the soggy adventurer beside me, cheerfully kicking his pink feet and waving arcs of water from his beaker, my heart welled with love. We were a merry team with simple needs. After five children I had learned to strip down baby paraphernalia to the bare bones: all Oakley needed was my milk, a few jars of Gerber baby food, clean nappies, cool clothes, sunscreen and *The Best of Disney* blaring on cassette.

From time to time we passed small settlements of mud huts with unkempt thatched roofs patched here and there with tin or plastic bags. Along the roadside, children rode listless donkeys laden with yellow plastic containers slopping water with each swaying step. Sporadically, bony long-horned cattle ambled across the tar road causing Oakley to yip with glee. Presently, I saw a man standing on the side of the road. He was wearing a smart button-down, mustard shirt and sharply ironed creases ran down his shabby brown trousers. He seemed to have appeared from nowhere, and I stopped to ask him if he needed help.

'Dumela Mma, ke a leboga,' he thanked me in Setswana.

I had taken some lessons in Setswana in the Africa Centre in London, but my understanding was limited to a few useful phrases.

He told me he was going to Francistown – the town I planned to spend the night in and explore in the morning. Oakley had fallen asleep, and, strapping his car seat into the back, I made room for my new companion beside me. He had no luggage, just a plastic bag from Spar and a five-litre container of cooking oil. After I'd offered him some water we set off.

It seemed rude to ask him where he had come from but for the life of me I couldn't work it out; we had passed a settlement two hours ago and the road ahead was empty, and the bare land on either side was melting into heat haze.

'Are you pressed for time?' I asked, 'I travel slowly I'm afraid. I don't want to miss anything.'

He laughed and said he kept Africa time.

'What's that?' I inquired. He seemed surprised but did not answer.

His name was Wilson and after exchanging a few pleasantries in English we drove on in companionable silence.

After a while we passed a huge mound of earth carved into a point out of which grew a straggly branch. 'Termites,' he said, 'very interesting animals. They live in eusocial colonies. Very interesting societies.'

'Eusocial is a very specific word. Have you studied biology?' I asked.

'Ah yes, at the University of Botswana.'

'How utterly riveting. It's my passion.'

Within minutes we were communing on the joys of Darwinism, and our mutual admiration for Richard Dawkins. An inspiring schoolteacher had given Wilson a copy of *The Selfish Gene* and it had motivated him to complete his secondary education and apply to university. For me it was *The Extended Phenotype* that had generated a life-changing epiphany.

'I hadn't realized how hungry I was for a fresh perspective until I read that book... I just devoured it,' I said eagerly. 'It inspired me to study biology and to look at the world refreshed by a deeper understanding. It changed me.'

Wilson smiled and nodded.

'On the first page Dawkins describes looking at a Necker Cube,' I said, remembering the frisson I had felt reading the words. 'You know the picture of the 3D cube that flips when you look at it for long enough. It's an illusion; both images are different and equally valid. I like that notion. It comforts me. Looking deeper doesn't necessarily mean you find something truer but you'll see something you hadn't seen before.'

'What is true in one place may not be true in another,' he commented.

'Exactly,' I said, looking out at the spacious and frankly pretty dull landscape, and relishing the shifts in my mindset that would influence me when I understood the land better. How was it possible not to fall in love with Botswana when, within hours of arrival, on the side of the road I had come upon such a kindred spirit?

The miles rolled by, and kicking off my shoes I nestled into the position that would become part of my muscle memory: my big toe light on the accelerator, my left foot propped up next to the gear lever and my right elbow resting on the window frame. Peace.

I remembered the first time I had read *The Extended Phenotype* – words resonating through me like a poem I could feel, but couldn't understand. I read all through the night, from time to time stirring the fire in the inglenook fireplace. Our old English cottage in Gloucestershire was night-time quiet: flames licked through hissing applewood, popping sparks and releasing sweet resin. The smell of young wood, wet wellington boots and child was soothing. Oakley was a cluster of cells (a secret even to me) and the others were asleep upstairs. Fifteen-year old Emily in her attic bedroom, most probably with one sibling or another snuggled in beside her. Angus in the room next door, warm on his mattress squeezed into a narrow landing under the elm eaves: his nesting place of choice. As I read, thoughts stirred in my head like smoke rising from a peatbed. I needed the oxygen of understanding.

Over the next few months, I devoured GCSE and A Level biology textbooks, I acquired a ticket to the Bodleian Library and I read every paper cited by Dawkins in *The Extended Phenotype*'s extensive bibliography. Then I hired a maths tutor to help me unravel mathematical language that stumped me. When I came up for air I was empowered. Dawkins had handed me a compass and given me the means to ask directed questions. Questions are what fascinate me: answers are only stepping- stones on which we rest to catch our breath.

'I know Richard Dawkins,' I said, 'I wrote to him to ask him a question and he replied.'

Wilson looked at me in shocked admiration.

'I know,' I laughed, 'I was pretty astonished too... not only did he reply but he was kind enough to teach me. That small person asleep in the back attended some pretty amazing lectures, tutorials and conferences while he was slopping around inside me, all thanks to Richard. His wife Lalla and I became good friends too.'

At that moment Oakley woke refreshed and burbling for food. I pulled over, and sitting on heat-softened sand Wilson and I shared water and a packet of Simba crisps while Oakley suckled.

'Why did you choose to live in Botswana?' Wilson asked.

'Ah, you won't believe me but it's true. The day I decided to move to Africa I opened the *Times Atlas* on the relevant page, shut my eyes and let my finger drop. It landed on the Congo, and after a moment's reflection I thought best not – so I tried again and that time my finger landed on Botswana. Boom – done.'

He looked at me incredulously: sometimes the truth is hard to take.

'What work will your husband be doing here?' he inquired.

It was a perfectly reasonable question, but not an easy one to answer.

My five children have three different fathers: none of whom would be coming with us. I kept it simple.

'It'll be just the children and me, but their father will be coming out to visit.'

I remembered trepidatiously telling each of the fathers my plans and to this day I celebrate their generosity of spirit. None of them was obstructive or unreasonable. All of them were concerned and anxious, but this resulted in helpful discussion.

Emily's father, Peter Bourke, was worried about her A Levels. Fair enough. We came to a compromise, and we put her on a correspondence course.

Travers, Angus and Maisie's father had worried about logistics.

'Any normal person might have chosen France or Italy... plane-wise that would have been one helluva lot easier but what the hell. Go for it. Why not?' he said. 'I'm moving to LA to give it a go. Why should you have to stay stuck in England if you don't want to? The kids will love it. But let's get them inoculated against everything that moves.'

Ian McNeice and I had fallen in love when we were both actors at the Royal Shakespeare Company, and we had a long and happy relationship living in our cottage in the Cotswold Hills. Over sixteen years, four siblings joined my daughter Emily. Ian's paternal love has been a unifying force in our family, for he has consistently given equal emotional succour and stability to his biological and his non-biological children.

I want to keep the story rolling, but the astute reader may be pondering where Oakley's father fits in. In time Ian and I split up as lovers, but continued living together: noble in principle – tough in practice. I had an affair with a younger man who came to live with us – very *Jules et Jim* and utterly ludicrous. Oakley is the sublime product of a relationship I do not regret, but that never had a future. There, that's the nutshell, and it's more information than I shared with the dear Wilson, whom I regaled with questions about Botswana until pinpricks of amber light sprang up across the scrubland as evening fires were lit in scattered settlements.

In the distance, I could see a faint glow in the darkening sky and Wilson told me that was Francistown. We parted company on the outskirts of town, and though I never saw him again I remember him with fondness.

4

Comeragh Road, London 2010

Oakley's room smelled of boy sweat and old socks. I buried my face in his pillow. I want to die. No, you don't, those days are over. I turned my head and saw the children's faces staring up at me from the floor. I picked up the ripped passport pages willy-nilly and put them on his table. Later. I'll sort them out later. He loved his siblings so much. What had driven me to tear them up? I must have known it would hurt him. What twisted version of reality had I inhabited at that moment? I didn't want that reality to be part of me but it was. My hands had ripped up little snippets of their recorded history. What possessed me? Nothing. Nothing possessed you, Kate. Take responsibility. You did that. And what did you say to Oaks? Don't let the memory come. Take responsibility. Don't look back. I hate London. Take responsibility. You made a promise. This is your last chance. They didn't take your soul. You didn't let them take your soul. I want to go home. I want the good times. I can hear a hippo grazing outside. Don't look back.

5

On the Road, Botswana 1994

The morning sun revealed Francistown to be a rather unlovely, functional town, so I decided to press on in my quest for somewhere to live. Whizzing down the road that cuts through the Kalahari and runs along the edge of the Makgadikgadi Salt Pans, I experienced a version of joy that was new to me. I was travelling on the surface of a planet that was spinning in space-time, and yet I did not feel small in its vastness: I felt connected.

Gazing down at Oakley I saw an expression on his mobile, squashy little face that I had not seen before. He seemed ironed; it was as if the big sky he was gazing on was expanding his mind and smoothing out his creases. I will never know what was going on inside his wordless head, but I will always remember the look on his face.

I continued on until we reached Maun – an unprepossessing town on the edge of the Okavango Delta. But trundling over the bridge that spanned the rapidly evaporating Thamalakane River, I felt like a Labrador who had found its basket. Maun smelled right. The air was lush with stagnating water and nutrient-rich animal droppings, faint wafts of diesel and hot rubber added complexity, and a lingering note of woodsmoke and hot cinnamon bound the aroma into scent so intense it made the hairs on my arms stand up.

Within two days I had rented a house, put down a deposit on

a 4×4 car, and enrolled the children in Matswane School. Boom – job done. The Round House was downriver, a few kilometres out of town, and surrounded by a glorious tangled garden full of citrus trees, trailing vines, wild sage and snakes. Inside it was a bit of a wreck, but it had potential. The owner promised to give it a lick of paint, sort out the Heath Robinson wiring and mend the broken shutters on the cracked windows.

A few days before I was due to leave Maun I got a telephone call from Debbie Peake, the woman who had helped me to find the school and who would become a dear friend.

'Kate, I think you should get in touch with Anne Sandenbergh... she started up an NGO called Women Against Rape. It's early days – she might like your help. She's rallying the troops in town now – now. I'll give you her number. She's quite potty... I think you'll get on well,' she said drily. 'Oh and Kate... go into the Delta. Take the opportunity while you're here, there's nowhere like it. I'd take you myself but I'm off to South Africa tomorrow and won't be back before you leave. It's been nice meeting you. Tsamaya sentle.'

I am a great believer in walking through open doors, so, despite having no idea how I could help, I called Anne. She sounded terse. During our brief telephone call, she asked crisp, pertinent questions – homing in on two facts. One: I had worked as probation volunteer in a maximum-security male prison for several years, and among the prisoners I visited were men who had committed sexual crimes. Two: I had read all Alice Miller's work on the impact of emotional, physical and sexual abuse on children, and had read a wide range of cross-cultural studies on the subject. On hearing this she invited me to attend the W.A.R. meeting she was holding at her house that evening.

I arrived late – having got faintly lost – and the light was fading as I carried Oakley across the river-grass lawn, whereupon I was soaked to the skin by a series of sprinklers that sprang into action and I tottered around in leaky circles in the cool of the evening.

I knocked on the back door, which was opened by a rather fierce Motswana woman who clearly did not want to be disturbed. She was preparing food in the kitchen, and said yes this was Mma Sandenbergh's house, and yes she would tell her I was here. Leaving me dripping in the kitchen she returned moments later with a woman who had wild pepper-and-salt hair, snapping grey-blue eyes and a face so lined it looked like raku pottery.

'Ah Kate, so you've met Key?' Anne beamed. She was wearing a brown skirt, flat shoes and a large floppy cardigan that slid off her sloping shoulders.

'Come in, come in. Everybody's here. Sadly, Irene can't make it tonight, one of her children is ill. I wanted you to meet her. Do you need a towel?' she asked looking at my bedraggled state.

'No, no I'll steam away. No problem.'

Brushing away strands of unruly hair that had fallen across her bright eyes, Anne strode into an airy sitting room and introduced me to a gathering of ten people. My stomach clenched in horror when I heard myself described as an expert in counselling, who was moving to Maun and would be working with W.A.R.

'No, no I'm not,' I said weakly followed by 'Hello, hello' as my hand was firmly shaken by people who offered friendly smiles and warm welcomes.

Oakley noticed a large jar of neon-bright sweets on a side table and, wriggling out of my arms, he tottered towards it. Catching sight of this Anne nonchalantly handed him a fistful of candy, and made a friend for life. As an English mother a list of E numbers, dangerous colourings and preservatives swam before my eyes, but I threw caution to the wind, and Oakley spent a very happy time sitting on the floor devouring his first African sweeties.

The adults were offered more wholesome fare, and Key arrived with several delicious home-made quiches and huge bowls of salad: the meeting was conducted while we ate.

Before I could digest I had to clarify a few points.

'Anne, thank you for inviting me but really I'm not a counsellor.

I used to be an actress and I gave up my career to study biology. I'm not trained; I've just read a lot about the physiology of post-traumatic stress because I am concerned about the long-term impact of child abuse. I can bring over books and papers that might help and I think Alice Miller's work on child abuse is seminal, but I'm not qualified in any way.'

At this Anne roared with laughter.

'Well, you're a few steps ahead of us I can tell you. None of us here are qualified, Kate, well not in anything connected to counselling. Hilda is a missionary working with disabled adults and children in Thuso Rehab, Laura is an accountant, Ann runs a mobile shop in Seronga, and is helping us to reach out deeper into the Delta, and I run an aviation fuel business in Maun. I started up W.A.R. a short while ago because there is no help for women and children who are being abused. They have nowhere to go and frankly these days with HIV infection rampant rape is tantamount to murder. So, we are doing what we can. None of us have any relevant expertise.'

I learned that W.A.R. had no office, no vehicle and barely any funding, but this group of determined, inspiring individuals was already helping women and children around Maun. There were no cellphones in those days, and only a few people had landlines. Anne's house was the centre of operations, and most nights she was woken by someone knocking on her door passing on news that had been carried by 'bush telegraph'. She was a lifeline for women and children who had nowhere to turn. I listened in awe to stories that would soon become all too familiar. When I left a few hours later I was part of the team.

The next day I took Debbie's advice and drove out into the bush.

Was I reckless driving my baby out into the Okavango Delta? Yes, most probably. But I wouldn't change a moment of those two days. The Okavango Delta was soon to be our backyard, and what would be the point of planning to set up home an hour away from one of the planet's great natural wonders, if I was too timorous to drive there independently?

We set off early for Camp Okuti, the only camp that would accept children under the age of twelve. We packed light and I blessed Oaks for being a late weaner. A few kilometres out of Maun the tar road came to an end, and we slid about on the chalky calcrete surface until it gave way to thick, soft sand: we were getting closer to the Moremi Game Reserve.

There is no feeling comparable to the moment when you enter the space in which the wild things have dominance. Every cell fills with fear and wonder. Anyone who tells you they are not afraid in the bush is either a liar or an idiot. Fear is your best friend in wild places, and when it is married to understanding it will keep you alive. As I write, my body is remembering the subliminal fear I sensed every day for over eleven years living under canvas in the wilderness.

Oakley and I took our exploration gently, and I soon learned there are no *Out of Africa* giant vistas in the Okavango; it is a subtle smorgasbord of habitats: wild land and water are continuously sculpted by wind, rain, tectonic shifts, hippos, elephant, termites and harvester ants. On the outskirts of the Delta are vast tracts of Mopani woodland: the emerald-green leaves look like butterflies. I remember getting out of the car on that first journey and picking a leaf for Oakley, and as he bruised it in his soft fist I smelled for the first time the smell that would tantalize me for many years – I could never define it – cinnamon, soil and a yearning for something long-forgotten.

Our punctual arrival at Camp Okuti, two and a half hours after leaving Maun, elicited rather more interest than I had expected.

'They told me at Riley's you drove yourself,' said a stout, but fit and tanned, middle-aged man, dressed in khaki shorts and a smartly ironed monogrammed shirt.

'Hello I'm Kate ... yes it was a beautiful drive,' I replied, smiling sweetly.

'With a baby? Are you mad?' His tone was concerned, not accusatory.

'Oh, Oaks is a trooper,' I beamed, 'best traveller.'

'I was less worried about him and more about you. What if you had been charged by an elephant or had a puncture? Would you have known what to do?'

We'd had an alarming run-in with an elephant on the way and I had coped rather well thank you very much, but he was quite right about the puncture. I didn't have a clue how to change a tyre nor had I even bothered to check if I had a jack: I simply assumed Avis would have supplied all that was necessary.

John Seaman introduced himself and grinned at Oakley.

'Well, either your mother is very brave or she's a fool so for the moment let's give her the benefit of the doubt shall we,' he laughed, turning to me with a warm smile.

'Come and meet the other guests and wash up before lunch.'

He ushered me towards a thatched bar on the side of the lagoon from where I gazed out onto the waters of the Okavango for the first time.

Light breezes curling through papyrus reeds wafted faint animal smells across the surface. Oakley started to reach into my shirt for my breast, and I fed him standing up looking out on white and pink water lilies and watching a small pod of hippo twitching their ears as they wallowed partially submerged in the cool water.

Over lunch I chatted merrily with the assembled guests and Oakley behaved impeccably – sucking on home-made bread rolls and carrot sticks. But I noticed a cabal of guests gather around John before the afternoon game drive, and he walked away to do some hasty reorganizing. It transpired that no one wanted to travel in a game-viewing vehicle with a baby. A while later, the couple who had drawn the short straw clambered into the back of the open truck, and taking up their position they proceeded to cover the remaining space with their camera equipment, three pairs of binoculars, bird books and a rather bulky first-aid kit – leaving Oakley and me to travel up front with our guide.

His name was Johnson and his profound knowledge of the bush was matched by his Buddha-like patience. This was fortunate because the couple in the back never stopped talking from the moment we left camp. But they were enchanting to Oakley, who was in his element. His silky hair was soon stiff with sand dust and his soft, ruddy cheeks were roughened by dry patches caused by the desiccating heat; but every impala, bird or bush that Johnson pointed out caused his baby spirits to soar, and from time to time, unable to contain his glee he threw himself onto the floor of the truck in paroxysms of delight. Kept cool by moist cotton clothes and rehydrated by water or a swift suckle, he did not flag once.

'He's very good isn't he,' said my female companion. 'Who'd have thought a baby could cope on safari.'

It transpired that Oakley coped better than I did. During the night I was violently sick and on returning to my bed, after one of many sorties to the loo, I was somewhat perturbed to find a lizard the size of a small truck lying stretched out on the twin bed next to me. By that time I was beyond caring if I lived or died, so leaving the monster undisturbed I went back to sleep. I was awakened in the morning by a polite knock on the door and an invitation to come on the early-morning game drive.

'Hello,' I said faintly, 'I think I'll pass on the game drive but could you please help me to remove a rather large reptile.'

'Ah a gecko...' said a knowing voice.

'I think not actually... it's more along the lines of a Komodo dragon.'

I was pleased to see the look of surprise on my rescuer's face when he clapped eyes on the somnambulant beastie that must have weighed close to fifteen kilograms and took up half the bed.

'Ah that is a rock monitor. I have never seen one in a guest chalet before.'

'What a thrill,' I said, 'there's a first time for everything. Shall we boot it out now before it devours my child?'

The rest of the day was spent in camp; Oakley played in the coarse river grass while I listened to the birds and watched the water flow by. It was heaven. Romance seeps out of the pores of the bush but as quickly as it thrills it brings you down to earth.

'Kate, you're leaving first thing tomorrow aren't you?' inquired John, joining me for a sundowner, while we watched a herd of elephant slaking their thirst at the end of the day.

'Sadly yes. We have an afternoon flight to Gabs and then home. It seems unimaginable we have only been in Botswana for ten days.'

'Well I have a favour... one of our staff has got malaria – would you mind giving her a lift into town and popping her into Maun Hospital?'

'Of course,' I said feeling very flattered to be asked, and at the same time slightly appalled. My knowledge of malaria was based on Somerset Maugham's short stories and lurid accounts of blackwater fever in the tropics. I had visions of the poor woman falling into delirious rigours in the back seat, or expiring next to Oakley as we trundled through the bush.

However, in the cool of the morning she seemed only mildly feverish, and we loaded the car quickly with her belongings and the remains of her rations: Tastic rice, a sack of Iwisa maize meal, cooking oil, white sugar and a tin of Ricoffy. I made a bed for her in the back seat and Oakley sat next to me like a small pasha. They both slept until we reached Maun, and by then the poor woman's fever was raging. She looked very wan as I drove into the bleak hospital compound.

If anything was going to put me off moving to Botswana that hospital should have done it. Painted white and government-regulation duck-egg turquoise, a straggle of single-storey buildings was strewn across a dirty, sandy compound. Ripped plastic bags shivered in the branches of scraggly trees offering thin shade, and a shabby sign announced Outpatients and Emergency. A tin awning overhung a narrow veranda, and a few women were already waiting their turn seated on painted chocolate-brown benches. An abandoned table strewn with notes and a blood-pressure gauge indicated that someone in charge had been around. Leaving Oakley in the car I settled the patient on a bench and went to find a nurse.

I found her in the dressings room, sitting on a gurney, reading a copy of the *Ngami Times*. The floor was littered with used dressings in various shades of brown. Sticky dust had hardened in the corners of the room and the painted cement was marbled by smears of dried blood. Against the wall stood a metal trolley bearing several pairs of scissors, a large plastic container of Betadine and packs of sterile dressings in various sizes. The nurse grudgingly meandered off to see the patient, and I returned to the car where I sat for a while grimly gripping the wheel.

'Right. There we are then. It's no John Radcliffe,' I said referring to the hospital near Oxford where Oakley, and three of his siblings, had been born.

Was I mad bringing the children here? Could I live with myself if anything happened to one of them because I had placed them at risk? No, I couldn't. But were risks taken in Africa so very different from risks taken in England? Risks come in many forms. We take them every day and sometimes we fall flat on our faces and sometimes we soar. All the same, I thought to myself, some risks require more grit than others.

'Have you got grit Oakley Smokey?' I said to my sleeping babe, 'I think you have. I've seen it in your eyes. Let's do this thing. Let's go home and tell the others.'

6

Comeragh Road, London 2010

Sitting on Oakley's unmade bed I tried to piece together the events of the previous evening. I had thrown him out of his own home. In what reality was that deemed reasonable. He had told me a truth I didn't want to hear, and I lashed out like a demon. I pictured him downstairs in the kitchen hating me, and making baked beans on toast. I couldn't remember if I'd cleared up the mess from last night. My rage had begun in the kitchen. On his bedside table I noticed his copy of *Salt: A World History* – perhaps he'd finally begun reading it. Why had he been so resistant? Dear God we had school to do later. College applications. SA bloody T tests. Revise the Code of Hammurabi: 'to bring about the rule of righteousness in the land, to destroy the wicked and the evil-doers; so that the strong should not harm the weak'. The irony of that would not pass him by.

I wondered if Oaks had rung one of the others last night. Probably Angus or Travers. If so I would be dealing with their wrath later. Why was today different? Was I feeling the first blush of real shame? Blush. What a pseudo-romantic word to use, Kate. The first sodding blush. Who are you kidding? I looked at my phone – 9.30. Okay, we would be starting school late. I tasted metal in my mouth and felt it digging into my chest. My familiar cilice. Guilt.

Homeschool rule number 1: Whatever happens outside school is not brought into school. How easy it had been to keep that rule in

Botswana when life had been simpler. Purer. So, Louisa M. Alcott. Where were my Plumfield days? My wholesome days? Days that would have made any self-respecting transcendentalist proud.

7

The Mission House, Botswana 1996

'You do know they prayed for Trav's soul at Matswane today?' Emily said indignantly. She was helping her sister hang loops of strangler fig vines across the ceiling, while I was up a rickety ladder hanging swathes of sackcloth over the curtain rails. We had been in Maun for three months and had just moved from the Round House to the old Mission House next door to Anne Sandenbergh. It transpired the well that supplied water to the Round House with the glorious garden was gradually running dry. We had manfully bathed in sludge-brown water – not wanting to make a fuss for fear of seeming soft. But when we could stand a spoon in the thick muck that came out of the taps we called it a day and moved on.

'That teacher frightened the shit out of him, Mum. In front of the whole class – I'll have you know they were on their knees at the time – she told him because he didn't believe in God he'd burn in hell.' Emily was incandescent with rage.

'Yes, I know,' I replied, 'and I'm livid about it too. But the bliss of atheism is no heaven means no hell either. I've managed to calm the poor little soul down. But I shall be speaking sharply to Mrs B tomorrow.'

'It's a rubbish school, Mum.'

'I know but I want them to make friends. We've only been here for a while, they need to settle in.'

'All the kids go to roller-blading. That rink is their social hub. Let's face it, Maun's not a rollicking place,' commented Emily, clambering down from the table to admire her work. 'Maisie, let's get the fairy lights up now. We will probably blow the pathetic circuit but we can give it a go.'

All the lights had gone out the night before when I plugged in a couple of second-hand bedside lights for the children.

'I suppose if the worst comes to the worst I could teach them myself for a while until we come up with a better idea,' I mumbled through a mouth full of string.

'You?' said Maisie sharply.

'Yes me,' I said, trying not to sound defensive.

'But could you?'

'Could she what?' asked Travers wandering in from the garden for a drink. He was hazelnut-brown, streaked in dirt and wearing nothing but a pair of cotton shorts.

'Teach us at home,' responded Maisie, standing tiptoe on the table and stretching up to pin a strand of fairy lights to the vine. 'I can't reach... help me Trav.' Travers obliged, climbing nimbly onto the table, looking askance at our artistic endeavours.

'Why on earth are you doing this?'

'Because it's pretty and the house looks empty without any furniture,' said Emily firmly.

'Sacks Mum... really?' he commented drily.

'Not sacks... sack*ing*, and it will look heavenly by candlelight,' I retorted, standing back to look at the effect of inventive curtaining, graciously looped and tied with hemp string: the whole thing had cost just two hundred pula: roughly £10 in those days.

'Do you know enough to teach us, Mum?' asked Travers in all seriousness.

'I'll have you know that your mother is considered by some to be a woman of above-average intelligence.'

'Okay what's seven times nine?... Mum... quick... you don't know do you... Ha!' cried Travers triumphantly.

'Okay smarty pants, how long is the gestation of an elephant?' I challenged.

'That's easy,' replied Maisie, 'twenty-two months.'

The younger children pottered into the garden to swing on the strangler fig vines, while Emily and I ambled to the open-plan kitchen to chop vegetables and chat.

'Seriously could you?' she asked.

'I don't see why not,' I replied, 'I brought millions of books from home and we've got so much space here it would be easy to set up school. I really can't think of a viable alternative... apart from going back to England and that's not an option. We said we'd give it a year.'

I threw some potatoes in the oven to bake, and wandered out into the garden to ponder.

It was the first week in September. A soft wind was blowing the smell of decomposing cow from somewhere behind the house. Due to the drought, cattle were dropping like flies, and the evening air was rank with the sweet, bruised smell of death. I could hear Angus and Oakley playing somewhere on the riverbed.

Was it such a crazy idea to teach the children myself? They were losing confidence at school and their work seemed so dull. I helped with their homework, which seemed to comprise endless spelling tests, repetition of times-tables and reading from a dreary 'reading book'. In Travers' case this was an agony. Letters swam before his eyes, and it took all his powers of concentration to harness the markings on a page until they formed coherent patterns. Back in England, an educational psychologist had diagnosed Travers as severely dyslexic, a trait he had inherited from me, and we were told not to expect too much from him academically. Sod that for a game of soldiers.

Luckily, I had attended a lecture at Oxford, given by the linguist and cognitive psychologist Steven Pinker, who was presenting his book *The Language Instinct*. Pinker was boyishly ravishing, with piercing eyes, ebony curls, and a jaw so finely chiselled you could cut bread with it; frankly it took me a while to pull myself together, before I could concentrate on his words of wisdom. They were life-changing.

His book explores humankind's ubiquitous ability to acquire spoken language as compared to our post-Pleistocene literary skills. The ability to speak and write are poles apart. Darwin succinctly sums this up: 'For man has an instinctive tendency to speak, as we see in the babble of our young children; while no child has an instinctive tendency to brew, bake or write.'

Pinker, and later excellent teachers at Bruern Abbey School, liberated Travers and me by shining new light on an old problem: as a direct result we gained confidence. If I tried homeschool for a term, surely I could do no harm? It was worth having a go, and in our bookshelves lay the guidance I needed.

Later that night I settled down to reread one of my childhood treasures: Louisa M. Alcott's *Little Men*. Once again, I inhabited the walls of Plumfield, with shy Nat, rollicking Tommy, serious Demi and wild Dan. I imagined I was overhearing the warm Germanic purr of Professor Bhaer reading Plato's *Apology* to a roomful of eager young people who shared his joy in learning. Once again, I was sharing their higgledy-piggledy life, growing food in the garden, eating wholesome food at a noisy dining table, pillow-fighting at midnight and learning how to be a kind human under the watchful eyes and tender guidance of loving, liberating adults. Alcott's book is a generous celebration of her impecunious father's role in the nineteenth-century Transcendentalist movement.

As a child, I had no idea what a Transcendentalist was – I had never heard of Thoreau and his pond. But the power of Louisa May's characters had transported me away from the rigid 1950s education system that was stifling my spirit, and offered me an alternative view of the world. Instinctively I knew there was nourishing meat on fictional bones.

'I can do this. I can do this and it will be wonderful... I have no idea how... but this may be the most exciting thing I have ever embarked on.'

8

Comeragh Road, London 2010

I wanted to stay in Oakley's room for ever. I didn't want to go downstairs and face another regretful day. My ears thrummed. I couldn't listen to the pictures in my head. I couldn't. Don't make me remember. Coffee. I need coffee. Heaving myself from the bed, I went downstairs guided by the smell of toast. In my peripheral vision I could see Oaks sitting at the dining-room table. His back was to me. He was eating and reading. Silence. I filled the kettle. Listen to the water heating. Focus. Hear it gathering energy in the kettle, building to a crescendo. Followed by the tremulous diminuendo of trapped steam rising up inside its liquid self: failing to escape; then the screaming: liberation. Job done. I wish I were a kettle. What pretentious crap is that? You idiot. Be a person. Think. He takes his first SAT exams in October. There is still time. He's bright. He's broken. You broke him. Mend him. It's your job. Do your job you shithole of a human. No: he's not broken. Not yet. He's teetering on the edge. The liminal zone. One last chance. You've got one last chance. I'm Going To Need a Bigger Boat. Stop. This time is different. Use your head. Remember how to think. Walk it.

9

The Mission House, Botswana 1996

Having completed the children's evening ritual – supper, bath, removing thorns and bits of stick from feet, checking for violin-spider bites and reading bedtime stories – Ems and I were relaxing on the veranda listening to the bell frogs chime.

In time the moon would rise: to my English eyes it still looked upside down. It was early days in Botswana, and home was still Hollybush – our old stone cottage with an apple orchard and a stream – far away in a Gloucestershire village. Ian McNeice and I had moved there when Emily was four. She had gone to the local primary school, and graduated to the comprehensive school in the next-door village, where she made lifelong friends. Her growing tribe of siblings loved her and trusted her, and the hierarchy remained undisturbed in our early Botswana days: in time, the family would stretch its limbs and positions would shift.

'Did you remember to tell Neecie you've taken the kids out of school?' asked Emily; aged two, she had christened her stepfather Neecie, and the name had stuck.

'Of course, I sent him a long fax. Anyway, he's coming out for Christmas so we can discuss it then. The whole thing may have petered out anyway.'

'What did he say?'

'Worried about Trav's dyslexia of course, but very open to new ideas. You know what he's like – wants the details. But trusts me not to fuck up.'

Transitioning a relationship over a continental divide was taxing. Neecie and I were building new lives and respecting each other's right to independence, while at the same time being constrained by some complex parenting. For me it was easy: the kids had grown inside me. For Neecie it was subtler. He was Emily's stepfather by choice, Trav, Gus and Maisie's biological father, and the role he played in Oakley's life was untitled. We discussed many things before and during our separation, but some things never needed to be said: when it came to the kids we gave each other love and mutual trust. There were no rules laid down, no boundaries drawn, and no map for the future. We had enough confidence in each other to know we would carve a path around whatever obstacles came our way and work together.

Perhaps a bit of genetic dilution had caused other bonds to grow: the children were a fiercely united tribe. Travers had ceremoniously cemented Oakley's place in the family, and was ferociously protective of his youngest sibling.

'What are you thinking about, Mum?' Ems asked, 'is it Trav?'

'Yes, how did you know?' I smiled, 'I was remembering what he did when I brought Oaks home from hospital.'

'Oh, I love that story...'

Travers, age nine, had not been a fan of my pregnancy. His loyalty to his father was unimpeachable, and he was bewildered by the prospect of welcoming a baby that was not Neecie's. Indeed, when my waters broke early one morning Travers had become deeply distressed.

'I won't have anything to do with this baby. It's not Dad's. I won't talk to it.'

Pulling him onto what remained of my lap, I held him close, reassuring him he never had to speak to the baby that was at that moment cranking my cervix into life.

'I mean it Mum,' he was crying now.

'I know you do. No one is going to force you. But I shall be speaking to the baby from time to time and feeding it; if that's okay with you?'

He laughed for a second, but then the tears continued.

'Trav, babies are very blobby, they have simple needs. I promise, you don't have to do anything you don't want to.'

'Really?'

'Really truly.'

'The others can love it,' he said fairly.

'That's a plan. Each to his own. And I shall love you all.'

I held him until he settled.

Forty-eight hours later I returned home from the John Radcliffe – after a spectacularly gruelling labour and delivery. The children must have heard the car because as I was mincing up the garden path the front door flew open.

Travers was the first one out. Barely looking at me he took Oakley out of my arms, and, carefully holding his head, he walked into the house. I cuddled the rest of the troupe and, answering as many questions as I could without getting too medieval, we traipsed upstairs to find Travers changing Oakley's nappy on the changing table. Noticing he had lightly sprinkled antiseptic powder on the umbilical clamp, I had a welling of love, but when I saw what he had laid out for Oakley to wear I burst into tears.

It was the tiny olive-green Babygro that had been worn by my first child, Emily's brother Rufus, who died of a cot death when he was ten weeks old: all the children had worn it. I watched Travers deftly manoeuvre his new brother's arms and legs into the garment, neatly pop the poppers down the front, and carefully pick up the boy to give him a hug before handing him to me.

'He's in Rufus's Gro-bag. He's one of us now, Mum.'

Just then a deep grunt from a hippo moving up the lawn towards us broke up the party, and Emily and I wandered into the kitchen to snack on Philadelphia cheese and Salticrax biscuits.

'Do you know what you're going to do?' inquired Emily, eyeing the smart new stationery I had bought for school.

'Not a clue,' I replied.

'Aren't you going to start on Monday?'

'Yes.'

'You do know it's Friday don't you?'

'Yup,' I replied. 'I know I am going to hang our work around a theme, but nothing I have come up with so far feels right.'

'A project you mean?'

'Yes, I want to find one central idea that will inspire them and unite all subjects.'

The hapless hippo grazed gormlessly. The drought was by now in full swing and the river was no more than a puddle: dead cows and donkeys littered the flood plains.

Only yesterday the children and I had burned a rotting cow carcass because the stench of decomposing flesh had become unendurable. We doused it in petrol and set light to the cadaver. It had gone off like a bomb and a swarm of jewelled blowflies rose up out of the flames and hovered like a cloud in the heat-rippled air. The explosion had knocked Travers off his feet, and the smell of singed hair mingled with the odour of charred rot and petrol. The cow's remains contorted and twisted in the heat and, in horrified fascination, we watched fat, creamy maggots, wriggling in and out of the charring bones, devouring slivers of protein as if protected from the conflagration by some invisible shield. Come on Kate, focus – sod hippos and burning cows – think about school. I decided to get up early in the morning and go on a thinking walk before the sun rose too high.

The morning sand was night-cooled when I set off at a brisk pace. In time, I passed two boys on donkeys, loaded down by a motley selection of plastic containers that slopped fresh water in rhythm to their faltering steps. The boys' dusty limbs dangled freely, almost touching the ground, and the unwilling beasts were persuaded on by loud shouts and slaps. I snapped off a branch of sage and bruised a leaf between my fingers. Its pungent volatile oils were aromatic yet blurred by an acrid, bitter note that lingered on my fingers. Think. It was all very well Ralph Waldo Emerson saying, 'All life is an experiment. The more experiments you make the better', but I knew that a well-designed experiment was more likely to bear fruit than a hotchpotch of good intentions. Homeschooling was going to require more than my love to make it work.

The sand was beginning to feel warm beneath my bare feet when the edge of an idea tipped into a corner of my mind. I increased my speed, hoping that if I pounded the ground hard enough the thought shadow might shift position and become clearer. A few minutes later I realized that what I was looking for was hiding in plain sight... the sand beneath my feet was the product of deep history. Sand had once been rock. I would teach the children the story of rocks.

There are few things that can match the excitement of latching on to a good idea, and now that I had found my bedrock the questions started to flow freely. If I was going to help the children to 'see the world in a grain of sand' how was I going to make it enticing? How could I make Plate Tectonics come alive?

'Toffee Mountains... we will make Toffee Mountains', I yelled out loud, and in a flash I mapped out our first morning at school. We would boil the sugar to different temperatures, and make brittle slabs of toffee for the tectonic plates and softer, more malleable toffee would act as the mantle on which the earth's jigsaw would slip and slide. The children could squeeze out Fold Mountains and create Block Mountains and let the toffee cool slowly or plunge it into cold water to see what happened to the structure of the toffee. From there it would be a simple step to explain how igneous, sedimentary and metamorphic rocks were formed.

With mounting excitement, I realized I had the perfect book for us to share at the end of the morning: *Franky Furbo* by William Wharton. For those of you who haven't read it I won't spoil the story, but I can tell you it is about a family that lives in Italy – the mother homeschools the children and the father tells them stories about a fox called Franky Furbo who can speak all languages. At the heart of the story lies the dichotomy of fact versus fantasy. Is Franky a real polylingual fox moving through space-time, or is he a figment of the imagination? Can we believe our own eyes or is reality beyond the limiting scope of our senses? Sometimes to reach the truth we have to suspend our disbelief. Wharton would be a perfect guide for the children.

Another aspect that delighted me was that I could introduce language to the children from an evolutionary perspective; a fresh vantage point might help Travers to come to terms with his dyslexia. Moving through geological time we would take a look at the Rift Valley, and think about how the movement of tectonic plates had influenced human evolution. Fresh ideas came tumbling into my mind at an alarming rate and, pausing for a moment to take stock, I rested in the thin shade of an acacia tree.

In our adaptive landscape, during the Pleistocene, our ancestors weren't reading and writing, they were surviving using their wits. They were developing language skills that have been passed on to us in an unbroken thread. I knew I had to introduce the children to Stephen Pinker and his joyful book. He was the right man for the job. But it might be tough going for them, so I must prepare the class carefully.

The ground was by now uncomfortably hot and I hopped home, intermittently cooling my feet in scrawny patches of shade offered by a few sunburned bushes.

10

Comeragh Road, London 2010

I was not inspired to walk far. The cold comfort of cement suited my mood. I wore my hangover like a hair shirt, and did not plan to alleviate the misery with Eno's Fruit Salts. I wondered if this was self-serving martyrdom or genuine remorse.

What had precipitated this latest fall from grace? I had been doing well. Working hard. Making a plan. No longer isolated by desolate selfishness. The decision to move to London had been an umbilical one: instinctive, empathetic.

Two years ago Oaks and I had visited England to see family. We were due to fly back home to South Africa in a few days, and were sitting on the top deck of a bus passing by Harvey Nichols when Oakley let out a visceral sigh that shook me into awakening.

'I feel at home here.'
'In London?'
'Yes, I love it.'
'Do you want to stay?'
He laughed, 'Don't be silly Mum we're going home.'
'But would you like to stay?'
He looked at me through narrowed eyes. Was I testing him?
'Would you?' I repeated.
'Yes,' he spoke quietly. Perhaps it was too intimate a truth for me to hear.

The decision was easy and immediate. I only had one chance to raise Oakley. Most of his people were living in England now. He needed his people.

'Okay we'll stay.'

'Ha ha very funny.'

'No, I mean it. I'll rent the farm out.' I had a faaaarm in Aaafricaaa. I bought it after the accident. After Pieter.

'Stop it,' he was giggling now, 'we've got no money. Where will we live? How can we, Mum? Be sensible.'

'We Africans know how to "make a plan". I haven't got a frigging clue how we will make it, but isn't that half the fun? Or do you want to talk me out of it?' I laughed.

'No-o-o-o I don't. Mum this is amazing. Really, we can stay? Are you for real? You're crazy,' he said putting his head on my shoulder, 'I love you.'

'Me too. I mean I love you too, not me. I don't love me. Oh do stop droning. You could go to school here Smokey. Think of it – proper school with uniforms and bells.'

'You're joking aren't you?'

'Well, you could. I'm just saying.'

'Don't spoil the moment,' he laughed, 'that's a nightmare idea and you know it.'

11

The Mission House, Botswana 1996

On Monday morning, the kitchen table underwent its first transformation into the school table. The children cleared away the breakfast while I laid out our new school paraphernalia, and Maisie got the giggles.

'Do I have to call you Miss Nicholls?' she asked.

'That would be nice,' I replied.

'Will you be taking the register?'

'I think she ought to,' said Travers wiping down the area where Oakley had been sitting, 'she never remembers our names.'

'I had far too many of you. Now teeth, and let me get things organized. Come back in two minutes.'

The children clattered out of the room, and returned one by one wriggling and stifling giggles.

We all felt a bit awkward. Maisie examined the contents of her new pencil case. Travers fiddled with the plastic sheets I had bought to protect their work, Angus beamed at me encouragingly and Oakley, stark naked, trotted out into the garden.

'Right my darlings this is all very exciting but before we start I want to lay down a few rules.'

Maisie groaned.

'Not horrid rules Mais – sensible ones. Number one. Whatever happens outside school is not brought to the table So, if you are all piss-pots at breakfast and I'm livid with you I will not be livid in school. Equally if we have a bad day in school, when school's out all will be forgotten.

'Second rule. No homework.' This prompted huge cheers from my students, on whom I smiled beneficently before continuing my speech.

'With such a small class if we work hard we will be able to cover a lot of ground so... school in the morning and afternoons free. Third rule. I will work hard to make sure classes are interesting and I ask you to participate. If you try, and I can see you're trying, and you still don't understand something then I'll know I have to find another way to teach it. That's it. Those are the rules.'

I stopped talking and waited for someone to say something. To my astonishment they remained silent. No backchat. I had become Teacher Mum.

'Right... Okay then... let's get on,' I said, slightly nonplussed. 'I want to start with something I think you will find surprising. I want us to learn about rocks.'

Maisie's face fell.

'Mu-u-u-u-m that's so boring. I thought you said homeschool was going to be fun.'

'Exactly, it sounds really boring, doesn't it? But I can promise you that by the end of the morning you will be eating your words. Literally.' Angus looked at me suspiciously and I laughed.

'You will be eating rocks and loving it... but first I want to read you something.' I went to the bookshelf and pulled out *The Language Instinct.* Seven-year-old Maisie looked at me in horror.

'Mummy that's a grown-up book. I won't understand it.' I could hear panic in her voice.

'Trust me. I'm only going to read bits, and I know you will understand it because this man,' I said, thumping my fist on the book, 'is so totally on your side you won't believe it. Let me show you.' And I began reading carefully edited excerpts from chapter one.

Steven Pinker officially opened our homeschool:

'"As you are reading these words you are taking part in one

of the wonders of the natural world. For you and I belong to a species with a remarkable ability: we can shape events in each other's brains with exquisite precision."'

I paused for dramatic effect and the children waited for me to read on:

'"That ability is language. Simply by making noises with our mouths, we can reliably cause precise new combinations of ideas to arise in each other's minds. The ability comes so naturally that we are apt to forget what a miracle it is. So, let me remind you with some simple demonstrations. Asking you only to surrender your imagination to my words for a few moments, I can cause you to think some very specific thoughts."'

Another dramatic pause and the children impatiently urged me on:

'"When a male octopus spots a female, his normally greyish body suddenly becomes striped. He swims above the female and begins caressing her with seven of his arms. If she allows this, he will quickly reach toward her and slip his eighth arm into her breathing tube. A series of sperm packets moves slowly through a groove in his arm, finally to slip into the mantle cavity of the female."'

'Is that true Mum?' asked Angus, 'do they really get stripes?'

'You bet your sweet bippy... and the fact you've asked that question is part of the wonder. Listen to what he says next: "Think about what these words have done. I did not simply remind you of octopuses; in the unlikely event that you ever see one develop stripes, you now know what will happen next. True, my demonstrations depended on our ability to read and write, and this makes our communication even more impressive by bridging gaps of time, space, and acquaintanceship. But writing is clearly an optional accessory; the real engine of verbal communication is the spoken language we acquired as children."'

I looked at Travers.

'See what I mean when I said he's on your side. Before we look at spelling and grammar and all that stuff, I want us to look at how language evolved... you will be amazed by the role children have played in the evolution of language. Steven Pinker doesn't give a toss how you spell words – what excites him is that you have words in the first place. Listen to what he says: "This book is about human language. Unlike most books with 'language' in the title, it will not chide you about proper usage" – see, I told you he's not bothered about spelling – "For I will be writing not about the English language or any other language, but about something much more basic: the instinct to learn, speak, and understand language."

'When you were little you all learned to speak English, just as Oakley is now, but I'll bet none of you can remember doing it. You call this a table because you heard me call a flat bit of wood resting on four legs a table – the word is just an agreed symbol – if I had called it a kumquat you would be calling it a kumquat – or a bongwangle or a...'

There followed a riot of creativity, and as soon as new words for 'table' degenerated into the lavatorial I knew I had hooked my audience.

'But equally,' I continued, 'children will have come out with symbolic sounds for something... maybe a plant or an animal or something and the grown-ups will have copied them. We all call cereal "cillawool" because Oakley calls it "cillawool" – in our family we know what that means.'

'When did people first start talking, Mum?' asked Travers.

'Good question Trav. The truth is we will never know exactly – it didn't happen suddenly. What we call language is just a part of human communication and there are lots of ways to communicate. Inside our heads we think in pictures, memories, sounds, smells and feelings. Pinker calls the wordless language in our heads "mentalese". Let me show you wordless communication. Maisie get me that big book on top of the bookshelf please.' Maisie tottered slightly under the weight of Irenäus Eibl-Eibesfeldt's mighty tome *Human Ethology*.

'What does "ethology" mean?' asked Angus.

'*Ethos* means the spirit of a culture... "ology" means "study of"... so really it means the study of behaviour,' I replied as I opened the book onto a page that had a series of black and white photographs of a Yanomami toddler.

'Oh Mum, he's so sweet,' cried Maisie, 'look at him, he's just like Oaks.' The children pored over the photographs and were soon flicking through the book in search of more pictures of children at play. They were enchanted, and easily identified with the human stories Eibl-Eibesfeldt had so carefully recorded on film. Maisie turned over one page and recoiled.

'Oh, poor thing,' she said, looking at a series of pictures of a grieving Yanomami woman, 'what's happened?'

'What do you think?' I asked.

'Something horrid, look at that picture,' she said, pointing to one of the photographs, 'it looks like she's listening to something really sad.'

'She's hearing that someone has died,' said Angus, reading the caption at the bottom of the page.

'Mum look at her baby... he's crying because she's crying. These pictures are amazing,' Travers said seriously.

'Aren't they just?' I agreed. 'No words... just human emotions expressed on people's faces. The baby in that picture hears his mother crying before he sees her crying and suddenly he feels her pain; just as she feels her baby's pain. That's called empathy. It's when you get inside someone else's skin and feel what they are feeling.'

I noticed Maisie had turned to a fresh page, and was studying a pen-and-ink drawing of a rhesus monkey comforting her infant, and I could see from her face she had made the connection between the drawing and the photograph of a human mother and child. I didn't say anything.

'This term there will be no spelling tests and no written work. We are going to look at the evolution of language and communication *before* writing.'

'I know... I know what there was before writing,' said Angus excitedly, 'there was painting – cave paintings – people drew stories of hunting and things.'

'Exactly, rock paintings. That's why we are going to look at rocks because the story of rock is part of the story of people. Let's have a break now and then we are going to make toffee.'

The children dissipated like a mist, and, putting the kettle on for coffee, I watched Oakley pottering about in the garden. His curiosity was visceral: driven by primal instincts he explored his environment learning by cause and effect. He was storing information in a haphazard mental filing system that would become more sophisticated as he matured. He paused in his meander to poke a stick down a hole – I hoped that it would not aggravate a scorpion that might be resting in the shade. He hunkered down on his haunches utterly engrossed in his task, from time to time shifting his weight to improve his balance as he dug deeper into the sand; soon he started using his fingers, presumably to make the hole larger, but from that distance I could not see the finer details. Suddenly he got up, and, standing arrow-straight, he looked down at the hole, then, turning on his heels, he ambled off to explore some other element of our large garden. I don't know what he learned from that tiny experience. Perhaps he had stopped digging because he had lost interest, or perhaps he had felt a movement in the sand or a minute change in temperature had disquieted him. Perhaps he had been looking for something, and had discovered the hole was empty. I will never know. But his brief relationship with that hole in the sand would be stored, along with thousands of similar tiny experiences in his day, and form a part of a complex web of experiences that would for ever shape his mental landscape.

I called him in and for the rest of the morning we folded toffee into mountains and chopped brittle toffee into continental plates, and when we were finished the children lunched on Gondwanaland and Pangaea.

12

Comeragh Road, London 2010

I looked over Oakley's shoulder. He was marking a drill test. Slope-intercept equations. He was not happy.

'Bugger it.'

'Do you need some help Oaks?' I asked, sitting down beside him.

'No, but you do.'

'Nice.'

'Seriously Mum, you do.'

Don't shut down, Kate – keep open.

'Can we talk about this later, please.'

'There's nothing left to talk about. I don't want to talk any more.'

He picked up his books and left the room. A few moments later I heard his bedroom door bang. The boy was gone. The child who had been awakened by a lion's warm breath on his face was more afraid of me than the wilderness.

The telephone rang, and I knew who it was before I answered it.

'What the hell is going on Mum?' Angus's voice was harsh. 'The boy called me last night. He was terrified. What were you *doing*? When will this stop?'

My skeleton rippled like a mirage in his heat.

'You're going to lose him Mum. You're going to lose all of us. Do you understand? We can't do this any more. Mum I've stopped caring. Can you imagine what that feels like? *I don't care any more.*'

'Yes, you do.'

'Of course, I fucking do. We all do. But I'm so angry Mum – I'm so angry it makes me cry.' There was silence on the other end of the line. I waited for him to continue. He sounded weary, 'I'm angry for the boy – someone has to be angry for the boy.'

'You're all angry for him. He's got all of you on his side.' That came out petulantly – that wasn't what was in my head.

'Jesus Mum, listen to yourself. This is not a playground fight. Sides? On his side? Grow up.'

'It's not what I meant.'

'Nothing is what you mean these days. But the words we hear, Mum, the words we hear, they mean something to us.'

There was nothing more to say. There was no ambivalence. Can't wipe this slate clean. You need a new slate Kate. You need help.

'Hello,' I said to the woman at the other end of the line. 'Is it you I talk to?'

'We are all here to help,' her voice was professionally kind.

'I've not rung before.'

'I'm glad you have now,' her tone was neutral. Conciliatory.

'How can I help?'

'I hurt my son last night. I hit him.'

I paused and listened for the catch of breath on the other end... and... there it is.

'I'm sorry to hear that. How old is your son?'

'Sixteen.'

'Had you been drinking?'

'Yes.'

'Why don't you tell me about it. Let's start at the beginning shall we. You only have to tell me what you want to.'

'It happened eight years ago. It's embarrassing – really I should be better by now.'

'Oh goodness me, there's no timescale for healing. Don't be so hard on yourself.' Her voice was noncommittal – I think she'd been aiming for non-judgemental.

'But that's exactly why I'm calling you – to be hard on myself. I can't go around hitting my child and getting roaring drunk? I need help.'

'Knowing you need help is the first step to recovery.'

Oh, stop with the platitudes. This is not my first step nor my tenth nor my bloody twentieth. I have been climbing this mountain for years: I know every foothold and crevice intimately. I have nearly summitted many times, and then lost my footing. I can do this. Help me . . . but for heaven's sake get off your crappy script. Don't make her cross, Kate. Be nice.

'Thank you,' I said, 'you're being very kind.'

I could feel her purring.

'My dear most people in your position have taken up drinking. Some turn to prostitution.'

I couldn't believe my ears. Was she saying that my boy had got off lightly? Was she giving me permission to carry on because I'm in the sisterhood?

'Are you still there?' she asked.

'Yes,' I said.

Tell her you're frightened. Tell her you are losing your children. Tell her you want to be whole again. Talk to her. She does this for a job. She's going to say something helpful. Talk to her.

'Take your time,' she said.

I don't have time. Today is my last chance.

'Shall I send you some pamphlets?' she said presently. 'Give me your address and I'll send you our pack. It's got a lot of useful information that may help you.'

You do that. You send me a sodding pamphlet. If only I'd known there were pamphlets I could have saved myself years ago.

I gave her my address and hung up.

I poured the last of the whisky down the sink. A useless symbol of regret. Been there got that T-shirt. Eight years. Had it all been bad? No. Lots of good things had happened. If I added them up, much more good than bad. But the bad stuff had been so toxic. It had gathered into all my corners and congealed. I need a broom and a duster to whisk merrily. I need a tra-la-la Doris Day spring clean – a woman's touch can weave a spell, the kind of hocus pocus that she does so well – perhaps I should wear a gingham frock while I'm at it. It's not funny. I know it's not funny but how the fuck do I clean this up? I used to be the goody in my story. I used to be a nice person. Well, nice might be pushing it but I was connected. Super-connected. I could feel the vibrations of the tiniest movements.

I was powerful. Kind. I want to cry. Well don't. Just don't. Be fierce. To protect your children you've killed a black mamba with a machete. You drove twelve hours to get them to the dentist for heaven's sake: once through fire. Nothing fazed you. Be brave. I want to die. I'm so embarrassed. Fuck that shit. Don't look back. Look forward. Be brave. You can do this.

13

W.A.R., Botswana 1996

Anne Sandenbergh was right. Rape was tantamount to murder. HIV was first reported in Botswana in 1985, and by the time I arrived one in three adults was infected. In those days, the virus was referred to as 'the Tswana sickness' and it was decimating small rural communities across the country. The fabric of village life was being eaten away and family structure was dismantling. Bewildered illiterate grandparents were raising orphaned grandchildren, who were attending school and learning new ways to understand the world. The old ways and the new, mixing like oil and water. Botswana was changing.

It was, and is to this day, a democratic, peaceful country with a relatively good infrastructure and a stable economy. After a slow start the government acted responsibly and appropriately to the threat of HIV/AIDS, and formed strong collaborations with a variety of international bodies: all are determined to stall the rate of infection, and there has been some success. Today lives are being prolonged by drug therapies and free access to antiretroviral treatments. The rate of transmission at birth and through breastfeeding has been reduced. Extensive healthcare education programmes have been initiated and implemented, and sex education programmes aimed at adults and teenagers have become more sophisticated as communication technology has improved. But human behaviour has proved more powerful than sound governance and good science. In time, I was to understand why nothing was going to stop the Tswana sickness from moving through Botswana like a tsunami.

A wall of silence gave the virus unfettered access.

Child and infant sexual abuse exposes the dark heart of human sexuality: universally abhorrent, universally practised in secret. Silence and denial leave children unprotected. As a result, HIV was drip-fed into the heart of communities via their most vulnerable members. In the eighteen months I worked for Women Against Rape all the cases I handled were children. A few weeks after arriving in Botswana I attended my first case.

'Kate, I've had a message from the convent in Sehitwa, a woman needs our help.' Hilda was panting from running to my house. She was a warm-hearted Lutheran from the Faroe Islands, and she and her husband ran Thuso Rehabilitation Centre for the physically and mentally handicapped. Like me she worked as a volunteer for W.A.R.

'Come in Hilda, have some water, let's talk.'

'No time. It's a bad case Kate.'

'Aren't they all?'

'It's a child... the same age as Oakley.'

I went cold and I could feel corners of darkness curling up inside me.

'Are you all right?' asked Hilda.

'I'm fine,' I said, 'but Hilda I can't go... Ems is with friends... Sehitwa is miles away... I can't leave the kids.'

'No, no of course not. I'll bring them back with me. Henry and Dava will be delighted.' Hilda had two sons the same age as Travers and Angus and my children enjoyed going to Hilda's house. It was cosy, full of love and comfort, and they had a television with a video player: luxury of note.

Hurriedly, I was given instructions. I was to drive to Sehitwa, a village ninety-seven kilometres away, where I was to report to Sister Margaret at the Lutheran Convent. Irene Fergus, a Motswana midwife, would accompany me. On hearing this I was mightily relieved. I adored Irene – she had smiling apple cheeks, a gentle, unflappable nature and the patience to teach me the ropes. I still had so much to learn about my new country and its cultural mores.

'Sister Margaret has lived there for nearly forty years,' Hilda explained, 'she'll give you the facts and show you where to go... I wonder what you'll think of her?' Hilda grinned – my atheism was a source of mild amusement to her.

'Oh, and Kate, pack some nightclothes for the children, you might get stuck out there.'

'No, Hilda, I'll be back,' I said firmly, and Hilda raised her eyebrows: she knew my car.

BJ 196 was a temperamental vehicle. Emily and I had a knack for remembering her numberplate, and on the drive to Sehitwa Blow Job 196 excelled herself by producing startling guttural noises, and disconcertingly from time to time cutting out altogether. Every few miles BJ ground to a graceful halt and rested for a few minutes. Then, girding her loins, she was persuaded, by some rich Anglo-Saxon language, to proceed. We limped to Sehitwa energized by willpower. On finally arriving in the straggly village I didn't think about the drive back – hoping that the car would regain her spirits after a good rest.

Like so many small villages that sprang up along Botswana's roads, Sehitwa was no more than a scattering of mud-and-thatch huts with a couple of official breeze-block buildings thrown in for good measure. Irene knew the way to the convent, and we walked through the scrub where goats grazed lugubriously on wisps of desiccated grass. The place was quiet and unusually no children came running up to meet us. When we got to the convent Sister Margaret greeted us. She looked as if she had escaped from *The Sound of Music*.

She had the kindest eyes I have ever seen and a merry smile.

She was in her seventies and had hard, knobbly, working hands. Her sleeves were rolled up to her elbows, and had there been a dash of flour on her pert nose I wouldn't have been surprised. I am not a woman of faith but my soul has been enriched by encounters with those rare people who shine with human goodness: Sister Margaret was one of them.

'Thank you for coming so quickly,' she said, in an accent that was an odd mixture of Scandinavian and Setswana.

'No, no thank you for calling W.A.R.,' I said as she ushered us into her office. The room was plain but well equipped. The Lutheran convent was a comparatively modern, well-built structure; I don't remember many details but there were some good-quality wooden beams and the pristine tiled floors were cool on my bare feet. It wasn't a hushed space – it felt vivid and active.

The stalwart nun poured us some cloudy water from a jug and settling back into her chair she told us the story.

'It happened last night... I have known her mother since birth... she was born here in the convent,' she paused for a moment, 'I'm sorry... it's difficult for me... the people here are my family. I know him too you see.'

Irene and I said nothing. I pictured the moist-eyed, tough old nun arriving in Botswana as a young woman. What must she have felt finding herself in such a desolate place? I wondered where she had come from and what her blood family was like? I was humbled by the courage of a young woman on God's mission who had dug in and devoted her long life to this little community on the edge of nowhere.

'He raped a child.'

She could barely squeeze the words out of her mouth. I wondered if her God felt hidden to her: I hoped not, for her sake.

Then she beat her hands on her knees and got up briskly.

'I'll take you to her now. I can't get her to speak you see. She won't say anything and she needs to see a doctor.'

'The child won't speak?' I asked. The nun nodded.

'Neither will her mother. That's why I need you. You women at W.A.R. know what to do.'

I felt utterly out of my depth, and I was sickened to hear that the twenty-one-year-old man who had raped the child lived next door to her. The nun pointed out the hut where the child lived and left us to do our job.

A broken fence constructed of twisted leadwood posts and tangled wire surrounded the small compound.

'Koko?' Irene called from outside the fence. She called again but there was no reply.

We walked into the compound and knocked on the wooden door of the hut.

'Mma?' Irene's tone was calm, 'Koko Mma?'

'Did she say "tsena", Irene?' I whispered.

We waited for a reply but again none came. A pair of rather grubby curtains had been drawn across the window and we couldn't see if anyone was in. Reluctantly we opened the door and stepped into the hut uninvited.

It was sparsely furnished: a yellow formica table stood in the corner, on it was a small collection of cosmetics: a pot of hair relaxer, Dawn Fresh spray deodorant and a jar of Ingram's camphor ointment. Against the wall stood two green plastic chairs, one had only three legs, and by the bed, acting as a bedside table, there was a blue metal trunk on which rested a tin plate of half-eaten congealed meat and mielie meal; a few listless flies ambled about. The mother and child were huddled together under a thin blanket.

'Dumela Mma O tsogile jang?' I said using the formal greeting.

'Dumela,' replied the young woman, and holding the toddler in her arms she half-heartedly heaved herself up onto her feet.

She and Irene exchanged quick words in Setswana and I gathered from the mother's tone she was not happy to see us. She kept repeating 'Ke lapile, ke lapile' (I am tired, I am tired). I was not surprised she was tired after such trauma.

The young woman looked healthy, and no more than nineteen. Her dress was hanging open at the front revealing her breasts, her hair was neatly braided and her skin was clear. I imagined her a day ago laughing, pretty and vital. But today I could not find her face; it was hidden behind a blank surface. In time, she reluctantly led us out to her fireplace outside and, stoking up some embers, she set a kettle to boil. Irene sat on a plastic chair and I plonked myself down on a log near to where the child had been placed on the sand. She was wearing a pale cotton dress and her hair had recently been loosened from cornrows. Her nose was runny and her mother ran her hand over the child's face to wipe it clean. The child did not seem aware she had been touched.

She stayed where she had been placed and did not move. I asked the mother if I could hold her daughter, and the child was put into a stranger's arms offering no complaint. She no longer cared who she was with. I looked into her deep, blank eyes, fearing what I would see: shock had stripped away her connections with the world: how would such a small person find her way back? I held her close and lifted the corner of the feeling I knew so well. I could not join her because she was unreachable but I knew where she was: she was in the blackness: my under-the-table place. I wanted her to sense she was not alone but I knew she couldn't. I rocked her as I rocked Oakley when he woke from a bad dream, but I was only holding her body: the essence of her was somewhere else.

In Setswana, Irene explained the risk of HIV infection, and asked the mother if we could bring the child to Maun hospital for testing. The mother shook her head. I heard Irene's patient, kindly voice explaining how easy the test was, and how there were things that we could do to help. Again, the mother refused. Irene asked if the baby could be given antibiotics against STDs. Again, the mother said no. She was afraid that by taking action she would anger the rapist. She was afraid of her own mother – who would be ashamed of her grandchild. She was afraid of being ostracized.

She was afraid the man would come back and rape her this time. She was afraid of the world, and who could blame her?

'Irene, please ask her if she has been to the police.'

'Last night they heard the screaming. The kgotla police came,' Irene replied.

'Last night I heard the screaming,' I said out loud – Tracy Chapman's voice playing in my head.

'What?' inquired Irene.

'Nothing. Go on.' My inadequacy made my skin crawl.

The kgotla police were uniformed tribal police, and the chief's representatives in a village or ward: a ward being a collection of villages. The kgotla police offered effective law enforcement but they did not have power to prosecute serious crimes like rape or murder: those were under the jurisdiction of the government police. And in those days the government police would only initiate prosecution if the victim, or the victim's family, instructed them to do so. I knew the only hope we had of getting the man tried in court was to get the child's mother to Maun.

'Ask her if she will come with us to Maun to lodge a complaint with the police?' I suggested, but the mother understood me because she said no before Irene could translate: I could smell fear. The man who had attacked her child lived a few steps away, and the nights were long and dark and her door was easy to open. Rage at injustice was pointless in the face of such desolation.

With heavy hearts we left them, promising that we would be back the next day. I told the child's mother that Irene and I would go to the kgotla police to make sure they protected her at night. It was the first time I saw a flash of expression on her face, and she nodded to us before walking back into her house and closing the door behind her. Irene and I hurried over to the small police station and spoke to two young policemen. I begged them to guard the mother and child through the night and they promised they would. They were kind and reassuring, but as children they had played in the sand with the boy who grew up to be a rapist. We reported back to Sister Margaret, who was clearly disappointed we had achieved so little.

The drive back to Maun was miserable. We were depressed and frustrated, and the car continued to play up until finally it gave up the ghost thirty kilometres from Maun. It was dark and we were alone, and Irene seemed genuinely worried. I was simply irritated and concerned about how I was going to get back to the children. I poked about a bit under the bonnet, but no amount of twiddling with various wires and sprockets made a blind bit of difference. The road was empty for miles on either side of us and leaning against the car I waited for a car to come by.

'Do you know what's wrong, Kate?'

'Not a clue... sorry,' I said briskly, 'it'll be okay, someone will come eventually.'

Irene looked around nervously.

'Get back in the car Kate... there are wild animals out there.'

The night was still and quiet. Far away a pair of jackals started calling. Out in the darkness I heard a larger creature moving heavily through the scrub – probably one of many hobbled donkeys eking out a miserable existence in the semi-desert. The rhythmic intermittent trill of a scops owl reminded me of a telephone. There were no cellphones in those days, and I had no means of getting in touch with the children to let them know I was safe. I thought of the mother and child alone in the dark, huddled together, and hoped that the young policemen would be true to their word and stay awake. I knew Hilda would be looking after my lot, but I was worried about Oakley: he was needing me more these days. At two and a half he was beginning to be aware of the big world beyond his family: children always need extra reassurance in the months before they take the first steps on the long road towards independence.

In time, a car hove into view and several men piled out offering assistance. After some manly tweaking and thumping, the car burst into life, and having proffered gushing thanks we sped off merrily: only to break down again ten minutes later. An hour later a police car drove up into which Irene stepped resolutely She had had enough of BJ and my mechanical inadequacies. After speaking to the policemen in Setswana she told me they were going to drive her home, and she'd send her husband out to get me. This arrangement happened rather fast, and as they sped away I was left feeling somewhat bemused, mumbling oh ah, and wondering whether that was in fact the best plan of action.

Irene's husband never made an appearance. Thus, necessity required me to become intimately acquainted with the bowels of a stubborn engine. For the first time, I did what would become a staple activity. I undid every wire (there were many) and wiped each one on my skirt before reattaching it. I pulled out the spark plugs, blew on them and put them back. I topped up the oil and water and then, with Zen-like restraint, I spoke kindly but firmly to the engine and told it to get-me-the-fuck-home-to-my-children. It did.

Irene and I went back to Sehitwa every day for a week. The child remained quiescent, and the mother remained determined to protect her child with silence. The police in Maun told us they could not initiate prosecution without consent from the victim's family. Irene and I meant well, and we were gentle and kind, but our persistent presence was counterproductive. On the seventh day, we arrived to find the little house locked and empty.

No one had seen the mother and child leave.

No one knew where they had gone.

We never saw them again.

14.

Comeragh Road, London 2010

> 'But it was not your fault but mine
> And it was your heart on the line
> I really fucked it up this time
> Didn't I, my dear?
> Didn't I, my dear?'

Mumford & Sons were being played furiously upstairs.

> 'Weep little lion man,
> You're not as brave as you were at the start.'

My lion children had been so brave. *So* loyal. *So* clever. They had climbed inside my heart and fiercely held me close and kept me safe. They were not afraid. But in time my fear ate them up and spat them out.

> 'Tremble for yourself, my man,
> You know that you have seen this all before
> Tremble, little lion man...'

I wanted to go upstairs and hold Oakley, but I had lost the right to comfort my boy.

Hungry for something fatty, I went to the fridge and pulled out lasagne left over from last night's supper. I cut a generous slab, leaving enough for Oaks to have later. Before I had ruined last night, we had been so happy: listening to music and laughing and remembering our early days in London.

We had lived in a tiny flat: sleeping on a mattress on the floor. No money, empty fridge. One weekend we had survived on half a loaf of bread and two eggs. But we made a plan. I joined a tutoring agency and slowly built up some cash – often walking across London between clients because I didn't have the bus fare. With my guidance Oaks studied independently and networked. He made friends with ease and soon learned to live in the city. We were a good team.

Then the recession hit and I had to sell the farm at a loss. The money I had left wasn't nearly enough to put down a deposit to buy a property, so instead I invested in happiness.

I paid a year's rent up front for a comfortable family house in West Kensington and shipped our belongings over from Africa. We had a home again. Oakley was safe. The others came to stay, and the familiar smells and sounds of family wrapped us up like healing bandages. We were happy until I started late-night drinking again.

What was I getting out of it? Was I accessing some deep and hidden truth – in vino veritas? No. Was I enjoying myself? Beyond the first smoky sip of single malt there was little pleasure to find. Was I still enjoying the oblivion? The dark, numb space where only the echoes of feelings lived. I had needed that place once, but not now. I was present in my life again. I knew what I was doing was destructive. Why was I still doing it? With passionate articulacy all my children had individually begged me to stop, and therein lay the rub.

The worm of resentment wriggled inside me. The worm that emerged from deep inside my belly growing darker and fatter as it rose up past my sternum gathering momentum until it reached my throat in a scream of rage. DON'T TELL ME WHAT TO DO. YOU'RE NOT THE BOSS OF ME. The sweating sense of powerlessness liquefying my bones with fear. DON'T TELL ME WHAT TO DO. YOU DON'T KNOW ME.

London 2010

I wished I could shut out all the memories but they were vivid – brash – abrasive – rubbing like sandpaper on my conscience. The memories were intact. I was the one who had fragmented.

Eight years ago, I had shattered from the outside like ice in water. Differential expansion. Internally frozen, the warmth of love cracked my chilled exterior. I didn't melt. I wish I had. Liquid me would have been easier to contain. Instead slowly I grew colder, more powerful and like a glacier I ground down anything in my path. Chunks of me splintered and fell away, crashing beneath my feet, until there was no me left. I was a stranger inside my own body.

YOU DON'T KNOW ME.

15

Gomoti Camp, Botswana 1999

The snapping of branches, the smell of elephant, and the scurrying of acacia rats under the groundsheet placidly infiltrated my dreamtime. Sometimes I would stir when the tent walls billowed because a passing elephant had nudged a guy rope, or when a small herd, browsing on branches overhead, showered seedpods onto the roof. But when a child hissed 'Mum' in the night I shot out of bed naked, and in a seamless movement I was in the car – always parked an inch from the tent flap – ready for action. Sometimes I drove away a lion sleeping against a child's tent, or dispatched a cobra that had slipped in through a rip in the canvas, or pushed away a marauding hyena.

The quieter the whisper, the greater the danger.

16

Comeragh Road, London 2010

Oakley was quiet. A barrage of teenage rage would have been comforting. Apart from some door-banging he had been self-contained – aloof. His isolation was complete. He had reached his limit and stepped back from me to save himself. With shaking fingers, I typed two letters into Google. American Airlines flight information – thank you Google, not quite the AA I was after.

Shame made the nerves under my skin retract and I couldn't feel the tips of my fingers as they scurried across the keyboard. This shouldn't be part of my experience. This doesn't belong to me. I could feel my rage awakening again. I pushed it back down. Why couldn't I focus it where it belonged? Why couldn't I be angry with them? Take control. Panic. Blinding fear. Sweating. Find the address. Write it down. Do it. I can't see. Yes, you can. There it is. Write it down. What time? I'm so tired. Too tired to type. What time is the meeting? Write it down. I can't feel my hands. 6.00 p.m. Say the words. I can't speak. I'm slipping into the black. I want to go under the table. No. Stay. Don't go under the table. Be present. Say the words.

Oakley came downstairs and put his head round the door.
'You all right Mum?'
'I'm going to AA tonight. Oaks, I'm stopping now.'
The words were out.
'Oh Mum.'
Relief has a sound.

17

The Crocodile Farm, Botswana 1997

'Mum what's the matter with you?' asked Travers one evening while we were preparing supper together.

'I don't know Trav... I feel lost.'

'But things are going so well... I don't understand,' he said tasting the tomato sauce he was making for a pasta bake.

'It's *because* things are going so well Trav... it's utterly terrifying.'

'You're bonkers,' he laughed.

'No doubt.'

'Mum look at us. Great place to live, that we can finally afford.'

We had moved from the expensive Mission House, and we were living happily in a rustic reed-and-thatch cottage on a crocodile farm, twelve kilometres from town. The children ran feral amid the croc pens and along the banks of the Thamalakane.

'School's going well,' continued Travers, 'lion camp at the weekends and you've got a man.'

'Aha, that's exactly what I'm talking about. I am not defined by a man. You've got a man,' I repeated, furiously grating up enough cheese for a small army, 'I can cope fine without a man.'

Travers looked bemused.

'No one said you couldn't Mum... but he's nice and he loves you... what's your problem?' Travers's voice was gentle.

'I overcomplicate things. I can't just let things run their

course... I always end up making things more difficult than they need to be.'

'Do you love him?'

'Yes, I think I do.'

'Well, there you go then.'

The romance was new and scary.

Pieter Kat had begun a lion research project in the Okavango a few months after we arrived in Botswana, and we had bumped into each other from time to time in town. One day he invited us all out to his research camp in Santawani. I turned him down, and like an idiot I told Angus.

'You did what?' Angus was horrified.

'I said no. There's too many of us. We don't need him... we go into the bush all the time and see lions. Remember the magic of seeing our first lions, when Emily was still here, those females and cubs we saw with the buffalo. Who needs lion camp?'

'Mum you're insane. He's so cool. We saw him on the telly at Hilda's... he's doing amazing work.'

'Well, all the more reason not to clutter him up,' I said primly.

Angus wheeled away to inform his siblings, who were playing down on the riverbed. Moments later I heard them thundering across the garden, moving as one organism.

'Why did you say no to the lion man?' panted Maisie, bursting into the house, 'Why, why?'

'Mum that was just silly,' said Travers crossly. He was carrying Oakley, who had no idea what the problem was but was furiously nodding in agreement with his brother.

'I can't believe it. I just can't believe it.' Angus was in shock.

'Lions, Mum, at his camp. A *research* camp,' Maisie stood with her hands on her hips and her chin out, 'unbelievable.'

'Unleavable,' Oakley joined the chorus.

'Okay, okay, I get the message... if I see him again I'll say yes. Jesus you're nightmares.'

Falling in love is neither convenient nor particularly pleasant

– in my case it is usually accompanied by stomach-clenching anxiety and a runny tummy, but it is an experience that is best shared by two. From the outset Pieter's and my romance took place under the gimlet gaze of the children.

Our first trip to lion camp was damp and eventful. The first rains had fallen, and we arrived late covered in a fine coating of black cotton mud. My hair hung in dank Medusa coils down my sweat-soaked T-shirt.

'Welcome to Santawani,' said Pieter courteously, 'looks like you had some problems on the way?'

'We got so-o-o-o-o-o stuck, right up to the axle... you should have seen us,' exclaimed Maisie, clambering out of the truck, followed by a trail of empty crisp packets.

'Yes, yes,' I said hurriedly interrupting the flow of what I knew would be an interminable story. 'I'm sure Pieter knows all about getting stuck,' I mumbled, picking up detritus, while my filthy children launched themselves into camp: there seemed to be a lot more of them than usual.

Pieter looked in the back of the truck in astonishment.

'Is there any food left in Maun?' he laughed, lugging boxes of fresh food, soft drinks, wine, night-time nappies, loo paper and other paraphernalia to the camp kitchen.

'Well, we are quite a tribe and I didn't want to drain your resources.'

Pieter and I packed away the food and cooked while the children cleaned up in the chalet we had been designated. Soon a delicious lunch was laid out under a hibiscus bower, and I was instructed to wash by Travers.

I took a cool shower in the chaos left by my offspring. By now, they could change a tyre, run a donkey-boiler hot-water system, treat small scorpion stings with disdain and identify tracks in the sand, but none of them could pick a wet towel off the floor. I slipped into a white cotton skirt and sleeveless T-shirt and after tying my hair into a plait I looked in the mirror and twirled.

'Blithering idiot,' I said, checking my legs for smoothness.

'You look pretty Mum,' said Maisie brightly, as I joined them at the table, and maddeningly I blushed.

While we ate lunch, a herd of impala grazed on a haze of sweet new grass. Suddenly, one of them arched its back and, leaping into the air like Nijinsky, it sent the herd flying.

'Pronking,' said Pieter.

'I beg your pardon?'

'That leap... it's called pronking.'

'Well, whoever came up with that term should be shot,' I laughed.

'Shhh,' Pieter's tone lost its urbane charm, 'quiet everyone.'

He strode out to his battered 4×4 truck, and reaching into the passenger seat he pulled out some equipment and climbed gracefully onto the roof. After twisting some knobs on a receiver, he extended his right arm up high, turning the antenna this way and that, every few minutes fiddling with the receiver until it sent out a loud bleep, bleep, bleep.

'Chandon's here, very close, do you guys want to come?'

Sending their chairs flying, the children of Hamelin followed him into the ancient vehicle. Pieter drove slowly, steering with one hand while holding the antenna out of the window. The car twisted and turned as we followed the direction of the bleeping and as the signal got louder and louder I noticed he turned the volume down and adjusted the frequency.

'We're way off frequency now. Keep your eyes peeled, they're right here.' The children did not need to be told to be quiet. Holding their breath, their gazes penetrating the scrub.

'There... under that bush... I see them,' Maisie whispered, pointing to her right.

'Good lion eyes,' said Pieter, and she glowed with pride.

Chandon was lying inelegantly on her back, her lean, muscular body exuding power: I could sense the potential energy coiled in every cell. The radio collar around her neck seemed incongruous on a wild beast, and the bulky battery pack looked like a medallion under her blonde throat. Lying nearby were four young sub-adult females; one of them looked up as the car came to rest a few yards from them but the others didn't move a muscle.

'Sancerre,' Pieter smiled, 'always a bit jumpy.'

'Sancerre... Chandon... what's up with the wine names?' I laughed.

I saw no fear on the children's faces as they gazed at the lions so close by. Maisie was nearest to them and, resting her chin on the edge of the truck, she stared at the creatures as if she was absorbing them into her. Oakley was sitting on my lap and I could feel peace in his body as he leaned against me. He was three and fearless when he met the Santawani pride.

He was thirteen when he said goodbye to the lions he had grown up with: by then he knew the smell of fear.

18

Comeragh Road, London 2010

I showered, blow-dried my waist-length hair until it was smooth and silky, applied my going-out-somewhere-smart make-up, pulled on a pair of slim-fit jeans and a rather fetching black silk smock. If I was going to be among the meth heads and itinerants I was going to look damn good thank you very much.

'I'm off,' I called upstairs, 'there's some lasagne in the fridge. Don't know how long I'll be.'

'Good luck Mum.'

Twenty minutes later, alighting from the Underground train, my defiance melted with my bones, which barely kept me upright on the interminable walk to the church hall. My cheeks tingled with mortification. This should not be part of my world experience. This does not belong to me. How does this work anyway? What do I do when I get there? Do I join a queue and shuffle in with my head down?

The church was a functional early-nineteenth-century edifice, built in an anxious flurry of expansion that had been precipitated by promulgated doubt and declared lack of faith. Wandering around the building looking for the hall and a gap in the fence, I felt as unlovely as the drooping plane trees that grew grimly on the pavement. I spied a small group of smokers gathered outside an arched doorway and my ears buzzed with blood as I approached them.

'Hello, are you here for the meeting?' The man looked friendly.

'Yes.'

'We haven't seen you here before.'

'First time,' I mumbled.

'Good for you. Welcome. Go in and settle yourself. We won't start for another ten minutes. There's tea and biscuits.'

Functional metal and canvas chairs had been set out in curved rows in front of a formica table. Some people were beginning to settle, while others were still pouring tea from an urn, and helping themselves to iced biscuits. Everyone looked clean and tidy and spoke in calm, hushed tones. I wondered if by accident I had walked into a Women's Institute meeting, and any minute now someone would set up a home-made jam stall. A man standing nearby must have seen my expression.

'First time here?' he asked.

'Ever,' I replied.

He seemed surprised.

'Well you look good, for that. I was in a terrible state at my first meeting. Welcome. Sit anywhere you like.'

I'd seen the movies. I knew the mantra.

'Hello, I'm Kate I'm an alcoholic.'

It wasn't true but the lie felt good.

I listened to the stories. The rock bottoms others had reached. I was too numb to feel their pain.

19

The W.A.R. Office, Maun, Botswana 1997

'Kate, it's Anne. Can you stay in the office for another half-hour or do you have to get back to the children?'

She was telephoning from her office in town, and she sounded flustered.

It had been a year since I joined W.A.R. and we had slowly gathered momentum. We had enough funding to rent a soulless office in a new complex opposite the airport, we had a phone line, a fax machine and a kettle. But not enough funds to run a W.A.R. vehicle, and Anne Sandenbergh was still taking the brunt of the running costs and paying the two salaries for the non-volunteer citizen employees. Anne's vision was to have the organization run entirely by salaried citizens. But for now, the team was still predominantly formed of volunteers.

'Sure,' I said, 'the kids are here with me anyway.'

'Good,' said Anne, 'I'll be with you now – now.'

The children hated being stuck in the compound, and while Irene, Hilda and I had been discussing the financial and practical logistics for a series of countrywide school workshops they had been kicking a football around disconsolately in the dust outside. I went out to break the news.

'Darlings, sorry, sorry, looks like we'll be here a bit longer.'

'Mu-u-u-u-m it's so boring. Why can't we go home?' Maisie grizzled, her face smeared with sweat, 'I hate football so much.'

'Didn't you bring a book?'

'Mu-u-u-u-m it's not school time.'

'I'm really sorry, how about a Steers supper later to make up for it?'

'No money Mum... remember?' shouted Travers from the goalposts created by the boys' ragged T-shirts.

'Fuck,' I muttered, our limited funds were always delayed in transfer, and an earlier trip to the bank had been fruitless.

'Well sorry chaps you're just going to have to suck it up. Lion camp on Friday so life's not too tragic.'

Maisie entertained herself by launching a blistering attack on Angus, who was felled to the ground, and in moments they were all thumping the hell out of each other in a tangle on the sand.

I left them to it.

Ten minutes later Anne arrived, shaking with rage.

'I have just had a radio message from Ann in the Delta... that mobile shop of hers is a godsend, she gets to hear so much,' Anne panted as she poured a glass of water and scraped her hair back from her damp face, 'apparently the headmaster in a secondary school out there has got a girl pregnant.'

'You're joking,' I said.

'No joke. She's fifteen, so that's defilement for a start, and he's got her pregnant. As you know the education department's usual response is to *transfer* teachers who break the code of conduct to a more remote location.'

'More remote than the western Delta?' I was incredulous.

'You wait, Kate. When you go on that school mission you're planning you'll be amazed how isolated some schools are,' Anne's eyes were snapping with rage, 'but it should be easy to get this teacher removed because he came over on a British Council contract... they hate a song and dance.'

A cry from outside caused Hilda to glance through the window.

'It's mayhem out there Kate,' she laughed, 'do you want me to do something?'

'No, let them burn it off. They rarely draw blood.'

Anne turned to Irene.

'I think this may be a blessing in disguise... this case is high-profile and should get us a meeting with the Minister of Education. Irene, you and I will go to the education officer in Maun first thing tomorrow and Kate and Hilda will go to the school. I'll ask the Christian Mission if they can fly you out.'

The prospect of confronting a headmaster somewhere in the Okavango Delta caused me to blanch and Anne's blue eyes twinkled.

'Of course, if you'd rather not,' she mocked.

'Absolutely yes... I'm your man,' I said girding my loins, 'what about the girl, will we meet here there?'

Anne laughed mirthlessly.

'Apparently this happened a few weeks ago, and the girl has already been removed from school as per government regulations. Ann is still trying to find out where her mother lives. Her father works in Palapye.'

'I don't understand why she can't stay in school.'

Anne explained that it was policy for girls who became pregnant to be removed from school lest they set a bad example. If they wished to continue their education after giving birth they were free to do so when the baby was a year old, but they could not return to the same school. With no money, and in need of support from their family, it was hardly surprising that few young mothers took up the option of a second chance. Teenage pregnancy ended all hope of further education, and often resulted in a lifetime of grinding poverty.

There was a knock on the door and Travers stood in the doorway.

'Sorry to interrupt... Oakley's pooped himself, I've hosed him down, but I'm losing it.'

That concluded our meeting.

The drive home was miserable. The children had been

disgruntled for a fortnight, and I too was distinctly lacking in gruntle. Two weeks before, Emily had flown back to England to get work – before embarking on a gap-year trip around the world, alone. Maisie's heartbreak at losing her sister inflamed the missing of her father, and she was utterly wretched. Travers was bearing the brunt of being the oldest and finding his feet – with an aching heart and a snappy tongue. Angus was peacekeeping and fighting back the pain of missing his sister; and Oakley, picking up on everyone's misery, was crotchety and out of sorts.

And I was in mourning. Emily and I had been joined at the hip for eighteen years and she was gone.

Friends offered consoling platitudes.

'You've got to let them go you know.'

'They all fly off sometime.'

'You can't tie them to your apron strings for ever Kate.'

I knew all of the above thank you very much. At no time in my life had I ever wished to entrap my children. I had raised Emily to embrace her independence with open arms and a compassionate heart. But oh my goodness me, when a child leaves home the missing hurts in places you didn't even know existed. I was hungry for a big cuddle, and a warm shoulder to cry on.

Our little reed cottage was only twelve kilometres from town, but soaring summer temperatures and frayed tempers caused by dehydration made it seem much longer.

'I hate W.A.R.,' grizzled Maisie, 'and I hate Botswana. Get off me Oaks you smell disgusting.'

'Don't be mean,' I snapped.

'He's covered in shit.'

'Don't say shit.'

'Shit, shit, shit, everything is shitty.'

'Right. Do you want me to stop the car?'

'Yes.'

'Don't push it.'

'Stop the shitting car or I'll jump out.'

'I mean it Maisie.'

'I mean it Maisie,' she mimicked.

'I'm nearing the end of my tether Maisie... don't push me.'

'I'm nearing the end of my tether Maisie... don't push me.' She was on a roll and I was seething.

'Eloise, I mean it,' chimed in Angus, quoting from Kay Thompson's classic children's book, and I roared with laughter.

'Oh yeah, great, laugh at Gussie why don't you – you never laugh at my jokes,' cried Maisie.

'Oh, for Pete's sake give it a rest Mais,' I implored. I was sweating like a cheese, and my daughter had been pithily accurate on the ripeness of my youngest son.

'What's for supper?' inquired Travers in sepulchral tones, 'please not schnitzels again.'

'What's wrong with a...'

'Mum, Mum, look... look,' Oakley interrupted pointing wildly, 'hyena, hyena.'

And indeed, a slope-backed adult female hyena was lolloping along in the scrub not far off the road.

'Wow,' breathed Travers, 'look, look there's another one coming out from behind that sage bush.'

I pulled over and we gazed in wonder at the snub-nosed carnivores: like magic, peace was restored.

Two days later the Christian Mission flew Hilda and me deep into the western Delta in a four-seater one-propeller plane: I am of the opinion that planes should have significantly more than one propeller. Indeed, had it been up to me I would have walked naked through lion-infested bush, rather than take to the air in a tin can. The flimsy aircraft was buffeted by thermal currents, causing it either to drop like a stone or whiz upwards towards the heavens. Hilda tried to chat to me over the noise of the engine, pointing out the ravishing scenery below, and I smiled at her weakly while imagining vultures winging their way towards us and becoming entangled in our lone propeller. As the fifty-five-minute journey progressed my palms grew hotter and sweatier, my knuckles whiter and my lips stuck to my teeth. When, finally, we emerged from the plane onto a small airstrip cut into the bush I showed great restraint by not dropping to the ground and kissing the good earth beneath my feet.

Hilda was immaculately dressed in a smart skirt and silk shirt with an elegant pussycat bow tied loosely at her throat. I was dressed in a sweat-drenched cotton frock that clung to me in all the wrong places, and holding a large straw bag that I had forgotten to clean out which was full of baby wipes and hideous debris from my last trip into the bush with the children.

The village was set beside permanent water. Lush trees edged the wide river, and barefooted children played in the shade by the water's edge, casually dipping in and out of the crocodile-infested river to cool down. Had our mission not been so bleak I would have enjoyed the bush walk to the school, but I was terrified.

It was all very well marching into a strange school in the middle of the Okavango Delta to confront the head teacher, but we had no authority to do anything and he knew it. I was glad Hilda was in charge. She must have sensed my anxiety and she laughed.

'Come now Kate, you can't be afraid of one little man?'

As it turned out he was a tall, rangy man with pale eyes. He must have heard the plane arrive because he greeted us at the entrance of the school with a placatory smile, and an invitation to have a cool drink in his rather shabby office.

As he sat opposite us, protected by his desk and puffed up by self-importance, Isabella's words from *Measure for Measure* played in my head: 'Man, proud man, dressed in a little brief authority... like an angry ape plays such fantastic tricks before high heaven as makes the angels weep.'

Hilda got straight to the point.

'One of your pupils has made a complaint against you. You have had a relationship with a student and made her pregnant. This is in direct violation of the teachers' code of conduct and it is statutory rape.'

She knew that last comment was risky because, remarkably in 1997, there was no reference to statutory rape in Botswana's penal code.

The headmaster was unmoved and replied calmly.

'She consented and was happy to be in a relationship with me. There was no "rape" as you call it.'

'Happy to be in a "relationship" with her teacher?' Hilda snorted, 'You know what will happen to her don't you? You have ripped up her future. And you? You'll be packed off home to pick up your life again.'

At this he looked startled.

'I have a contract here,' he blustered, 'I have eighteen months to run on my contract.'

I could hardly believe my ears. Was it possible he thought he could keep his job after what he had done?

'Are you aware that members of your staff are sexually abusing children at this school?' continued Hilda, carefully negotiating thin ice.

'I was not aware of that,' he responded in an even tone.

'We have written statements from the children to say many of your staff are having sex with your students.'

'Statements?' he jeered, 'are you talking about messages in those ridiculous boxes you leave in schools?'

One of W.A.R.'s first actions had been to place padlocked wooden boxes in schools across Ngamiland into which children could post anonymous messages. The boxes were collected as regularly as our small team could manage, and after going through them we took appropriate action.

'Indeed, we are,' replied Hilda, 'the content of the box we collected from your school was serious enough for us to hand it over to the education officer in Maun.'

The headmaster turned pale.

'And for good measure,' Hilda was on a roll, 'photocopies have been sent to the Minister of Education in Gaborone.'

On hearing this the head changed his tack.

'Ladies...' he purred and I bridled, 'let me reassure you the students in this school you may be referring to are in fact adults. Many girls come here aged twenty to complete their studies.'

Anne had warned me he might use this as an excuse, and it was true that some secondary-school pupils were in their early twenties but that was not the issue.

'We received well over sixty complaints, would you say you have over sixty girls here who qualify as adults?' I asked sweetly and he said nothing.

Hilda proceeded as planned.

'Your school is not the only school we have had complaints about. And as I said we have registered all our concerns through official channels. You should expect a request from the education department for a hearing on this issue.'

At this the headmaster's skin flushed a pale shade of rose.

Three weeks later a hearing was convened at the school. At the time, I did not understand what an achievement this was. Anne had pulled out all the stops and a representative from the Ministry of Education flew up from Gaborone for the day, joined by Maun's chief education officer and his assistant. Over coffee in the headmaster's office the representative from the Ministry explained how the meeting was to proceed.

He made it clear that this was a government investigation, and, because W.A.R. had brought the case to the attention of the department, a concession had been made for members of W.A.R. to be present. Our comments would be welcomed at the end of the investigation, but we were not invited to participate during the meeting. There was to be a follow-up meeting in Gaborone with the Minister of Education at which W.A.R. had been invited to participate.

At the appointed time the government officials, Hilda, Irene and I settled at a long wooden table, set up in the shade of a hibiscus-flower awning. The silent students stood nearby, shuffling occasionally, waiting in the glare of the sun.

One by one they sat down. One by one names were taken, and dates of birth and places of birth were neatly transcribed on a list by the education officer's assistant. One by one they told strangers their most intimate secrets. Everything was recorded on sheets of paper. The meeting was conducted in English, Botswana's official language. The children didn't cry. And I squirmed in silent agony as I participated in what was an extension of the abuse these children had suffered. The endlessly repeated words still echo in my head.

'You say a teacher has had sex with you. Is this right?'

'Yes,' the replies were barely audible.

'Did he rape you?' The rolling r in the heavy Setswana accent felt harsh on my English ear.

So many haunted and confused faces. So many silences. Sometimes the education officer from Maun had to lean forward.

'You must answer,' he said to one bemused twelve-year-old girl.

I looked desperately at Irene and raised my eyebrows in a silent question. Should I intervene? Irene shook her head.

The child hung her head and said nothing.

'Can you tell me his name?'

The child answered and the name of the teacher was recorded on the list.

The rigid formality of the meeting was as stultifying as the heat. The morning wore on and the list of teachers' names grew. By the end of the morning some names had become familiar.

The last child to be seen before lunch broke down. Her body shuddered as she described what had been done to her, and tears poured down her cheeks. From across the table I watched a child's heart break and I could do nothing. When she left, her story was torn up.

'What are doing?' I said too loudly.

'She is an unreliable witness,' the representative from Gaborone replied 'she was crying.'

'But of course, she was crying,' I blustered 'she's been terrified, out here alone, I'm amazed more children haven't cried this morning.'

'It is not our culture.'

'Oh, please...' I said, again too loudly, too rudely, 'crying is a universal, please don't talk to me about culture.' Hilda took me firmly by the arm and led me away.

'I can't bear it Hilda... these children have no one to look after them. No counsellors, nothing.'

'They have us Kate,' said Hilda.

'But we're not *doing* anything,' I said desperately.

'Yes, we are. We are here. This meeting is because of W.A.R. A man from the Department of Education is listening to these children because we have listened to them. Do you understand what that means?' I shook my head.

'This is the beginning, Kate. These are good men, they care, don't be mistaken about that.'

'But they tore up her story.'

'One story Kate, they tore up just one story.'

20

Comeragh Road, London 2010

While I brushed my teeth in the bathroom I could hear Andrew Marr rabbiting on about something important on the television at the end of my bed. A few minutes earlier I had been listening diligently to his topical burble, but whatever thoughts I may have had on the matter had whizzed merrily into the ether never to surface again. I was dazed.

My first AA meeting the night before had been a baptism of some sort: certainly not of fire. It had been humiliating but otherwise rather bland. I had been neither disappointed nor inspired, but I had committed to a body outside my family: the children were released. I knew the fact of that. But I was still blinking. I couldn't look that truth full in the face.

It was Sunday and I had no plans. I was too numb to be active. I think the numbness might have been shock. Still in my pyjamas, I was pottering downstairs to make some toast when the front doorbell rang and I heard a child giggling. I opened the door and there was Emily with the brood.

My daughter's warm grey-blue eyes smiled at me. She knew.

'Hello Mamma.'

'Surprise Granny, surprise, Happy Mother's Day,' six-year-old Eliza chirruped, hopping from foot to foot with excitement.

Emily bustled in carrying bags, and a sleepy baby in her arms. Bella had recently woken from a long sleep in her car seat and her eyes were still adjusting to the light.

Emily laughed and kissed me.

'We knew you'd forget Mother's Day... we've brought everything with us... lunch all sorted.'

Eliza hopped restlessly from foot to foot. She had a mop of Titian-red hair and translucent white skin that shone pale blue when she was worried. She and Maisie were cut from the same cloth: they loved rawly – empathetic to confusion – fearless, gentle, wild and as vulnerable as baby impala.

'Go on Jack,' Eliza urged her older brother, who handed me a box of Cadbury's Milk Tray and hugged me for a long time. I breathed him in. And remembered... Maisie and Oakley had been with me on a supply trip to Maun when Emily called from England with the news that she was pregnant with my first grandchild. We were beside ourselves with joy and seven-year-old Oakley, who had only vaguely begun wearing clothes at the age of five, asked me to buy him a tie: apparently, imminent uncledom required the right attire. Driving back to camp the car was full to the gunnels with supplies, and several small children I was delivering to their mothers in the bush. Maisie was riding shotgun, and Oaks (wearing new tie and collared shirt) and the other children were bumping about in the back squeezed between gas bottles and loo rolls, chewing on warm Chappies gum and slurping on water bottles. The journey home was marked by our familial landmarks: Giant's Tree, Elephant Corner, Potato Man Termite Mound; and at Hyena Pan we were joined by Inferno – Oakley's favourite lion. His face was scarred and battered, he had lived a tough life, but he was a spectacularly chilled-out lion. He ambled along beside us, and from time to time his great body swayed up against the door. Rolling down my window I told him our news.

'Infy... I'm going to be a grandmother... can you believe it?'

He continued walking, unperturbed and disinterested, until he turned off to the right and wandered off into the bush.

Inferno and Jack are bound in my memory.

'Where's Oakley, Granny?' asked Jack while Emily and I unpacked the food in the kitchen.

London 2010

'Upstairs asleep... go and jump on his bed,' I replied, and the children stormed off, Jack lugging Bella in his arms.

'Nothing's changed has it Ems,' I giggled, 'there's always been a tumble of child around.'

'Since I was six,' she laughed. 'Mamma?'

'Yes,' I knew what was coming and shame made me hot.

'Oaks told me,' she said, 'I'm so proud of you.'

'Well, in that case you know I haven't got anything to be proud of.'

'No, no, not about that, he told me you'd gone to AA.'

'About time.'

'Just a tad,' she laughed, 'I'm so glad, Mum.'

'Me too.'

'Oh Mum.'

'Oh Mum what?'

'Just oh Mum.'

I hugged her. I was so grateful. My girl had bundled her kids into the car, and driven from Littlehampton to be with me. Active loving.

I loved the house she lived in happily with Jimmy and their children. Battered by sea winds and time, the eggshell-blue house stands in a terrace overlooking the Sussex coast. On stormy days, the old windows rattle and the odd tile flies off the roof while Emily's seaside children sleep unperturbed under the eaves. Her house smells of washing powder from a machine that rarely rests, old biscuits crumbled under cushions, hot toast, fresh towels, damp coats, baby bath bubbles, wax crayons, sea air and calm. Emily came out of my body calmly, and bustling into my broken heart she made me safe. Nevertheless, I slept with my hand on her body for a long time: just to make sure she was breathing.

'I suppose the family telegraph has reached Maisie. Did you tell her about AA?' I asked.

'No, probably Gus did. Call her, Mum...'

'Course, tonight... I'll call her tonight.'

But the little worm wriggled inside me. Resentment. Isolation. You don't know. I don't want forgiveness. You don't understand.

21

Santawani Camp, Botswana 1997

'I'm worth eleven cows. Don't you forget that,' Maisie said, mashing an avocado and a banana with a fork. I had been made this generous offer for my eight-year-old daughter earlier that week in the dried-goods aisle in Spar supermarket.

'If he'd thrown in a couple of goats he'd have had a deal,' I replied, exfoliating my skin with demerara sugar stirred into olive oil. I was wearing knickers, hair-removing cream on my legs, and a rather fetching silver-foil headdress was wrapped around my henna-slathered hair.

We were spending the weekend with Pieter again. The boys were out tracking the lions with him, and Maisie and I had stayed in camp for a beauty session. The children and I had just come back from a three-week road trip around south-east Botswana giving HIV/AIDS workshops at schools and in villages. It had been a worthwhile but arduous journey, and an afternoon chilling with my girl was my idea of heaven. To compound our goddess-ness, a banana cake was baking in the oven and home-made bread was proving on the bonnet of the car.

'What's that called... lobby... labby something?'

'Lobola. Bride price. A charming custom and one I shall be adhering to rigidly,' I said, applying the mashed avo and banana face mask liberally. Most of it slid gracefully down my sweaty cheeks and landed on my breasts in lumpy dollops, so I lay on my back on the floor trying to keep still so the fruit acids could have their way with my epidermis.

'Mum?'

'That's me.'

'Is Pieter your boyfriend now?'

'I guess – sort of.'

'Have you told Emily?'

'I sent her a fax, and then I called her.'

We had had a long, intimate telephone call during which she had demanded all the details: with no stone left unturned.

'Mum?'

'Mmm.'

'Why is Travers allowed to drive in the bush by himself?'

'Because…' I said sleepily, the excess of the mash was pouring down my neck in rivers and my head was slow-roasting in the tinfoil, 'anyway he's not allowed to go far.'

I'd taught Travers, Angus and Maisie how to drive on the old airstrip near Santawani. By now, lion camp was our second home. The children and I were learning the ropes. Tracking the lions meant we were often miles from home in rough terrain – in those days we had no car radio. If anything happened to me out there the kids had to be able to get back to camp: driving was an essential skill.

'It's not fair.'

'He's older than you, that's why.'

'Why?'

'Why is he older than you? Don't be daft.'

'No. Why's he allowed? And Gus. It's not fair. At school they are both ahead of me because I'm stupid.'

'You are *so* not stupid.'

'I am. I don't understand anything,' she was winding up for a meltdown.

'Bollocks,' I sighed, resigning myself to the fact the beauty session was not going to be relaxing. 'Dearest child of my heart – you are eight... I know, nearly nine,' I corrected myself hurriedly, 'and working wonderfully for your age. In fact, far ahead of many your age and you are heaps more talented at art than anyone – you can't keep comparing yourself to the boys... who are older... or you'll go potty.'

'In the bush we're all the same.'

'What do you mean?'

'We all know the lions. We can all do whisker patterns and track. I see things before the boys,' she was close to tears, 'I see things they don't see. In the bush we're all the same. Sometimes I'm better.'

'Oh Maisie.'

'No, Mum, you don't get it,' her frustration was palpable, her hands were fists and her amber eyes were flecked and furious, 'just because they are stronger and can lift gas bottles and things and do things and change tyres by themselves they think they're the boss of me.'

She was right. It wasn't fair. I hated being patronized by macho men in khaki shorts, and it happened to me all the time. Being patronized by much-loved brothers must be even worse.

'Right,' I said, heaving myself up from the floor, 'let me shower all this shite off and then we will make a plan. That cake smells ready to me. Whip it out will you.'

The cake was perfect. Risen. Billowy. Golden-brown.

Scraping off hair remover and unwinding the silver foil from my head I pondered the pros and cons of letting Maisie drive by herself. It was risky for sure, but during a driving lesson she had already coped with an elephant charge without panicking, and shown herself to be good under pressure. Life in the bush could get claustrophobic, walking alone was out of the question, and she was old enough to need space for herself. Maybe it was time. Slathering the cowpat of henna with shampoo, I turned my face up to the rose and turned on the tap. Nothing. Henna was dripping down my body and congealing with unguents on the floor.

I fiddled with taps and banged on the pipes hoping to shift a water lock, but to no avail. There could only be one reason.

'Maisie, is Darrel out there? Don't go out... just check if you can see him from the door.'

I heard Maisie open the door of the thatched kitchen chalet and roar with laughter.

'Err yes... he's *right* here... in fact you should be able to see him from your window.'

Suddenly, the smell of elephant mixed with apple-scented shampoo. Darrel was an amiable beast with a penchant for drinking out of our drain and detaching the water pipe.

'Darn it.'

I waited patiently for him to move off, before stepping out stark-naked to reattach the water pipe and continue my shower. I wondered if Pieter would approve of me allowing Maisie to go on short trips alone. My style of parenting was not his cup of tea. So far this was not a problem, but we were still in the heady days of romance.

One thing was for sure, before any child was let loose in the bush alone they had to be able to change a tyre safely and independently. With no radio in the car even short trips were risky because punctures were a regular occurrence.

'Maisie,' I said, drying my hair in the sun, 'I've been thinking. If you want to drive alone you've got to change a tyre with no help – start to finish – *capisce*?'

'Really Mum... are you serious?' Her lion eyes were shining.

'Yup, let me get the bread off the bonnet and into the oven and then I'll watch you. I won't say a word. No help. You've got to remember all the steps. You've done it enough times with all of us so you should be fine,' I said, putting the bread in our ramshackle gas oven. My bread always turned out like concrete but I lived in hope.

'Right Mais, the front tyre on the passenger side has got a slow puncture so it needs to be changed anyway. Off you go.'

My young daughter eagerly lugged the hi-lift jack out of the back of the car – it was almost as tall as she was and weighed fourteen kilos. Resting it up against the bull bar she moved on to the next step (loosening the wheel nuts, but not removing them). Her hands weren't strong enough, so she had to stand on the wheel spanner and bounce on it. She did the same for each wheel nut. Her hair was getting in her eyes and sweat was flying. With the nuts loosened she returned to the hi-lift and my stomach clenched in anxiety. Hi-lift jacks are indispensable tools, but they are not user-friendly and if a finger gets trapped in the locking mechanism you can kiss the digit goodbye. Maisie fitted the lip of the jack under the bull bar, and slipping her fingers inside the mechanism she locked it firmly before pulling down on the lever and lifting the car. Using two hands and straining every muscle she hauled on the lever until her feet almost left the ground. She kept on pulling and releasing until she was happy she had lifted the car high enough.

Standing back and taking some deep breaths, she tied her loose hair into a knot and moved round to the tyre. It was then she realized she hadn't taken the new tyre out of the back of the truck. With the car balanced on the hi-lift she knew this had to be done carefully. Grabbing the tyre rim with both hands she slid it gingerly onto the ground. With no one telling her what to do, her confidence was soaring. She rolled the tyre nonchalantly over to the passenger side with one hand. She never once looked at me – she was determined and bloody-minded, and my heart was bursting with love for this steaming, tenacious small person.

Next, she removed the previously loosened wheel nuts and heaved the punctured tyre off the bolts. Then she grabbed the new tyre, and kneeling down on her haunches she balanced its weight on her knees. Taking a deep breath she heaved the bulk up onto the wheel bolts. By now her arms and legs were quivering under the strain. The tyre slipped off three times before she managed to hook it onto all the bolts at the same time. It was painful watching her try to get the first wheel nut on... it slipped from her sweaty fingers and the tyre fell away from the wheel bolts onto her knees for the fourth time. But she was fighting for her independence and she was not going to give up. Panting for air she pushed the tyre back on the bolts and fumbled with the wheel nut once more... I could see she hadn't got it on the thread. Tears were pricking in the back of my eyes, but I kept my mouth shut and watched as the nut fell off again.

Maisie was by now scarlet with exhaustion, but she never asked for help. It took her two more goes before the tyre settled into place, and she let out a deep sigh. Reaching for the wheel spanner she partially tightened the wheel nuts. Then she slipped the hi-lift out of gear and, heaving on the lever, she brought the car back down. Then back to the wheel nuts for the final tightening with the spanner.

'Alternate nuts, remember...' I whispered.

'I know, Mum,' she snapped, standing on the wheel spanner and stamping down.

'Done. Mum. Done.' She looked mighty in her faded cotton dress, purple in the face and glowing.

'Girl Power Mais the Daze. Fucking Bush Girl Power.'

'No swearing... Mum... no swearing,' she laughed, rolling the old tyre to the back of the car and heaving it onto the tailgate. Job done.

'Men in khaki – eat your hearts out!' I yelled as we hugged.

My girl took me out for a spin, and we sang 'Wannabe' by the Spice Girls all the way to Jackal Pan.

Back in camp the bread burned to a crisp – much to everyone's relief.

22

Comeragh Road, London 2010

Not drinking was easy. I just stopped. Of course, sobriety produced clarity but within that lay confusion. I was a living oxymoron. Unprepared and ready. Afraid of how much there was to face and eager to face it. Puzzled and certain. Newly defined and blurry round the edges. My energy was no longer generated by fission. My nucleus was no longer unstable and easily split when bombarded. I was powered by fusion. Bonding. Isolated.

'Mum?'

'That's me.'

'Are you going to a meeting tonight?

'Yup.'

'Will it be okay if David and India come over later?'

I loved Oakley's clever, warm, non-judgemental friends.

''Course – I'll bung a French roast in the oven before I go.'

'Thanks mum. You're the best.'

I made banana cake.

23

W.A.R., Botswana 1998

'We are just scratching the surface,' I cried, bursting with frustration.

Anne, Hilda, Irene and I were having a planning meeting, and things were getting heated.

Lack of funding was crippling us and W.A.R. was embattled by its own success. Local and national government were actively involved now, and a 'cottage industry' was rapidly evolving into a serious NGO. As the word spread, more and more women and children were coming to us, and our resources were stretched beyond our capabilities.

Passion alone could no longer fuel the work.

'Every single school we visited had children who made complaints about their teachers. It's an epidemic.'

'HIV/AIDS education is paramount,' Irene insisted.

'But we've got to get a better handle on child sexual abuse,' said Anne, 'the recent data shows an increase in infection in prepubescent children. That's a serious warning sign.' Maternal transmission of HIV accounted for infection among babies, but not for prepubescent children. Children were seroconverting long after the window period that could account for transmission at birth or through breast milk.

I was tired. It had been a tough few weeks at work and homeschool was challenging my mental resources – most nights I was up until the wee hours preparing classes. Fighting back exhausted tears, I tried to keep calm.

'Child abuse is pandemic... it's our species' darkest secret, and here in Bots this nonsense that sex with a virgin 'cures' HIV is making matters worse. Irene, you're right, education is crucial, but we must extend our focus – we've got to help these children.'

Hilda gave me a hug. She and I had been helping a mother whose six-month-old baby had been raped to 'cleanse' a man. The baby was still in Maun hospital being treated. Her reproductive system destroyed.

'We need to raise awareness. If we are going to get the funding we need... we have to raise awareness,' Hilda said turning to me. 'Kate, do you have contacts who might help us in England?'

I thought of all my friends, and realized how rapidly we had disconnected. Soon after arriving in Botswana I faxed long, rambling letters back home to my friends, but our points of reference were changing so dramatically that finally it made me sad, and so I stopped. I got very few letters from England. Communication was cumbersome. At that time, the boy who would one day bring us Facebook was the same age as Travers, and probably sharing similar concerns about the condition of his epidermis. But we had a landline telephone in the W.A.R. office, and that would have to do.

'Yes,' I replied to Hilda, 'I'll call people who might help. First, let's prioritize need, and I will try to raise some dosh for specific tasks – at the least I can ask someone to write an article about what's going on here.'

I called a well-known theatrical producer to ask for funding for W.A.R., and we had a jovial but fruitless exchange. I telephoned various thespian chums who listened sweetly to my pleas for help, but most of them were far more interested in hearing about Travers and Angus's recent attack of malaria.

'Oh my God. Oh, how awful. Are they all right?'

'Yes, they're fit as fiddles. Darling, I'm ringing because we desperately need help.'

'Oh, I know, too awful. You are being marvellous. War Against Rape, what a good name. Tell me, what did you do? Was the hospital ghastly?'

'What?'

'The boys?'

'Oh no, I nursed them at home.'

'Oh my God how terrifying.'

It had been. One late afternoon Travers had spiked a sudden temperature, accompanied by a blinding headache, and I had whizzed him over to our Nigerian family doctor, Dr Patrick, who tested Travers for malaria. Angus developed the same symptoms a few hours later.

Advised by Patrick I nursed them at home, with regular visits from him.

'Kate, you can do this,' he told me, 'they will be happier at home. You caught the signs so quickly, the medicine will work fast.'

'But they keep being sick, Patrick, how will they keep the medicine down?'

'If they keep it down for thirty minutes it will have assimilated. If they vomit before that time then redose them. I'll come by again later.'

My poor feverish boys lay side by side, delirious and puking through the night. It was terrifying and empowering. I was learning to cope with everything Botswana threw at us. I ran a tight ship, keeping charts on which I monitored times of doses and recorded their fluctuating temperatures half-hourly. If they climbed too high I wrapped them in tepid damp sheets, and my poor boys shivered miserably in my arms. The next day Patrick laughed when he saw my immaculate charts hanging at the end of the beds.

'You can see for yourself they are getting better. Excellent nursing, Mma.'

Three days later the boys were swinging on strangler-fig vines as if nothing had happened.

Back in the office I made countless phone calls to friends who listened kindly to my pleas, but they were disconnected from my reality. Anne was supportive of my attempts at fund-raising but slightly irritated: the cost of international calls was mounting. They all had a similar theme, and in truth I handled them badly.

I called a well-respected journalist I knew vaguely. He was not interested in prepubescent infection – too upsetting for the readers – they would switch off. However, he was intrigued by the sexual abuse at schools.

'How many cases did you say?'

'In one school, nearly three-quarters of the staff were mentioned by the girls.'

'The school in the Delta?'

'No, that was another case. The headmaster got a student pregnant but other staff members were also involved.'

'All these are ex-pats?'

'What?'

'All the teachers – you said the head was on a British Council contract.'

'Yes, but not all the teachers are expats.'

'Ah well, in that case we have a problem.'

'I'm sorry I don't get you.'

'I can run a story on expats abusing students but not citizen teachers. Too touchy.'

'So, you're telling me that if poor little black girls are fucked by nasty white men it's a story, but black on black doesn't count.'

'Calm down.'

'Don't tell me to calm down. I've driven every inch of this country. These kids are isolated – real isolation – schools in the middle of nowhere – no phone – no radio – no one to help them. Sometimes teachers even pay the child's parents... can you believe that? Poverty is brutal. Girls are being used and abused, and you are telling me that because their abusers are black they have to suck it up.'

'You called me, Kate. If this is how you speak to people you are asking for help you need to change your tone.'

'I don't understand. I just don't understand,' tears of rage bursting out of my eyes, 'we're flying by the seat of our pants here, in the middle of a pandemic, we need cars – we need fees for lawyers – we need a safe house – but most of all these kids need advocacy. People need to know.'

'Look, I understand your frustration, but I'm telling you the story won't run.'

'Well, thank you very much.'

I hung up.

Fund-raising was not my métier.

But a call with an old friend was the one that sowed a seed of doubt that festered and confused me for months. I told her about the last trip the kids and I had made down to schools in the south-east.

'I don't know how you do it? I'd be far too scared. You have taken such a risk.'

I felt an unspoken judgement. She was concerned for my children's education, and their health and safety, and to be fair she had a point.

Homeschooled, malarial, and tracking lions at the weekend: it was a far cry from the life they had been living in the Cotswold Hills. But hells bells – as Ray Bradbury advised, living life at risk is jumping off a cliff and building wings on the way down... we were jumping off cliffs and growing feathers. We were strengthening, each of us in our own way.

'It's hard to explain,' I said, trying not to sound defensive, 'but here people just get on with things... when the shit hits the fan you just make a plan.'

'But what if Oaks had got malaria?'

I couldn't reply. I had been petrified he might get infected. At his age malaria would have been even more dangerous.

'He's so little, Kate.'

'There are lots of little kids here,' I snapped, 'lots of Oakleys. What makes him so special?'

'Don't be ridiculous.'

'Look, I'm trying to get help for kids who have no one to vouch for them. We have to do something.'

'But Kate what about your *own* children? Why aren't you thinking about them? Stop trying to save Africa and think about your own poor benighted kids.'

I hung up: it was becoming a theme.

My friends were right. And they were wrong. They were muddled. And so was I. I was doing good work, important work. Was I being a good mother? I couldn't say. I raised no money.

The truth was that energy and passion were not enough. I didn't speak Setswana, I wasn't a qualified counsellor, I had no training in social work, I had no relevant expertise and yet I was working closely with traumatized women and children, running HIV/AIDS education workshops, helping the police to improve the way they processed rape victims, and having meetings with government ministers. I was doing things I would never have been able to do in my own country without years of training. I was trusted and I took my responsibilities seriously, but was my loving kindness a form of arrogance? Months later matters came to a head and I tasted humble pie.

Things were looking up. Anne had acquired funding from a Scandinavian foundation, and wisely had engaged an experienced fund-raiser to ensure W.A.R. could continue to expand. She arrived shortly before the International Women's Day meeting in Maun at which the Minister of Health was to give the keynote speech. The meeting had been arranged cooperatively by W.A.R. and two locally run women's groups, among them the Young Women's Christian Association.

We had hired a large hall with a dais, and on the morning of the meeting chairs were neatly arranged in closely packed rows. On either side of the dais two rows of more comfortable seats were set out for local dignitaries, among them the mother of the chief of Ngamiland. The chief's mother was tantamount to royalty. The House of Chiefs is similar in function to the House of Lords in the UK. It serves an advisory role in legislation related to tribal law and custom. It has eight hereditary permanent members representing the Tswana tribes, and selected members who serve a five-year term.

When the doors opened, women, and a smattering of men, respectfully took their seats and animated chatter fell to a polite murmur as one by one the dignitaries were shown to their seats, among them Anne and Irene who were W.A.R.'s official representatives. Irene and I smiled at each other from across the room. W.A.R. had come a long way from the higgledy-piggledy group of well-intentioned individuals Anne had inspired.

The meeting was opened by a prayer, and after some typically lengthy introductions the Minister of Health was welcomed to the stage. She gave a thoughtful, insightful speech about the role of women in Botswana. She discussed the need for a re-examination of cultural mores in the light of HIV infection, and she was impassioned on the power of sexual and general education for girls. She made it clear that domestic abuse and sexual crimes against women and children were not only legally and morally repugnant under both customary and judicial frameworks, but presented a clear and present danger to the overall health of the population.

The Minister spoke with clarity and wisdom, and when she paused only the distant chug of a diesel truck on its way out of town disturbed the peace. The room was hot. The windows were closed against the dust that wafted softly across the compound, stirred by lazy breezes that rose briefly and fell away as if exhausted by the effort. The smell of woodsmoke on skin merged with freshly cleaned, neatly ironed clothes and sweat. I looked at the rows of flat, hard-working feet, many clad in Sunday-best lace-up shoes, some in unlaced canvas plimsolls, tongues flapping open. Bare legs, little knotted scars, small burns: stories written on skin. Tired tears ran down my cheeks. Relief. The Minister had the power to effect change.

In time, she invited questions from the floor, and one by one women voiced their concerns and were given direct answers. I beamed a smile at Anne and Irene, and we nodded to each other. The Minister was being purposeful and honest: she offered no pseudo-comforting platitudes. More and more women stood up to voice their concerns: mothers, wives, girlfriends and grandmothers who were caring for orphaned grandchildren. Shocked, illiterate old women stoking their night fires and waking up to a bewildering new world. And then a man stood up and spoke, and he was listened to in quiet respect.

'Today you speak too many words. Read your Bibles. The Bible tells us. She tells us all we need to know. Eve, she committed the first sin. You women are paying for the sin committed by the first woman. God tells us you must pay for Eve's sin. That is all you need to know. This is God's will.'

Even the dust stopped stirring.

'Women are guilty. You carry Eve's guilt.'

I looked across at Irene: her calm face was implacable: where was her rage?

I looked at Anne: her blue eyes were sharp and her mouth was set hard but she didn't speak. My eyes scanned the room in desperation: all eyes cast down; wordless; no voices speaking out against atrocity.

The man continued speaking but boiling blood muffled my ears; the new fundraiser for W.A.R. was sitting near me, I looked at her with burning eyes: we must speak out. She looked straight ahead. The man continued, no one stopped him: God's freaking will... rape... brutally... babies... a virgin's organs bought and sold... stop talking... be quiet... you monstrous human being... My rage mounted until I could stand no more.

I stood up.

'I'm sorry but is no one in this room not offended by what this gentleman is saying? Is it possible that we can accept that God condones the cruelty meted out to a baby who is at this moment in a cot in hospital a few hundred yards away recovering from an attack so brutal I will not describe it. God condones the rape of a two-year-old child whose soul was stripped from her body by brutality? God condones the uncle who bought his niece for her body parts. On International Women's Day we listen to a man who tells us our gender, our babies, our daughters, deserve to suffer violence at the hands of men because a mythical Eve ate a freaking apple. Is anyone else as offended as I am?'

The silence was deadly. I chilled to marble.

'Well, I'm sorry but I can't stay in a room where a man speaks such an abomination.'

My footsteps made the only sound in the room, and the door seemed a long way away as I walked up the aisle and left the meeting.

The next day I was summoned to the W.A.R. office and hauled across the coals for my rudeness. I was a representative of W.A.R. and I had been disrespectful in front of a government minister, the Chief's mother, and in front of the Christian women's groups who were helping W.A.R. Anne Sandenbergh admonished me for not respecting cultural values and common courtesies. Oh, how it hurt. Oh, how unjust it felt. But I sucked it up because she was right, and I would have walked through fire for that woman. I learned a brutal, conflicted lesson. I was a guest in a country that I was learning to love deeply, and embedded in the nature of my new home was non-confrontational communication. I had to learn to temper my passions: no matter how much it hurt. So, I went to the YWCA and apologized in person, and I wrote a letter of apology to the Minister and I apologised to each member of W.A.R.

But humble pie tasted so bitter it made me gag.

24

Comeragh Road, London 2010

I was feeling nauseous. Watching telly in bed, propped up against soft pillows, I had finished an entire packet of Real Devon Cream Toffees while Grissom, and the shatteringly handsome Warrick, cleaned up Las Vegas. I could hear music drifting down from the roof garden. Oakley and chums at play. It was late and time for a Nytol One-A-Night.

Today had been dreary. After three months, the AA meetings were becoming monotonous. I respected them and took them seriously but the Higher Power thing was an issue. I had been told not to think about the HP as God – someone even suggested I think about it as an Oyster card, for fuck's sake. What on earth did that mean? The meetings were still helpful. The men and women were brave but the HP thing was lurking deviously. If I took the twelve steps, at some point I would be required to acknowledge that I was powerless. I would be saved if I turned my will over to a mythical notion. No. Never. I knew what powerlessness felt like. I could taste it. I was not powerless over alcohol. I had control over what entered my body.

I flicked channels. *Bones*. That's what I needed, or an old episode of *Grey's Anatomy* – let's see what grumpy Meredith is up to shall we? Someone was being sick in Oakley's loo. Clambering out of bed, I pottered onto the landing. A wan child was still heaving. I waited until she had finished. She was not a regular on the scene. She had been silent during our riotous supper earlier that evening. She must have weighed about six stone. A thimble of alcohol would have been enough to set her off.

'Sorry Kate. I'll be off now.'

'No, my angel you are not going anywhere. You can barely stand. Sweetness and light, sleep on the sofa downstairs. I'll make you up a bed.'

'No, my mum, I must... oh crap...' She slid back into the bathroom to finish off.

I got clean sheets and a pillow and made up her bed on the sofa.

Shortly, the bedraggled little soul was standing in the sitting room doorway with her coat on ready to go.

'Your mum will not be grateful if I send you off in this state. Trust me it's a mum thing. You're staying here tonight.'

'She'll be livid.'

'What's her number? I'll text her.'

The child look terror-struck.

'You want her number?'

'When telephoning it's a pretty standard part of the procedure.'

'What will you say?'

'That you are totally arseholed, and have puked all over my house while singing old sea shanties,' I laughed, 'don't be daft. I'll just say it's too late to send you home and you're snuggled in safe. She'll read between the lines. She can get in touch with me if she's worried.'

This thing of not having parents' numbers was new to me. When Emily was a teenager we used landlines, and parents were in contact with each other simply and undramatically. Now, getting a parent's cell number was considered invasive. Cellphones had fractured regular wholesome parental connections. I had no contact with Oakley's friends' parents. He went to their houses and his friends came to me, but to this day I have never met a parent. Their children are an important part of my life, I have grown to love Oakley's close friends, but I have never been to their homes. Outside my own home London was cold. Impenetrable. Unwelcoming. For Oakley it was warm. Alive. Oozing with potential.

I had to flip the Necker Cube.

Oakley came thundering downstairs looking for his friend.

'Sorry Mum... so sorry.'

'No prob. But just how much have you all been drinking up there? I bought you guys beer but no one could get pissed on what I supplied.'

The irony of the situation was humiliating. Oakley rose above it.

'Dave brought half a bottle of vodka,' he said shamefaced, as if I was a regular parent: not a woman he had seen so drunk she was barely human.

'Well that'll do it. She's fine. I've texted her mum.'

'Can the others sleep over? They'll text home.'

I kissed him goodnight.

He knew the answer to that question.

I was a fully fledged London parent, dealing with fledgling urban teenagers. But I still didn't have a fully fledged life. If Oakley got into university I would have to work like a carthorse to fund it. London would have to be home for a long time. I had to find a way to love it.

I can do that.

I have control over my heart.

I have control over my body.

I have the Power.

25

Santawani Camp, Botswana 1998

Pieter and I were straining, free, abandoned, locked into a pulsing rhythm. The vibrations rippling through my bones intensified almost to an agony. As we were reaching a crescendo lions roared outside, and I laughed until I hiccuped.

'Well, that's a first,' I rejoiced, flinging my arms out wide, 'coming to a roaring lion – eat your heart out Meryl Streep.'

Pieter grinned and leaning over me reached for his cigarettes. He kissed me lightly before lighting up and I snuggled into the crook of his arm. We lay back listening to the cacophony of roaring, counting the guttural grunts that followed each thunderous gut-straining bellow.

'Hear that?' Pieter purred. 'Listen. One, two, three, four, five, six, seven, eight, nine, ten, eleven and twelve... there... that's Bordeaux.'

For a second I was entranced by the eroticism of a man who knew the wild so intimately.

'Oh, what bollocks, you have no idea which one that is?'

'No really... listen. They roar differently.'

He was right, they did. After a while the roaring grew fainter as the males wandered off into the night.

'Seriously, can you tell which is which by counting the grunts?'

'Seriously? No. But I do recognize their roars. Poor boys they're fussing about something – there's probably some nomad knocking around. We'll go out tomorrow and look for tracks.'

'Darn it I've got a planning meeting. I've got to go back to Maun early. We're doing a workshop with the Bushmen near D'kar on Tuesday. For God's sake don't tell the kids you're tracking for nomads, they'll be livid with me.'

'Do you have to go?'

'Must. There are only two of us doing the workshop. Lots of logistical crap to sort out.'

Pieter snorted, and stubbing out his cigarette he took the torch from his bedside table and went outside. I could hear him peeing in the sand.

'Workshops. They're a total waste of time you know,' he called out to me, 'time and money down the drain.'

I heard the car door open and close and he came back with an old squash bottle half filled with water.

'Thirsty?' he asked, handing me the bottle. The tepid water still tasted faintly of Oros squash. Though I had been in Botswana a few months longer than Pieter, he had lived on the continent for years and understood Africa far better than I did. In many ways I found his cynical world-weary experience alluring but also it pissed me off. This was my journey. The children's and mine. I felt defensive. Quarrelsome.

'W.A.R. is doing amazing work. It's heartbreaking. You have no idea.' I was irritated by my inarticulate platitude and so was he.

'What's going on out here in the bush is pretty heartbreaking too. Let's face it the whole continent is heartbreaking. But bleeding hearts don't solve problems here Kate.'

'Obviously. But you have to care. To participate you have to care. I care intelligently, Pieter. I'm not just a bleeding heart. I'm learning on the job.'

'I know you are. I see how hard you work. But you must be prepared. These NGOs thrive on people like you and they spit 'em out when they are done.'

I had already felt the spittle: when I walked out of the meeting on International Women's Day I had no allies.

'And your kids, Kate,' Pieter interrupted my thoughts, 'what about them? I suppose you'll be taking them to D'kar.'

'Of course.'

'Have you thought about the impact your work is having on them?'

I deflated and curled up in a ball. I thought about it all the time. It didn't matter where in the world I lived, balancing motherhood, work, self-enrichment and self-empowerment was tormenting. Why doesn't anyone tell you that from the moment a baby emerges from your body guilt will be a constant factor in the equation of your life? Pieter was right, there was an imbalance between the children's needs and mine.

Raising the children in Botswana was powerfully and positively catalysing their development. I could see their compassion, wisdom and pragmatism being enriched by living unsanitized, visceral lives in an energetically developing country. However, due to my work the backdrop of their life was sexual violence. I knew in my gut that their exposure to my work was too raw. But I was still driven.

I was actively participating in real change. Anne and I had recently come back from a constructive meeting in Gaborone with the Chief of Police. He cared. He asked questions. He was a good man who used his power proactively. After careful discussion, he gave his permission for W.A.R. to work with the Maun police and help them to develop protocols for processing rape victims when they reported an attack. This was a huge step forward. If the workshops went well in Maun, and the local police gave positive feedback, we could extend the programme nationally. Currently, there was no cohesive system in place, and it was imperative that victims were taken to the nearest hospital to be tested for HIV and medicated against sexually transmitted diseases. Ironically, the prevalence of HIV/AIDS prompted the government to take affirmative action for victims of rape and domestic violence. Without the virus, I suspect progress would have been much slower.

Uncurling my legs, I stretched out and my feet touched Pieter's. They felt cool.

'I know, I know,' I sighed, taking in a few deep breaths. I stroked his forearm and examined his fine hands. Ballet dancer's expressive hands, with a thread of engine oil under each clipped nail. I brought his right hand to my lips. Smelling his musky skin. I wanted him again.

'Just give me time. It's a lot to process.'

I rolled over and looked into his eyes.

He stroked my hair and began kissing my neck.

Somewhere in the darkness a child vomited.

And that, as they say, was that.

26

Comeragh Road, London 2010

'You're round the bend Mum.' Travers was Skyping from America: he was anxious.

'Tell me something I don't know,' I laughed.

'Seriously, you've got no money, you're scratching a living tutoring when you're not teaching Oaks. If he gets into college how the hell do you expect to pay for tuition?'

'Something will turn up. I'm a firm believer in Mr Micawber's excellent philosophy.'

'Why doesn't he go to uni in England? He'll get a student loan,' said Travers, practical as ever.

'UCSB has been his dream ever since you got in. He's going to get the same chances you all got. Anyway, in the UK he'll be lumbered with student debt... marvellous system.'

'But at least you'll get help.'

The pleasure of having direct conversation, without the undercurrent of pain and fear, warmed me like a hot bath on a winter's day.

'Trav you were born worried my angel child.'

'Well, someone has to,' he giggled, 'dear God my family.'

'Anyway, we've got to get the little bugger in first, and at this rate he's not going to make it. So that will be a relief to one and all.'

Oakley was having a very jolly time in London, and as a result his recent work had been appalling. The normality of that was heaven.

'Mum?'

'That's me,' I knew what was coming.

'Are you still going to meetings?' his voice was gentle, concerned.

'No, my darling, I've stopped. The God thing was getting too much for me.'

'God? I thought AA was non-religious.'

'Ostensibly, but it's lurking.'

'Does that matter if it's helping you?'

Good point. Yes, it did matter, I was my own master, but now was not the time to discuss it.

'Trav, I promise if I feel myself wanting to reach for a bottle I will throw myself back into the rooms with gay abandon. Truth is I really and truly don't want a drink any more. I don't even think about it.'

Travers's face looked worn. A shadow of the dark days fell over him.

I shut my eyes and the image of him standing in the doorway at the hospital ripped through me like a bullet.

'I know, Mum, Oaks has said things are really good. He's happy again.' The warning in his voice was crystal-clear.

'I know,' my voice was small.

I could feel the flood of regret, shame and responsibility crashing against the dam I had erected. Dams are good. They have a purpose.

'Oh Mum,' he was hurting, and he was so far away. I wanted to reach out, but we were too raw to touch each other, and so we prattled on for a while, talking nonsense, reminiscing about camp and the lions. Botswana always peppered family talk.

'I need to go now, Mum. It's been lovely talking. I love you.'

'You too my angelest. Tsamaya sentle.'

'Go siame Mma.'

I quit Skype. I was exhausted.

Isolated.

I needed to think. Thoughts were struggling to be seen but I couldn't connect to them. My cheeks seared with shame. It had been easy to stop drinking. Why hadn't I stopped before? Why don't I understand? I'm clever – this should be easy. I'm so tired. Stop. Breathe. You can do this. It's a simple question. Break it down.

London 2010

Drinking hurt your children. You knew. Why didn't you stop? You love your children. You didn't love being drunk. Or is that a lie? Was there some part of being drunk that you needed? You don't need it now. I can feel muddle coming. My ears are throbbing with blood. Stop. I can't see. Wait. Be patient. You're not going to get it now. But something is coming to the surface. There is a picture. In the darkness.

27

D'kar, Botswana 1998

D'kar is a small town close to the Namibian border, and the drive was hot and dull. The ambient temperature was forty degrees, and everyone was coated in fine white calcrete powder blowing in through my open window. Reduced to sticky stupors, the children sagged in the back seat eating Simba crisps and drinking cold Coke from the cooler box. Irene was snoring beside me, her head resting against the window she kept firmly shut. I liked long drives – they gave me time to think.

There had been anonymous reports of domestic violence in the Bushman community, and the Kuru Development Trust had invited W.A.R. to give an HIV/AIDS workshop for the women. The Trust had been providing support and capacity-building initiatives for the Bushmen for ten years. Recently an art project and museum had been opened and the Trust was in the process of developing a preschool programme for Nharo-speaking children. Neither Irene nor I spoke Nharo and an interpreter was going to help us. The Trust had kindly offered to put us all up for a couple of nights while we ran the workshop. It was the first time the children and I had encountered a Bushman community, and in preparation Angus had given us a presentation at school, delivered in his best formal tone:

'The Kalahari Bushmen, or Kung San, have lived a hunter-gatherer lifestyle for over a hundred thousand years. Their ancient culture is rich in legend and practical skill, derived from living almost symbiotically with plants and animals in the unforgiving landscapes of the Kalahari. Two thousand years ago, when the Bantu-speaking peoples started to migrate into southern Africa, the Bushmen were pushed gradually further into the harsher arid zones where they maintained their cultural identity, but over the years they have become increasingly marginalized. Like so many indigenous hunter-gatherer societies the Bushmen's skills and egalitarian social system were undervalued within rapidly developing nations. Botswana is a country that prides itself on tribal tolerance and integration but in reference to the Bushman the pejorative term "Basarwa" is commonly used.'

As we travelled through the bleached landscape my respect for Bushman skills intensified.

'Imagine finding food out there, Mum. There's nothing,' Angus murmured sleepily.

'I was thinking just the same thing Gussock. Imagine understanding the land like that; reading stories in the sand in trails left by insects and birds or whatever. Mind-boggling.'

'I was reading that when they hunt, nothing from a carcass goes to waste,' Angus continued quietly, 'because they respect the animal for its essence. They empathize with it when they are tracking. In the book, they said it's a spiritual relationship. Is that like God for the Bushman?'

'Yes, sort of.'

'Did you ever believe in God, Mummy?'

'No. I tried to. But no one is born believing in God. They learn it. I was sacked from Sunday school. Did I tell you that?'

Angus roared with laughter.

'Shhh you'll wake the others,' I whispered, 'my mum was furious. I was expelled because I asked too many questions.'

'How old were you?'

'Five or sixish,' I sighed, remembering the humiliation of being sent out of the classroom in front of everyone, and being made to sit on the stairs until my mother came to pick me up.

'What sort of questions, Mum?' Gus was wide awake now.

'Oh, I dunno, things like how big was the boat that carried all the animals and why didn't the lions eat the rabbits? How did Jesus walk on water, did he have special feet like a duck? Nothing momentous. I was just curious.'

'What did they say?'

'Well nothing really. If they'd have said it was magic that would have made sense to me. But they said it definitely wasn't magic, and so of course it made no sense at all.'

'If they had said God was magic you would have believed?'

'Oh yes for sure... I understood magic... all children do.'

Magic makes sense to us as children, and it plays a powerful role in our emergent reality. Embracing fantasy and magic is a required precursor if we are to understand the truth of the invisible world around us. Our reality is constrained by the limits of human senses, but childhood magic and fantasy help us to develop the muscles we need as adults to wrestle with powerful, intangible ideas. The giants in science and literature had (and have) profoundly active and resilient imaginations that can stretch an idea across untravelled terrain: expanding the boundaries of human understanding.

'But would you have gone on believing in God?' asked Angus.

'Probably not – in much the same way I stopped believing that hedgehogs did ironing and sand fairies granted wishes,' I laughed. 'Anyway, in answer to your question I never believed in God because I never found the idea very exciting. If he wasn't magic – he couldn't be real.'

'But magic isn't real, mum.'

I looked in the mirror at my boy: his sun-whitened hair, his sun-dried skin, smeared with sticky slicks of Coca-Cola, his warm blue eyes that saw the world calmly. He had slipped out of the space where magic and reality are intertwined, and briefly I felt sad. Growing up happens in privacy, in quantum space, neural connections arising, shifting, editing, pruning: electrochemical penetralia.

'No, my angelest it isn't. But magic is part of our journey. For Oakley a speaking fox is easier to believe than the reality of standing on a planet spinning at a thousand kilometres an hour.'

'Miles mum. A thousand miles.'

'Yes, yes but you get my gist. The truth is hard, Gus – wonderful but hard. We need to walk through the back of a few wardrobes till the time is right.'

'So, is God like that?'

'Yes – but the trouble is you're not expected to grow out of him.'

Suddenly the car lurched alarmingly to the left and skidded across the road: a blowout puncture.

'It's a sign,' Gus giggled.

Travers and Maisie woke when the engine stopped, and piling sleepily out of the car all hands were on deck. Working efficiently and in silence we had the old tyre off and the new one on in five minutes.

A few miles later steam billowed out of the radiator, and pulling onto the side of the road, we waited for the pressure to abate until it was safe to unscrew the radiator cap.

'Bone dry!' exclaimed Travers, examining the tank, 'I topped it up before we left – so we've either got a leak in the hose or a hairline fracture in the tank. BJ is a pile of junk,' my twelve-year-old mechanic muttered, tightening the jubilee clips on the hose, 'the water in the jerry will be baking-hot so we can pour it in now. Grab it from the back, Gus,' Travers instructed.

'There'll be a garage in Ghanzi, we can sort it out there,' I said.

'No way Mum,' Travers cried indignantly, 'they'll rip us off for sure. Better to keep topping up and wait till we get home. Melissa's dad will sort us out: he's a brilliant mechanic.'

Brian Schreiber worked in one of the local garages, and his

enchanting diminutive daughter was among the band of close friends the children shared. A few years later, when my internal gasket blew, Brian's non-judgemental kindness would be a lifeline for Maisie.

'If we need a new one Brian will know where to get a recon rad,' Travers continued.

'Recon rad... bloody show off,' Gus mimicked his brother while tipping water into the tank from our antediluvian jerrycan.

'How long will we be in D'kar?' asked Maisie.

'A couple of days,' I replied.

'*Days?*'

'Yes days... why do you think we packed a suitcase you backward child?'

'What suitcase?' asked Angus.

'Are you all simple? The only suitcase we possess. Get in all of you... now,' I snapped. I was cross and worried; there was no money to pay for a new radiator, recon or otherwise.

'There's no suitcase in the back, Mum. Irene's holdall but no suitcase.'

'Oh, damn all dancing footmen. I can see it all now... I left it on the bed at home... piss and piss and double piss.'

Nothing coalesced the children faster than me making a mistake.

'Mu-u-u-u-m.'

'We will simply have to suck it up and make a plan. I'm sorry and all that jazz but nothing to be done.'

Maisie giggled, 'Irene and Oaks are still asleep... do you think they're dead?'

'That or immune. Let's hope the latter,' I said, grinding the gears and speeding away.

28

Comeragh Road, London 2010

There's a place I went to when I was drunk, where I thought I was the truest version of me. It felt real: the answers were there. Sometimes I found a tangible fragment of truth – or I thought I had. I had to tell someone, so they would know it too and look after it for me before it dissolved like gallium in water.

Night after night I had woken Angus from his elephant sleep and shared my incoherent ramblings.

I sat on the sofa in West Kensington and made myself remember.

I wanted to cry but some tears are too frightening to release.

The more connected I became, the more I understood what had happened to my children. Strangers had fragmented me. I had shattered my family.

Healing is unendurable. No one tells you that.

29

D'kar HIV/AIDS Workshop, Botswana 1998

The stifling room smelled of new cedar wood, cheap pine disinfectant and sweat. Three rows of white plastic chairs had been set out in a semicircle. The older women chose to sit cross-legged on the tiled floor. They were adorned with ostrich-egg beaded necklaces and colourful hand-painted headscarves. The younger women sat on chairs, and a few stood in the back close to the door.

Irene and I worked well with the interpreter, and we covered the ground faster than I had expected. The women had listened attentively to our presentation on HIV/AIDS and had participated by asking questions; I had done my 'How to Put on a Condom' demonstration, using modestly dimensioned bananas picked from Anne Sandenbergh's tree, which generated riotous laughter. Irene and I were approaching the more delicate part of the workshop.

Opening out the discussion to domestic violence and rape was always a challenge. We had been invited because allegations of abuse had been brought forward, but in a public forum we had learned from experience to expect silence or denial. The support W.A.R. had been given by the Commissioner of Police had empowered us, and we had more confidence that women would be better defended and protected by the system. But that made little difference to women living in tight-knit communities, where shame, guilt and the fear of being ostracized were powerful censors.

'I'm going to tell you something that I don't often share.' I paused and waited for the interpreter. I had learned that reliable interpretation was made easier by short soundbites.

'When I was a young child, I was sexually abused by a teacher in my village school.'

A few seconds later there was a small gasp, the interpreter had been clear.

'I'm telling you because it is important that we share our stories. Sadly, my story is not rare.'

The older women looked at the floor but some of the younger women nodded in agreement.

'Talking about bad things is hard. Sometimes it's easier to pretend bad things haven't happened, or to keep them secret.'

I waited for the interpreter again.

'It's our right to keep secrets if we want to. But now because of HIV/AIDS, keeping secrets about rape and violence is dangerous.'

The room was so quiet I could hear a bird chirping in a tree outside in the compound. I kept very still and waited.

'We are here to listen to your stories,' said Irene, 'we are here to help you if you need help.'

No one spoke. One of the older women took off her headscarf, shook out the dust, and retied the hand-painted fabric with skilful fingers.

Silence: then a young woman called out from the back of the room and a few heads turned. The woman stood up slowly, her hands holding the hem of her cotton dress, her face an implacable mask. The older women cast their eyes on the oxidizing banana skins left over from the condom demonstration: no one was laughing now. Stretching her arms high above her head, the young woman slowly removed the navy and white printed dress and let it drop to the floor. She was naked but for a pair of white cotton kickers. She turned around, and her back was striped raw with lash marks.

'Last week. He did this to me last week,' she spoke in English. I could hear air being sucked through teeth. The heat in the

Scandinavian custom-built chalet was becoming unbearable. It was only 11.50 a.m.

Another woman spoke, in Nharo: then another and another and another. I had expected more reticence. But the women were becoming increasingly animated – nodding in agreement, shaking their heads in acknowledgement. Sharing secrets together under a tin roof, not sitting alone under the stars. So many women hoping we could get them the help they needed. A social worker from Ghanzi was joining us at lunchtime – she had good ties with the community and the local government-run clinic. She would be effective.

Was I wrong to be relieved the women were opening out about gender violence? Was I wrong to be relieved that my explanation, of how an invisible virus destroys the immune system, had made sense to them? For the demonstration, I had used white rice and red kidney beans to represent white and red blood cells, and tiny black lentils for the HIV virus: the virus that forced shame to come out into the open. So much pain in one space. What a bitter triumph.

And then I saw Maisie standing in the doorway – staring at the wounds a man had carved on a woman's body. She looked bewildered and I felt sick.

'Mummy?' she used her best don't-interrupt-mum-at-work voice, 'Travers says can you come. It's Oakley. I'm so sorry.'

'Go Kate. It's all right,' Irene smiled at me. 'I'll see you at lunchtime.'

I apologized to everyone for leaving early, and, taking Maisie's hand, we went to find her brothers.

The compound was empty. A trestle table had been set up for lunch under a canvas awning – jugs of Oros orange juice and water were warming under the futile shade. A brown mongrel wandered across the yard and settled, panting, under the stoop of the single-storey wooden dormitory chalet. The smell of woodsmoke and cooking meat wafted from somewhere. Lunch was on the way. Maisie, barefoot, led me towards the museum, picking her way through creeping devil thorns, taking care to plant her feet on bare patches of sand between the low-growing weed with its pretty yellow flowers and vicious seeds.

'Is that poor lady why we're here Mummy?'

'Yes Maisie, she is.'

'I see,' she held my sweaty hand more tightly so it didn't slip from her grasp. 'Mum?' her voice was small, hesitant, 'will I get this HIV thingy?'

My daughter was afraid she might contract a disease that children her age back in England had probably never heard of – let alone been in contact with daily. I had been so busy teaching other people I had failed own my child.

'No, my darling you will not,' I replied staunchly, 'none of us will. It's not something you catch like a cold.'

Then and there, sitting on the sand, I taught her the fundamentals of the immune system; using devil-thorn seeds, some droppings a helpful goat had deposited earlier, and yellow flowers.

'HIV is a virus and oddly enough it looks a bit like this devil thorn – with pointy bits sticking out. Viruses are not living things. Can you remember the seven criteria for living things?'

'Nutrition, excretion, reproduction, growing, sensitivity, movement and r something,' she relied promptly.

'Well remembered – respiration is the r you're looking for. Viruses can do all that but they can't reproduce by themselves so they catch a ride in other cells. HIV burrows into a white blood cell just like this,' I explained, plunging a devil thorn into a sun-dried goat pellet, 'the virus carries a coded message that tells the white blood cell to replicate more viruses and soon the white blood cell bursts,' I said, squeezing the goat pellet until it broke apart, 'and out pop lots of HIV viruses that go and infect other white blood cells.'

'Are they in everyone's blood?'

'No, Maisie. The virus has to get in first and it's not easy. HIV can't survive outside the body. It's not lying about on the floor or floating around in the air. It can get into you if you touch the blood of a poor person who has HIV, with an open cut or wound on your hand and their blood mixes with your blood. That's why I always have doctor gloves with me.'

I kept latex gloves in the glove compartment in the car, and always had a box of them at home.

'Do lots of people have it?'

'Lots.'

'Children too.'

'Yes, Maisie children too.' I rummaged in my canvas bag for a bottle of water. 'Here, we need to top up.' We shared the bottle. Long ago Maisie had got used to drinking water with 'bits in it' – often the soggy remnants of a Simba crisp.

'There is another way the virus can get in,' I continued, 'if a man or a big boy has HIV the virus can be in stuff called semen that comes out of big boys' and men's willies. That's why condoms are so very, very important.'

'I know what a condom is,' she giggled.

'I know you do. But they don't just stop babies being made – they stop the virus getting in as well. Just like wearing doctor gloves really.'

'So, none of us are going to get it?'

'None of us my darling one.'

'Good,' she said cheerfully, 'I found a digger-wasp nest this morning – do you want to see it?'

'I'd love to but let's sort out Oaks first.'

And off we pottered.

'Angus says the wasp lays her eggs in an insect she's paralysed, and the lava eat it alive.'

'Some species do, other wasps lay eggs and bring food into the nest every day.'

Maisie looked at me with bright eyes.

'I'm going to see if she brings food,' and she sprinted away, hopping from foot to foot on the midday sand. I watched her until she disappeared into the scrub to find her wasp and laughed: one minute HIV/AIDS and the next digger wasps.

The Oakley drama was nondescript and bowel-related.

'That child has an arse like a tap,' Travers grumbled, 'the museum is really interesting – we've been learning about poison arrows – the poison is squeezed out of the lava from a beetle... it's so cool – but I have to keep taking Oaks out. He must have eaten something bad.'

Oakley looked fine to me, naked and wild, he was playing inside a grass Bushman hut that had been built behind the museum for display.

I found the facsimile hut disquieting. The compound was functional, clean and efficiently run by good people doing their best to empower the Bushmen by keeping ancient practices alive, while at the same time preparing them for the challenges of integration into an increasingly westernized Botswana. But in those days the project was depressing. The Bushmen lived in a separate compound away from Kuru: ghettoized like so many first people.

'Well, better out than in,' I said brightly, 'as long as he keeps drinking water, no worries.'

Lunch was a sombre meal. The social worker was surprisingly indolent and unconvinced that domestic abuse was an issue worth addressing. She conceded alcoholism was rife among the disenfranchised community, but she had had no recent reports of rape or domestic crime. I couldn't believe my ears.

'Well, come to the meeting this afternoon and you will meet women with serious grievances,' I said hotly, but Irene shook her head.

'I don't think so Kate. They will not speak this afternoon.'

'What do you mean? That poor woman who had been lashed and the others were very open.'

'The old women will silence the younger women. You wait. This afternoon will be different.'

It was.

I don't remember what I spoke about – it didn't matter anyway because an impenetrable wall of silence had gone up. Everyone was polite and I assume the translator was honest, but I might as well have recited 'The Jabberwocky'. An hour before the appointed time Irene called the meeting to a close.

Women silenced women.

Suffocating in frustration and suppressed rage, I drove to the tiny village up the road and bought handfuls of warm banana Chappies from the tin shop.

I chomped furiously on the bubblegum until the flavour disappeared and the gum became hard.

'Voices have got to be heard. There must be a way.'

Talking out loud helped me to clear the clamour of rage in my head. I stuffed two more Chappies into my mouth and rolled them around so the dusting of sugar melted on my tongue before the artificial banana flavouring was released.

How can women tell their stories and stay anonymous and safe?

Think.

And to whom do they tell their story?

Who can make a difference?

I chewed until I had an epiphany.

The chief of the whole country that's who.

The President.

Irene and I brainstormed on the drive back to Maun and we came up with a plan. Women could write to the President for help. They could speak freely because there was no obligation to sign the letter. Access to PO boxes was not widespread, but health clinics and tin shops were. If the women delivered their letters to these local centres nurses and shopkeepers could safeguard them and post them all on a specified date to ensure optimal impact. I suggested a title for the exploit.

Post a Letter for Justice Day.

30

Comeragh Road, London 2010

There were steps leading up to a small grey patio at the back of the house. The walls were covered in gravestone ivy, sticky pads on aerial roots seeking the cracks in the bricks: stretching them to breaking point. Untended paving stones were smeared with green slime. The landlords had planted immense pots of broad-leafed functional plants that I was required to nurture. Something had to be done.

Flowers make me happy, my favourite flower is germander speedwell but it grows wild in grassy fields, and can't be bought in London's garden centres. So, I bought pots of blue campanula and honey-scented alyssum and tubs of rosemary and thyme, apple mint and lemon balm. I wound flowering courgette, jasmine and tomato plants around the fence, and planted troughs of lettuce for the slugs. Pots of chives, garlic, sweet william and pansies filled in the gaps and by the evening I had transformed the patio into a Beatrix Potter tumble of colour, which over the next few years self-seeded into a sweet-smelling muddle. This London home had a purpose.

Empathy returns in incremental steps. The consequences of conscience are harsh. Promethean repetition. Healing does not expunge – it exposes. Healing does not exonerate – it challenges. For atheists there is no forgiving God to fall back on. There is no promise of redemption. There is sadness. It's an appropriate feeling. Of course, I don't feel it all the time. But when it finds the cracks I let it in: to remind me.

I knew each child would crack in one way or another. Not now. It would take time. They would break when it was safe. They would break when I was strong enough to hold them. There was no time-scale. Instinct would guide them. My task was to be ready.

31

Santawani Camp, Botswana 1998

'What did you say?' Pieter asked bemused. After a hot, tiring day tracking in Mogogelo pride territory, we were sitting around the table in camp tucking into a hearty vegetable and red kidney bean casserole and the porcupine was rustling under the table on his nightly forage. The children picked up their feet, and popped their heads under the table to watch the gentle creature huffling about between our chairs muttering in low tones.

'Letter for Justice Day,' I replied enthusiastically, 'we are asking all the women in Botswana who have a grievance related to domestic and sexual violence to write to the President.'

'Well good luck with that,' Pieter laughed, 'how on earth do you expect the odd letter to make a jot of difference?'

'That's the point,' I continued, 'it won't be the odd letter. It will be thousands all posted on the same day. Anne's got the radio stations to cover it and the kids and I are off to Mochudi and Gabs to spread the word... so empowering. Anne is—' I stopped. Pieter's attention was elsewhere.

'Well, will you look at that... hold steady, Oaks.'

The porcupine had stopped foraging, and was gazing quizzically at Oakley who was holding out a slice of aubergine. 'Stay still,' whispered Pieter, 'and Porky just might come to you.'

We held our breath, watching the animal tilt its head from side to side, summing up my small son. Oakley's hand stayed steady, and he made soft encouraging sounds – his trill voice unusually low and calm. Wriggling its backside the porcupine rustled up to Oaks, sniffed a couple of times then, taking the vegetable gently between its teeth, it retreated back under the table to devour it.

'It didn't snatch. Did you see that?' Oakley cried, his clear blue eyes shining with delight.

The children cleared the table and Pieter put some more wood on the fire. The sight of his tall, lean body lit by the sparks from an African fire was so ludicrously erotic it made me laugh. The blend of woodsmoke, Pieter's skin, sweet wood fermenting in fresh elephant dung and wild sage was enough to make me want to tear my clothes off then and there. Pieter must have felt it too because he kissed me like we kissed in bed: freely.

'What are we going to play tonight Mum?' called Angus from inside the kitchen hut. 'Botticelli or the Hat Game?'

'Not the Hat Game!' yelled Maisie, 'you always choose stupid people I've never heard of... it's not fair.'

Pieter released me from his arms.

'Seriously?' he laughed.

'I should have used protection. I can only apologize.'

After heated debate we played charades until the children peeled off to their tents one by one at the allotted time. In the bush, Oakley went to bed at the same time as Maisie because it wasn't safe for him to be sent to bed alone. In a few months Travers would be thirteen; thus, under family law, he would be allowed to go to bed when he liked, and drink coffee. Finally, the last tent zip was pulled down, the last goodnight was called and the last 'one more' kiss was blown. Pieter and I were alone.

He poured two large whiskies and we sank back in our chairs looking up at the stars. It was a quiet night: just jackals calling in the distance, something small scuffling in the bushes, the crackle of the fire and a child turning over in its sleep.

'This is my favourite time,' Pieter sighed, taking my hand and

Botswana 1998

kissing my open palm. 'What were you saying earlier, before we were so rudely interrupted?'

'About what?'

'W.A.R. stuff.'

I didn't want to talk about W.A.R. stuff – I wanted him – I wanted this life.

We sat in silence and watched the fire die down.

32

Comeragh Road, London 2010

'Oh my God kill me now,' I cried, thundering downstairs into the kitchen to join Oakley who was cooking supper.

'I have had an afternoon from hell – whoever invented GCSEs should be hung, drawn and quartered,' I growled, taking a Diet Coke from the fridge, 'the dulth of teaching alkanes and alkenes to children who couldn't give a toss is beyond endurance.'

Oakley giggled, grating cheese over a pasta bake and putting it into the oven.

'My child, I have never loved you more, I am starving,' I cried, 'I didn't have enough money on my Oyster, and my arsehole bank refused to give me a five-pound overdraft, so I had to walk all the way back from Golders Green in the pissing rain. I am a shadow of my former self.'

Thanks to the sale of the farm, rent was paid for the year, but living in London was shockingly expensive and the bills were mounting. I had no credit rating and no overdraft facility – so money meant no money. But the house felt like a warm pair of arms. Oakley and I were living in easy companionship, neither of us digging up the past. It was a fallow time: nutrient was accumulating in an undisturbed household.

'I've got some funds on my Oyster, you can take that tomorrow Mum.'

'Thanks darling I'll need to. I have classes in Ealing and Knightsbridge and I think another one might be confirmed in Regent's Park – here's hoping.'

London 2010

I went to set the table, which was strewn with damp paper and spilled coffee: a visual cliché depicting the agony of writing the personal statement. Tidying his work away, I lit the candles for supper. College applications and SAT exam preparation were taking up most of Oakley's time now, and his well-developed grit was standing him in good stead. But how do you encapsulate who you are, in no more than seven hundred words, when you still don't know who you are? My brave boy, who had been through so much, had no points of reference to show him how outstanding he was: his life was merely his life, lived without arrogance or self-promoting pride.

The dining room glowed with light from the kitchen and the fairy lights I had strung up in the patio. The table was squashed between our tumbled bookshelves and the old dresser I had bought in Jo'burg, after the accident, when Pieter was still in my heart.

Over supper Oakley devoured most of the bake. He had just touched six foot and was still growing – almost overnight his body had turned into a man's.

'How many colleges can I apply for?' he asked.

I knew which college he wanted in his heart of hearts, it had been his dream ever since the day Travers had been accepted; during our Midas years in camp – when everything we touched had turned to gold.

'I think we can run to five,' I said, applications were expensive and we had to pick carefully. 'Go for the ones you really want, and then have a safety net just in case everything goes tits up.'

'I'd like to have a couple of runs at my SATs and SAT subject tests too if possible. I can use my best scores.'

'No sweat.'

Oakley laughed. 'I love the fact we're worried about the application fees.'

'Let's worry about getting you in first. I'll worry about tuition fees later. I'll find a way. You just focus on passing the exams, and the quality of your applications.'

'Writing the PS is miserable,' he said, munching on garlic bread, 'the truth is I don't know where I belong, and until I had to write it down I'd never thought about it.'

'We're a global family now, everyone's all over the place.'

'This is about me Mum,' he snapped, 'not my family. I'm English but I feel African. Botswana is my home but to my London friends it means nothing. They don't want to know what it was really like. They just want to hear *bush* stories.' I knew what he meant. I had the same problem: people just wanted me to reaffirm BBC wildlife documentary romanticism. Reality was of little interest.

'Back in Botswana I was Little English Boy,' he continued, using his perfect Setswana accent, 'even though I had no memories of England before that Hollybush Christmas when I was seven. Then living in Jo'burg, learning Zulu, so helpful for applications,' he grinned, 'Carlow Road felt like home, Mamma... I loved that house. We all spent time there. Ems and the babies. Then the farm... that was never home to me... it never felt like home,' his eyes clouded over, 'I don't know where I belong.'

So many homes in his short life: he was trapped on my path. One I hadn't chosen. No one would choose that path.

'Feeling rootless. Maybe that's what you should write about?' I suggested.

'Maybe.'

'Leave it for a bit – let your ideas sediment,' I advised.

My heart ached for him. I had a sense of what he was going through. He liked London but I felt like a stranger in England: lost and useless. Lion researchers were pretty much top of the list of non-essentials in the heart of the great metropolis. I had become an expert in lion reproduction, and with growing concern I had observed a subtle, but definable, reproductive vulnerability in Africa's most iconoclastic species. Any serious work on lions needs a minimum of ten years – we were just getting into our stride when everything was taken away – so pointless – petty and capricious. If it hadn't happened, would we still be in camp? If it hadn't happened? Stop, Kate. Not now. This is about Oaks.

London 2010

What had he said? 'It's about me not my family.' He's untangling himself: they all do at this stage. For the first sixteen years children are along for the ride on their parents' journey, and then they start carving their own path. It's scary. They've got to learn how to work their compass. In the bush I had to walk away from the aluminium body of the Land Rover to use the compass – even non-magnetic metal subtly interfered with the reading. Oakley needs to walk away from me, so I don't interfere.

This is my fifth time round. I've got this.

'I'm going to a debate tomorrow, dearest child of my dreams, at the Royal Geographic: explorers pondering costs and benefits of exploration. Come. It might open out a fresh perspective.'

It did. Listening to Ed Stafford talk about his trek from the source of the Amazon in Peru to its mouth in Brazil inspired Oaks to re-examine his own journey. The Okavango was his river: from babyhood he had glided in wooden canoes through water lilies over pods of hippos – once we had all been tipped up by a hippo – fortunately onto the riverbank and not into its gaping jaws. Oakley had fished in muddy water with sticks and bent hooks, and the annual flood had marked the passing of his years. From babyhood to eight years old he had lived a wild life on smooth water. But aged eight he had been caught in a rip tide that tore us all apart and a year later, just as we were beginning to tread water, we were swept away again: away from Botswana and the lions to an urban jungle in South Africa.

A few weeks later he showed me his personal statement.

I still have a copy: I put it in a plastic sheet to protect it.

33

Botswana 1998

Lion Research, Box 66, Maun
Fax to Emily from Mum

Darlingest of all the Emilys,
I miss you so much I could burst. Thrilled your work in London is going so well. Your last letter made me laugh a lot. So proud of your tenacity and hard work – funding your own round-the-world ticket is a big deal. Slightly crapping myself at the thought of you wandering the globe alone but I know you will suck the juice out of every second. Things this end are great.

WHOOP WHOOP LION CAMP NOW HOME: see new address above.

The final move to Santawani Camp done during biblical storm, so all the mattresses I had strapped to the roof of car arrived in camp like soggy sandwiches – but books and children dry. School all set up in the kitchen hut – I bought the bookshelves and cosy bits and bobs so it looks like home. Tents comfy with our beds in them – no need for all our heavenly PEP store blankets, as sweltering rainy season upon us.

Our first night as a proper lion family was interesting. Woken up by shattering thunder. Jove clearly not pleased and hurling lightning about with gay abandon. Convinced the children would be smitten in their sleep, I leapt out into the tempest, stark naked, to sort things out.

With lightning dancing around my feet I rolled down all the window flaps in the tents. Tiny knots and wet fingers not a good combo. Finally had all windows protected and then I noticed the flysheets were straining under the accumulating water, and remembering what P had told me about how important it was to keep flysheets taut, I heaved the sagging canvas up and tipped about a million gallons of water all over me. At which point a hyena whooped close by and I legged it back to our tent. P looked at me in wild amaze, and rolled over mumbling something about me being out of my mind. So, all in all a great first night!

The kids are thrilled to bits and love being proper bush children. I promised to drive them to rollerblading in town every Wednesday evening. Vital they keep in touch with chums. P did lots of eye-rolling, as it's nearly a two-hour drive to town in the rainy season. Anyway, he's not doing the driving so can't see what the prob is. As you know there is a slight diff in our approach to parenting ha ha! Gus has christened him Murdstone – which on a bad day is not far off the mark. Oh, but on a good day he is bliss.

I ache to hear your voice – this global family lark is all very well but not being able to chat with you at will is miserable. The children miss you like crazy, but Maisie in particular misses sister time. They all loved your last letter, but if you could send a special one to her it would be mega.

Trav has taken on the mantle of being the 'oldest' and is driving them all crazy with his bossiness. He means well, and he is being so diligent at school it brings tears to my eyes. He is simply the best and chivvies the others to start school on time and behave at the school table. He is setting a brilliant example and truly, bar the odd strop, school is going beautifully.

Maisie had a small conniption the other day and stormed out of class (the drama was about where the sodding stratosphere went on a model they are making of the atmosphere) but Trav went after her and must have done some magic because she came back all sweetness and light.

Oh, you would have died laughing.

The other day I built Oaks a wigwam, and hung a buffalo skull from a lion kill over the entrance – a bit stinky but Oaks loved it. He made a real den with blankets and odds and sods he scavenged. Then I caught him striding across camp wearing nothing but a francolin feather headdress and a natty pair of green knicks, with something stuffed down the front of them:

'Oaks?'

'Yes.'

'What's in your knickers?'

'Nothing.'

'Can you come here please?'

Down the knicks were a packet of Pieter's cigs and a lighter.

His plan had been to smoke a peace pipe in his wigwam.

P not quite as amused as I was.

Working hard lioning every day. Trav is the best at navigating around the study area. I am still getting hopelessly lost, which is pissing me off, but it's brilliant that Trav is shining in the field. He has a gift for detail and P is genuinely impressed by him. Trav's confidence is growing day by day which is vital because he is still battling with his reading and spelling, and despite working his arse off Gus is always a few steps ahead. I have to be scrupulously fair when I'm marking their work, and boy it can be heartbreaking. I see the labour Trav puts in preparing for a test and Gus just does a quick bit of revision in the back of the car and always scores higher. Not by far, but he's top of the class. Trav very sanguine about it, and Gus never gloats so no drama, but it must hurt. But when we are out with the lions things even out beautifully, and everyone has skill sets that we rely on as a team. Maisie sees everything – the other day we were driving home and she was reading in the back of the car and mentioned casually there was a leopard in a tree. Indeed, there was, hidden high in the branches, how she had seen it in her peripheral vision is beyond me.

I am reading every scientific paper written on lions till my eyes bleed. It's fascinating reading but some stuff is frustrating the hell out of me. As you know I am very mechanistic and I am reading lots of statements about lion behaviour with very little mechanistic justification. However, I'm keeping my trap shut until I have finished reading them all, and done a bit of pondering. But questions are mounting. I am riveted by every aspect of this work but I'm still learning so many of the basics of field research that, for now, it's best to put my head down and learn how to patch an inner tube.

Pieter took me through the process the other day and though I was trying my best to pay attention I find him so impossibly sexy when he is doing all that 'manly' stuff that I just melt into a puddle. Who knew your hardcore feminist mum was a blithering 19th century maiden.

Things at W.A.R. going well... they have some proper funding now. It's taken on a new lease of life. We have a lawyer now, and several people, who I think joined after you left Bots, are currently in training to be counsellors, all Motswana, so that's brilliant.

Pete going away next week and I will be in charge of lioning. I must say I find it a bit daunting but bugger me sideways it's exciting.

What a life-changing time we are all having.

I am so-o-o-o-o-o-o happy.

Write soon huge love and a million kisses.

Mamma xx

34

Comeragh Road, London 2010

Work. Bills. Food. Sitting on an Underground train eyes front. Mind the doors please. Wet floors, watch your step. I was safe in the fear of London's streets. I was challenged by city life, and challenge is always a good thing.

One day I went to Westminster Abbey and paid for an audio guide. I was startled to hear an old friend's voice in my ears: Jeremy Irons had been a comfort to me when my baby son Rufus died. Jeremy was one of the few friends who talked about it. Most of the others were too scared of the sorrow. He was an excellent guide and I enjoyed his company, and the stories in the stone and the motes of dust spinning in slivers of spangled light. The soft echo of footfall, and the hush of death inside a monolith, soothed me. Standing in front of St Edward's Chair, on which British monarchs have been crowned since the 1300s, I was moved. Yet, it didn't make my heart soar with wonder. Instead I wondered why we celebrate clinging to tradition. Does an action have value merely because it has been done before? I came out blinking in the late-afternoon sunlight and looked at the anachronism of Parliament. It should be a museum. Thinking about a New World should be done in light and space, not huddled in old rooms reeking of smoke and polish and old people's breath. Weighed down by history I heaved a great fuck you, and walked home along the Embankment.

Why was I feeling a scratch of anger again? Why was I feeling lost in my own country? There were so many petty rules, so many precautions, so many little ways of limiting personal freedom. We are all born anarchists, we learn to conform and speak in shibboleths, and that's reasonable. But in addition we are urged to be afraid of anarchy, and I resisted that instruction with gathering energy.

Anarchy is not lawless – it functions under natural laws. It is self-regulating and organically responsive to change. It has compassion and reason. Anarchy celebrates personal freedom and urges decentralized cooperation. Anarchy is not a chaotic system – it is constrained by morality, justice and personal responsibility. It is alive, constantly re-evaluating, anarchists do not get comfort from the status quo. London is nourished by the status quo, despite its undeniable diversity, energy and creativity: it is still rooted in the Changing of the Guard at Buckingham Palace. London feeds on the dust of pomp and circumstance: it chokes me.

The smell of the river was comforting. The sweet rot of water reminded me of home, the river was going to be my refuge. London had to be home for the foreseeable future so suck it up Kate, and make the best of it. It doesn't matter where you are. You have a job to do. Alice Miller the shit out of this.

I had first read Alice Miller when Maisie was a baby.

Miller's unsentimental, practical and uncompromising insight into children's hearts and minds was painful reading. She was a Swiss psychologist and psychoanalyst whose seminal book, *For Your Own Good: The Roots of Violence in Child-Rearing*, offered the hurt child in me advocacy that healed my heart. It also caused me to tremble as a parent of four young children. Looking at the world through a child's eyes revealed the many ways a child could be hurt by poor judgement and lack of empathy. I devoured all her books and metaphorically Alice took my hand and guided me through the jungle of child-rearing. I slipped and fell many times, and apologized to the children when I was unreasonable, unfair, cross or misunderstood them. They knew I was fallible, but they trusted I would never lose sight of them. But I did. I did.

Pounding the pavement with speedy steps, the anger was rising again. Don't be angry. Take the long route back. Think. The river is beautiful in twilight – lights on the bridges – a lone rower sculling rhythmically against the current – a plastic bag full of air spinning in an eddy – an old iron barge full of rubbish trundling towards its depot. The river is living history, older than the city, replenishing, purposeful. When the Abbey has crumbled, the river will still rise and journey for two hundred and twenty-nine miles to the sea: as inevitably as the shifting plates beneath my feet will go on splitting and binding continents, spilling lava, cracking open the earth and making mountains. Toffee Mountains. Our first day at school. All that time ago when the children were small.

 I remembered pounding the sand tracks behind the Thamalakane River pondering on what hook I should hang our first class. Rocks hiding in plain sight. My step quickened with my understanding. The children. Hiding in plain sight. Grown up now. Kind. Forgiving. As loving as ever. Perhaps even more so, but not healed. Thoughts came like splinters. Pictures in my head. Sounds. The sound of Emily's voice when I told her what had happened. I heard it now. Her pain. And I wasn't there for her. Travers in the doorway. Mourning for what he had lost. How did he know? Angus struggling to keep ahead – to understand what I couldn't. A young brain burning with old thoughts. And Maisie. My breathing came too fast, too shallow. I leaned on the wall overlooking the river and tried to remember the order of the bridges: which came first, was it Battersea or Chelsea? Which was the pretty one? The one with the paint? Breathe. Maisie was fourteen. She'd been fourteen for a month when it happened. Her path into womanhood all fogged up. I can't redo that bit. I can't take back that time. Shining a light into her pain is going to be unbearable. Fuck that. Alice Miller would hold no truck with self-pity. Look at the child. Get inside her head. Walk in her shoes. You couldn't then – you can now. Be prepared. Jesus there's a lot of them. Five. So many stories. None must get torn up. Each paragraph must be revisited. Oakley's story was easier in the beginning. I could manage his eight-year-old needs: we were a fierce team. But he was there all the way through:

no escape, clinging to a broken person, loving me and battling. Flying high at each new breakthrough: relishing each happy day. Doggedly swimming against my stream each time I spiralled downwards, until he was exhausted. Each one of them has splinters of childhood stuck in their hearts. And when they are ready I must pull out the thorns. I pictured them at the Mission House lined up on the sofa after bath time like Russian dolls. Bare feet presented for inspection. One day I had pulled out a thorn as thick as a matchstick from Oakley's ankle. He had been so proud: it was the biggest thorn ever.

Time to go home now. Heaving myself away from the wall, I walked on. My step was steady. The anger had gone. The air was cool and refreshing. There was an easy rhythm in my stride, and then I felt someone coming up behind me and I faltered. He was too close. Looming. Driven by terror an animal sound rose up inside me contracting my throat. I could feel the heat. My legs buckled and my vagina desiccated. He passed by. Innocent of what he'd done. I breathed away the panic. I thought I'd got through that. Maybe that will always happen. Brush that fear away as you do a fly.

I had been angry earlier because I was afraid.

Walking in the children's shoes was going to hurt, and it would hurt for ever.

35

Santawani Camp, Botswana 1998

'Something doesn't make sense to me,' I exclaimed, 'if it's true that lions don't go back into their regular reproductive cycle until their cubs are one and a half what is stopping them?'

'Go on.'

'What do you mean go on? I'm asking you a question.'

'Develop it.'

I was sitting on the sand by the fire drinking a glass of Johnnie Walker. Pieter was in his chair – he never huddled on the ground.

'Develop it,' I mimicked, 'that's very pompous, Dr Kat.'

'Not at all. It was a perfectly reasonable request. What could be delaying oestrus?'

'That's just it, I can't find any sensible mechanistic explanation that might delay oestrus. Poor nutrition? Scratch that, there is plenty to eat. Regular suckling? Scratch that, females suckle sporadically and some females don't suckle for days at a time. Phenomenal suppression due to dominance hierarchy? Scratch that too – not applicable to lions who live in fission – fusion groups. I can't find any biological mechanism that could suppress oestrus for nearly a year after the cubs are weaned.'

'So maybe there isn't one.'

Wriggling my toes into a patch of fire-warmed sand, I poked the fire back into life. I loved watching the sparks flying in the cold night air: woodsmoke curling into my hair.

The lions' behaviour was a source of endless fascination. As any self-respecting lion researcher should, I had read George Schaller's seminal work *The Serengeti Lion*, and every scientific paper written so far on lions, and it was becoming clearer that some aspects of lion behaviour in the Okavango did not fit into the model presented by long-term studies of East African lions. Differences in behaviour or 'culture' were perfectly reasonable given that the populations were responding to diverse ecological pressures.

Even in our study, prides had their own 'cultural' practices. The Mogogelo pride hunted throughout the day – often snacking on baboon. The Santawani pride hunted at night, and their thoughts on baboons were akin to mine on the Christmas sprout: to be avoided at all costs. Once we saw a baboon fall out of a tree and land in a crumpled heap in front of the Santawani pride – who stepped neatly over the bemused animal and walked on without a backward glance.

Lions are adaptable: historically they had ranged successfully across Africa, parts of Europe and Asia and they had learned how to 'make a plan'. However, an aspect of female lion reproductive biology puzzled me. It had been suggested that females entered a pseudo-oestrus. And I had racked my brains trying to think of an environmental pressure that could have driven Nature to select in favour of false oestrus.

The moon was waning and the stars were running wild. The only sound was the spitting of the fire. A sudden kerfuffle broke the peace, and the walls of the boys' tent billowed as someone from the inside was punching the canvas trying to break through. Ripping open the zip Angus rolled onto the sand screaming in terror.

Running over to him, and careful not to touch him, I spoke calmly.

'It's Mum, Gus. I'm here. It's Mum. You're safe.'

I knew not to touch him while he was caught up by the horrors in his head.

His eyes were blazing with fear and he looked around him desperately.

'It's Mum, Gus. You're safe. Can you hear me?' I spoke neutrally, careful not to break into his space harshly. Slowly the craze of his night terror faded and he stopped writhing.

'I'm going to touch you now. Is that all right?'

His eyes were glazed and his cheeks were burning red. I stroked back his hair and he flinched briefly before relaxing.

'It's Mum, Gus there's nothing to be afraid of now.' I took him in my arms and rocked him while he came back into consciousness.

Travers was standing in the tent watching his brother, concerned yet sanguine: he was used to such disturbance. Since toddlerhood in Hollybush Cottage, calm, unflappable Angus had had night terrors, and they continued unabated.

'What was it this time Gus? A bear, a snake?' inquired Travers.

'Dunno... can't remember. Sorry Mum.'

'Don't be silly my darling, do you want a cup of hot Milo?' I asked.

'No... back to sleep,' he mumbled, 'sorry everyone. All right now.'

'Is Gus all right?' murmured Maisie sleepily from her tent.

'All fine. Go back to sleep now.' I tucked the boys back into bed, zipped up their tent, and wandered back to the fire.

'Do you worry about that?' asked Pieter who had observed the escapade from his chair.

'Of course I do, but I've been told he will grow out of it. I have no idea what triggers him. Sometimes he can go for months without one, and then bam out of nowhere a whopper like that one.'

'We've got to be careful about that. He can't go gallivanting out of his tent like that... it's dangerous if there's something around.'

The pronoun 'we' warmed me. Sharing the children was not

easy – boundaries were stepped over – expectations were confused – territories were unmapped.

I kissed him on the top of his head.

'I love you Dr Kat, quite a lot actually.'

'Shall we go to bed?'

'Yes, but I want to carry on with what we were talking about before we were so rudely interrupted. Oestrus – I'm riveted.'

Later that night I lay awake thinking.

There are few sights more enchanting than a tumble of females and their cubs, wildlife documentaries thrive on the saccharine, but they obscure the darker, less romantic reality of lion motherhood. The notion that Nature is perfect obfuscates a simple and defining fact of life: all Nature has to be is good enough. Perfection is an ephemeral aesthetic construct. Lion mothers were not perfect. All the cubs in the study were identified with minute accuracy, but they were not given names until they were a year old: the reason was simple – less than half made it to their first birthday. Life is tough in the wilderness and maternal behaviour was at times laissez-faire. Not all females were negligent, far from it. Some were very nurturing, but others had a take-it-or-leave-it approach to small cubs.

Only the other day, we had watched three adult females wander across Baby Jackal Plane at dusk, leaving five twelve-week-old cubs out in the open alone and unprotected. We waited for one of the females to return, but they all continued on their merry way disappearing into acacia woodland without a backward glance. The next day we found the females on an impala kill: not a cub in sight. The baby lions had been left to sort themselves out: learning starts early in the wild. Twenty-four hours later they had rejoined the adults. Oakley was overjoyed.

I needed to pee. Easing myself out of bed I tiptoed out of the tent, shining my torch around into the darkness before squatting down. Balancing on my haunches I kept shining the light until the last dribble; it would be foolish not be aware of my vulnerability.

The children always woke each other and had a pee partner: a rule they never broke. I kicked sand over the urine, and before slipping back into bed I wiped the sand off my feet.

My mind was racing, something I had seen that week had puzzled me. One of our study prides had two cohorts of cubs aged three months and five months. All the females were lactating, and thus supposedly not in oestrus and sexually attractive. So, why had one of the collared pride males paid a visit to the family and attempted to mate with a lactating female with five-month-old cubs? She flattened out on the sand doing all she could to make her vagina inaccessible, but he was persistent. He forced entry and the other females attacked him ferociously: roaring, biting, cuffing. He darted off and then whipped back for a further attempt. This time he was summarily dismissed and skulked away into the undergrowth. A lion who was not due to return to her reproductive cycle for a year had smelled sexy to him: oestrogen was Chanel No. 5 for lions. The smell of her sex had driven him to flehmen; a lip-curling, teeth-baring, neck-stretching involuntary ecstasy. There was nothing pseudo about that oestrus. Her urine elicited flehmen for several days.

The night air chilled the canvas walls. Rolling over, I lay against Pieter's back to absorb his warmth, and lulled by his peaceful breathing I fell asleep.

Over breakfast we had a family meeting.

'The females sniff each other's pee,' said Angus, helping himself to several vegetarian schnitzels, 'and they do flehmen too, not just the males.' He looked up as Pieter joined us for coffee.

'Mum wants us to record what happens when the females sniff each other's fannies and pee,' continued Angus.

'Oh she does, does she?' remarked Pieter drily. 'Well as it happens I think it's a good idea so we will add that to the list of obs.'

His patronizing tone irritated the hell out of me, but I sucked it up. It would take time for me to earn my spurs.

'Among females with cubs and occasionally during pregnancy,

sexual behaviour has been recorded,' I quoted from a paper. 'Schaller mentions it too, so do Pennycuick and Rudnai, but only in passing. Also, pre- and post-partum mating have been noted: so there must be elevations in oestrogen.'

'There is a non-invasive way you can test for steroid hormones,' Pieter paused to pour himself more coffee, 'it's not been done much in the field but we could discuss it with someone I know at the Smithsonian.'

'What do we test?'

'Poop. We can test for levels of steroid hormone metabolites in poop. If you can collect enough regular samples you might be able to gather enough data to look at estradiol peaks.'

And so began the lion crap years, and I would not change one glorious, malodorous moment. Merry evenings spent wading through carefully labelled bags of poop, to be sent away for hormonal analyses, offered insight into fluctuations in parasite load and into the lions' diets. To my amusement we found they regularly snacked on small birds, springhares and other small prey: *amuse bouches* to keep them going between large kills.

36

Botswana 1999

Lion Research, Box 66, Maun
Fax to Ian McNeice from Kate

Darling Neecie,
You won't believe this but we have moved *again*. Santawani Camp was taken over by new management, and they evicted us because they wouldn't allow children under twelve on the site. A ghastly man, in knee-hi powder-blue socks and gynaecologically short shorts, gave us 24 hours to quit. Charming. I hated him until he told me he had seen a child crushed and killed by an elephant – at that I mellowed – what an awful thing to witness.

Anyway, the kids were mega as always. We all offered to go back to Maun so Pete could stay in Santawani, but he wouldn't hear of it. So, we packed up lock stock and barrel and high-tailed it to town – where we camped in Audi Camp (you remember that nice place with the pool we went to when you were here last). I was doing my usual 'It'll all be all right' lark but inside I was packing it.

Anyway, you won't believe what happened next. P and I were in Spar doing some rather lugubrious shopping for supper when we bumped into Karl-Heinz Gimpel in the tins and dried goods aisle. The darling man heard our tale of woe and promptly offered us some space behind a safari camp he has just put up on the

Gomoti River. We arrived in Spar gormless and homeless, and left stuffed to the gunnels with gorm and with a sprightly spring in our step.

Two days later we drove two cars piled high with our possessions into Gomoti, and when I saw the spot we had been allocated I felt desolate. I had brought our kids all the way from the comfort of Hollybush to sweet fuck all.

Home was a patch of sand.

The clearing was surrounded on three sides by dense palm scrub – making it impossible to see if predators were lurking in the scrub – it was far more dangerous than Santawani.

Pieter drove over to the edge of a thicket where some tired acacia trees had battled against elephants. One had been bent over but it was still rooted in the sand creating a wonky living arch. Like our storm-ripped apple tree in Hollybush... do you remember?

Pieter said it gave us the best shade, which was bollocks because I had parked under a huge twin-trunked camelthorn acacia tree with wide-spreading branches that offered a generous pool of shade. I was too tired to argue... apparently he wanted to save it for a greater purpose... that's where we will put a mess tent... one day... when we get funding. Ha bloody ha.

Oh, but this will make you so proud, Neecie. While I was sitting in the car being Mrs Gummage, all lone and lorn, Maisie was clambering over the tailgate of Pieter's truck pulling a rake behind her. I watched our nine-year-old girl walk over to the fallen tree and busily prepare the ground for our tents. Working systematically, pulling the rake behind her and retracing her steps a rake's width apart, she worked doggedly in the heat until the ground was nearly as smooth as marble. What a girl we made, Neecie.

Mojo returned – I whizzed over to join the boys who were unloading the tent poles. When Maisie had finished raking, Pieter and the boys dragged one of our metal tables upside down over the raked patch to create a silky base for the tent floor. Putting up Meru tents is not hard if you know what you're doing, and Pieter gave clear instructions. We had three to put up before nightfall: one for us, one for the kids, and one for storage, books and project equipment.

Maisie and Oakley were too short to be much help putting up the tents, and I was too busy struggling with rusty tent poles to notice what they were doing. In time, I heard hammering and looking up I saw Maisie had created our kitchen underneath the arched tree: she was hammering nails into the trunk to hang up the saucepans. Oakley had been seconded to unpack the boxes and bin liners containing our cutlery and plates, and he had laid out bottles of dried herbs in neat rows on the metal table they had set up under the tree. So bloody resourceful.

I hooked up the fridge to the gas bottle so we could keep the poops frozen. Yes, we still have lion crap freezing in the freezer – what Health and Safety would say I have no idea. We are working on a new system, and have sent away for desiccant so we can dry the poop. You won't be surprised to hear I unloaded all the books (despite some derogatory comments re prioritizing). A home is not a home without books.

By nightfall glowing hurricane lamps were hanging from the trees, hot water bottles were warming the beds, Pieter's vegetable curry was cooking on the stove under the Kitchen Tree, the books were lined up in the bookshelves ready for school in the morning, and a lion was roaring from the other side of the river.

I hope beyond hope that Gomoti Camp will be home for a long time.

We are all longing to see you, and your last care package was a huge success. I have picked up an old TV/VCR, which we can run on solar power – so much excitement about your new DVDs.

Love to you and Cindy,
Kate xxxxxxxx

37

Comeragh Road, London 2011

'I miss the smell of rain.'

'Me too,' I sighed.

Maisie was calling from the tiny terraced house she rented with friends in Stoneybatter, Dublin. She was preparing for her graduating exhibition at the National College of Art and Design, and finalizing her BA thesis on olfactory art.

'I heard a lion roar last night Mum... from the zoo... long roaring like Inferno calling from across the river. It took me right back to Gomoti,' she sounded sad. 'Mum, what's the name of that book you read us when we were little... the one about the Neanderthals?'

'*The Inheritors* by William Golding,' I replied.

'That's the one. I loved that book. The family don't use words... they share pictures in their heads... they "see" the forest with their feet and noses... that's what I remember when I was a child... but everything is slipping now.'

The sharp rawness of life gets blunted when survival no longer depends on reading messages carried on the air. Smell traps a memory, like amber captures a fly, but as time passes the context fades leaving behind a displaced feeling: a sense of yearning for a moment that is lost in our internal universe. I had read Maisie's unedited thesis, and in it she used a word that was new to me: *Sehnsucht*: a word more powerful than 'nostalgia'. She wrote:

'When I was a barefoot child I lived in a tent in the Okavango

Delta, Botswana, in an environment close to the one in which our species evolved. I could smell rain in the air a day before the first drops fell on parched earth. I could smell the sweetness of death from a lion kill, carried across kilometres by the wind, as easily as I could smell the elephants that nightly browsed the acacia branches above my tent. The smells of the African bush are stored in my sensory memory and are conjured by thoughts, visual images, sounds, tastes and feelings, but of all my senses smell evokes the most profound emotional memories. Sometimes language is unable to describe the potent power of sensory experience and the German word *Sehnsucht*, meaning inconsolable longing, best encapsulates the confusing amalgamation of the evanescent and the everlasting that lies at the heart of our olfactory memory.'

I wondered if each of us would always feel an inconsolable longing for Botswana: if the feeling of 'coming home' would always be expressed in the scent of a mopane leaf crushed in my hand.

'Gussie's here, Mum, he came to see me... we collected elephant shit from the zoo yesterday.'

'I beg your pardon,' I laughed.

'It's for my installation... just an impression of camp, nothing obvious... I asked a perfumier to create the smell of rain... it was fascinating working with her... defining each element. Cindy helped me to source old canvas... it smells just right, like my old Meru, and inside the canvas I'm playing a video I made... images of trees... movement... fading in and out... things you almost see but don't... I dunno... does that sound crap to you?'

'Utter bollocks, why on earth you can't do nicely framed pictures of sunsets and giraffes is beyond me,' I teased. 'I am longing to see your exhibition Mais... I will be there at the opening with bells on.'

'I'm scared, Mum.'

'Of course you are, because you care. But I'm not. I read your thesis Maisie: it's brilliant.'

'No, it's not,' she snapped – her usual knee-jerk reaction to praise.

It was an outstanding marriage of the arts, humanities and science, in which she examined the work of olfactory artists and architects; cross-cultural differences in relationship to smells; historical shifts in human responses to smell, and recent studies on the olfactory neural network and its direct connections with the limbic system. Of the five senses the olfactory system has the most direct pathways to the hippocampus and the amygdala – structures in the limbic system responsible, respectively, for memory, the fight-or-flight response and emotions. Maisie's examiners shared my opinion on the quality of her work, and a few weeks later she was granted a first-class degree.

After our phone call, I sat staring at the faded face of a young lion hanging on the wall: a picture Maisie had drawn for me as a birthday present long ago, using what she had at hand – an old mascara stick. She had always spoken through her hands, and in the smudgy shadows she had articulated the innocent sadness of fleeting time and lost hope. Lions were teetering on the edge of existence: on the threshold between what was and what is to come.

Lying back on the sofa I pictured all the lions that had passed through our lives: hundreds and hundreds of them. And the cubs... so many... most of them had died. In our study area too many adult females had died without replacing themselves... a rate of attrition that was not sustainable. Maisie had watched their complex stories unfold and during her childhood she had observed the edges smudge between lion and human domains. She described the conflict between man, cattle and lion in an animation called *The Buffalo Fence*: images gradually erased frame by frame, as lions are being erased population by population.

I felt deflated: life in camp had been so full of hope... so full of energy. Day after day gathering data... learning... sharing information with the government. Believing our work would make a difference.

The children never tired of putting the lions first: so many times we had risen in the night when we had heard a lion calling – just to check its ID. If it was a nomadic male moving through we would ID him, and biopsy him so as to add his DNA to our growing database.

Pieter was a highly experienced geneticist, and not only could DNA verify paternity, but also we could build a picture of the degree of relatedness across prides. My observations had revealed that at times pride males were cuckolds. Combining meticulous observational data with genetic evidence was going to be revealing.

Getting a biopsy was time-consuming but reasonably non-invasive. We shot a dart into the lion's hindquarters and the dart bounced out pulling with it a small plug of flesh. The dart had a fluffy red tail attached to it that made it easy to retrieve the precious samples. We had tiny plugs specially designed for the cubs. We sampled many hundreds of lions. Thousands of patient hours... it seemed so pointless now... I lay back on a pillow remembering the baking-hot hours in the car with the children... eyes glued to binoculars... whispering whisker patterns... recording the colour of their little noses: pink, pink spotty, grey or black... IDs of the cubs required infinite patience... hidden in the grass or tumbling over the females in search of a teat... there... that one... write down its number I have the shot... the children not moving a muscle as I aimed for the tiny safe target on the cub's hindquarters... grass blowing in a sudden breeze obscuring my line of sight... a female getting up to pee and all the cubs shuffling places... redoing all the IDs... waiting again... for the clean shot... if in doubt leave it... don't disturb the peace unnecessarily... there's always another day. Take your time... I thought we had time.

After years of gathering genetic data we sent off our carefully stored, irreplaceable samples. I remembered our excitement waiting for the results. Months went by. No news. The lions kept their secret stories.

It began to rain. Odourless London rain. I went downstairs to cook supper.

38

Gomoti Camp, early December 1999

The candles were wilting in the summer heat, and I was marking schoolwork and listening to the familiar night-time burble: vigorous tooth-brushing and spitting, the glug of water bottles being filled at the sink; someone pattering to the bookshelves; someone squirting Tabard insect repellent, sending spindrifts of toxic chemicals into the air that would cause mosquitoes to hold their noses and rush back home to mother and someone impatiently revving up the car.

'Night Mum.'

'Night my angels.'

Two more last kisses from Oakley, then the children bundled into the car and chugged a few hundred metres to bed: from time to time a lion or two meandered through camp, and the children would wait in the car until all was clear before unzipping their tents and settling in for the night. It was early December and a stirring in the air carried the distant smell of rain. Putting down my pen I breathed in the mossy nourishment. Winter dust had made way for cotton-mud, and halcyon skies were blackened by thunderclouds. Sweet new grass drew the buffalo out of the permanent swamps, and the lions followed the herds across the flood plains. Waterlogged soil hidden under feathery grasses made tracking the study animals a precarious business. It was rescue season.

Earlier in the day a class on Fraunhofer lines had been interrupted. I had begun the class by laying out a bowl of carrots and green apples, and talking simply about how different objects absorb and reflect different wavelengths of light, and I was in the middle of reading an excerpt from 'Bar Codes in the Stars', a chapter in *Unweaving the Rainbow* in which Dawkins poetically explains how elements in the stars absorb different wavelengths of light, when Pieter's voice crackled over the camp radio.

'Gomoti, Gomoti come in.'

Pieter's tone over the airwaves caused the children to scatter into action without need for instruction: he was ratty so he must be stuck.

Angus answered the radio.

'This is Gomoti, where are you Pieter?'

Travers was already at the workshop collecting the tow chain.

Oakley was filling water bottles and Maisie was packing up sunscreen and biscuits.

'On the Mogogelo past the horseshoe near the bush where Vouvray had her den last year. Bring the chain. Tell the mother to take care at horseshoe it's very boggy... for God's sake don't get stuck too.'

I giggled. The heat made him cranky, but I loved the nakedness of summer.

It was a pretty standard extraction: after digging under the tyres and laying down some wood for traction, the chain was attached and with a few tugs from Land Rover 2, Land Rover 1 slid out of the mud as easily as a milk tooth from a soft gum. The children and I were soggy, and even cool Pieter looked a bit moist around the edges. Despite it being 40 degrees in the shade, he was wearing long trousers and laced-up boots, but his shirt was off and his smooth skin was dimpled with evaporating beads of sweat. His working smell made me ache and, sending the children on ahead, we drove home alone: we took our time.

From the kitchen table I could see Pieter's reading light glowing inside our tent – he was still awake – I sighed. When I had finished going over the children's essays I would take off my cotton dress and strip-wash alone in the kitchen, then I would spray Yves Saint Laurent Y onto warm skin, and slide into bed beside him, brushing my body against his, and we would have easy summer sex and laugh. But a deal was a deal. The kids always delivered their work on time, and I always marked it the same day.

I settled back to work surrounded by an allurement of nocturnal companions: creamy lacewing moths fluttered around flames that cast a puddle of light on the tablecloth, in which swayed a gathering of emerald and copper-spotted praying mantises, their eyes trained on glinting Japanese beetles. Small powder-blue moths landed briefly before flying off towards the moonlight; and black beetles, the size of pinheads, zigzagged through the throng hoping for the best. A few dusty stink bugs released a sharp smell of rotting grass and hastily I put a plate over my heavily diluted glass of brandy – one tiny beetle landing in a bowl of food could transform even the tastiest dish into raw silage.

Despite some creative spelling, and a few grammatical errors, the children's work was shockingly good. Indeed, I had to reread each piece to make sure I hadn't over-romanticized. It was hard maintaining objectivity, and to help me I used a marking scheme that enabled each child to identify problems and progress. Marks were allocated for content, vocabulary, grammar and presentation. They took pride in making their work look good: artistic Maisie set the bar high. Against the onslaught of paper wasps I protected their work in plastic sheets. I have years of irreplaceable written history stored in a white trunk at the bottom of my bed.

The term's project was to write and illustrate a 'book' of anecdotes and recipes, to be printed on home-made elephant-shit paper and sold in the local safari camp to augment pocket money. Making paper from the fibrous, sweet-smelling excrement was a craft project and a biology lesson. Ellie poop is rich in germinating seeds and partially digested branches: an inefficient digestive system means elephant only absorb about 44 per cent of what they eat. They use their stomachs for storage and digestion takes place in the gut – most of it in the hind gut via fermentation. The bush offered endless means by which to teach a blended UK, US and South African curriculum. Oakley soaked up information like a sponge and by the age of ten he had informally covered the whole GCSE biology curriculum without even breaking into a sweat.

The children had embraced the project with alacrity, and after a few weeks had been inspired to write a chapter book. Frankly, I felt they were over-ambitious but naturally I supported their effort, and that night I was marking their first attempt. They had divided the chapter into three parts with a common thread: Life in the Bush.

Rereading Travers's section, the hairs on my arms stood up: he had found his written voice. The pictures in his dyslexic brain were reflected by evocative words describing a morning game drive.

A thought was gathering in the corners of my mind, and, watching a praying mantis hunt, I pondered. Soon a hapless moth wandered too close and was snatched up – fluttering in a resolute grip, the creature was delicately manoeuvred this way and that. The expression in the predator's eyes was apologetic and it ate with the utmost decorum – its antennae waving like a feather in an Ascot hat, and its paws bent neatly downwards with a whisper of an outstretched pinky.

An hour later, scented and still damp from my wash, I slipped into bed. Pieter was asleep. The air in the tent was heavy with heat – maybe there would be cooling rain tomorrow. I lay against him lightly and he woke.

'It's you,' he said sleepily.

'In person not a picture,' I laughed.

'Work done?'

'All sorted,' I said, kissing his lips, 'I've had an idea.'

'Tell me about it,' he murmured into my neck, 'later.'

It turned out to be a good idea. It changed the children's lives. But it would be some time before we learned how.

It was a busy month: end-of-term exams, lioning and rainy-season preparations. Drainage pits were dug, tent flaps were repaired and tied down and plastic sheeting was stretched across the open walls in the kitchen.

Everyone who lived in camp was busy. Stephen spent a great deal of time in the workshop mending tyres; Lettie and Rhoda spent a great deal of time watching the sky and hurriedly pulling down clothes from the clothes line before black clouds burst over camp. Clothes and light summer sheets had to be ironed to kill botfly larvae, and a huge mosquito net was hung up in the mess tent under which we snuggled when watching videos. But high winds and biblical storms could not dampen spirits, for Emily was coming for Christmas and the Millennial New Year: the countdown had begun.

The day before Christmas Eve we got to town early. We had a lot to do before the Air Botswana plane carrying Emily landed at 3.10 p.m. It was a burning day, not even a wisp of cloud floated in an azure sky.

Pieter, Travers and Oakley picked up gas bottles, diesel, inner tubes; got two tyres fixed and popped into the garage to check up on some rather ominous knocking in the Land Rover pickup's engine.

Angus, Maisie and I went to the bank – and spent hours in a queue long enough for the average reader to complete *War and Peace* and get a head start on Gibbon's *Rise and Fall*. Finally, melting, and clutching much-needed pula, we drove to the air-conditioned heaven of Maun Food and Produce to stock up on Christmas rations.

MFP was bristling with Christmas goodies: painted biscuit tins depicting snowy Victorian scenes, chocolate Father Christmases, boxes of mince pies decorated with holly, Christmas puddings in gold wrapping tied with red ribbons, Shereen Oake's delicious home-made jams, gloriously gaudy baubles, sparkling lights, frozen turkeys, and mercifully no sprouts.

Maisie called to me from the opposite aisle.

'How many boxes of mince pies Mum?' she cried, 'you're the only one who eats them.'

'Three: two for me, one for Farmers,' I replied. 'Farmers Christmas' was an Oakleyism that had entered the family lexicon long ago.

Soon our flotilla of trolleys was lined up at the checkout piled high with staples, Christmas treats and Ice, Ice, Ice.

'Did you remember the carrots for the reindeer?' asked Angus.

'Bugger it no – go and grab a sack.'

While Maisie and I loaded the car with dry goods, Angus loaded the frozen and fresh food into three large cooler boxes and laid bags of ice on the top before closing the lids tightly. There was little hope the frozen food would still be frozen by the time we got back to camp, but at least everything would be cold. The freezer in camp was beaten into submission by summer temperatures, and manfully did its best by pretending to be a fridge. While the others faffed around in the back of the car squeezing bags of loo paper into what space they could find, I opened the bonnet and topped up the radiator with water.

'Agh shame man. What are you feeding – an army?' a familiar voice boomed from behind me: in a small town there are few strangers.

'Nigel Cantle as I live and breathe – I thought you were in the bush,' I said giving him a hug. He was a good friend and managed Starlings Camp upstream from us.

'Where's Pieter?' he asked, looking around, 'I saw that scarred male this morning on my way in, one of the three males that have been wandering about recently.'

'Inferno? The boy with the bashed-up nose, where did you see him?'

'Near my camp by the bend in the river, you know where your kids like to catch barbel, by himself.'

'Interesting, we haven't seen the other boys for a while,' I said, 'what time?'

Botswana 1999

'Seven-thirtyish. You'll tell Pieter?'

'Yes Nige I will,' I grinned. In all the years I did lion research, I can count on one hand the times when anyone in Maun directed a statement about the lions to me. I knew Nigel meant no harm by it – he was a bluff man, who'd cut off his right arm if it would help someone. Five years later his kindness touched my life unforgettably when, close to midnight, on a late September night, Nigel drove into camp to deliver news that would mark the beginning of a long goodbye. But today, unbeknown to us, good news was winging its way across cyberspace, and in a few hours my sweaty children were going to get a surprise that would transcend all Christmas presents.

By 3.00 p.m. we were at the airport. The children incidentally lined up in order of height, noses pressed against the glass, eyes scanning the sky for Emily's plane. It landed on time, and as she disembarked she looked up at us, standing in our usual place at the window, and beamed a smile. As one body her siblings rushed down the stairs and hopped about waiting for their sister to emerge. The greeting was entrancing – our final departure was not.

The knocking sound in the engine proved to be quite significant, and we had to wait for a vital part to be welded: it might have been quicker to have had it hand-woven by Buddhist monks. The welding machine was on the blink, and had to be repaired before our repair could be done; and that repair exposed another flaw that had to be addressed before we could safely move off. Anyway, it gave us time to have a good family quarrel about who was going to drive back in the big car with Emily. Angus, the peacemaker, agreed to go with Pieter in the pickup on the proviso that Ems didn't share any exciting news until we were all in camp.

Driving out of town at dusk we came upon a funeral cortege, and as was customary I pulled the car over and stopped. We bowed our heads as the procession passed by, and people walking home on the roadside dropped to their haunches in respect.

'It's still bad then,' said Emily.

'HIV? Yup, more than ever these days,' I sighed, 'Anne Sandenbergh was telling me that instead of slaughtering cows people are slaughtering goats now... for funerals.'

'No!' Emily was shocked, she knew that it was disrespectful to honour the dead by providing goat meat at a wake. It was a tradition that all relatives attended family funerals – no matter how distant genetically and geographically. Some had to travel for days, and naturally they needed to be accommodated and fed. Cattle were the cornerstone of family wealth and pride. The drought and cattle lung disease had been decimating, and already impoverished families were battling.

'Families are being hammered from all sides,' I said grimly, 'the young are dropping like flies.'

'Brown died last week,' Travers announced.

'Who?' asked Emily.

'Oh, of course you don't know,' he replied, 'he was a guide, Pieter said he was going to be a great conservationist. It happened so quickly: some people just get it and die. Boom like that,' he snapped his fingers.

'You don't need to be so callous about it,' said Emily sharply. Glancing in the mirror I saw Travers's brown eyes widen in shock, he looked hurt.

'I'm not Ems, I'm just...'

'He's not callous Ems,' I said hurriedly, defending Trav, 'he's just telling it like it is. Brown died very suddenly and it was shocking. The kids knew him well.'

Ems slumped in her seat.

'Water everyone... you're all snappy and dehydrated.'

As always, we stopped at the tin shop in Shorobe and bought warm banana Chappies and then settled into the journey home merrily chewing and playing car games. In time, lulled by the chug of the engine Oaks fell asleep, his head resting on a cardboard box. An hour out of Maun I saw a lion, and then another and another.

'Oh, the cubs, the cubs, it's the Santawani pride you know Ems,' cried Maisie, 'that's Sancerre and Moët, and there's Amarula... do you remember Ems?... they had the cubs that died when we were still living in Santawani... do you remember?'

Emily didn't reply. She was gazing at the lions milling around the car – all her creases smoothed. She had the same look Oakley had had as a baby – long ago when we were driving through the Makgadikgadi Pans.

'Oh Mum,' she whispered.

Travers took the GPS coordinates and recorded the sighting in the data book, and grabbing my binoculars from the glovebox I checked whisker patterns: never assume you know who the lions are: always confirm.

'Shall I track for the boys, Mum?' asked Maisie

'Yup might as well,' I agreed, 'wait for the girls to move off first.' And while my youngest daughter clambered onto the roof to track, I held my oldest daughter's hand. I had missed her to an aching.

'Anything?' I called up.

'None so far.'

I sighed – I was longing to get back home.

In time I heard a faint clicking and... 'Oooooo,' cried Maisie, 'I've got Médoc but far... towards camp actually.'

Those were Médoc's golden days – before he got sick.

'Camp or Santawani?'

Maisie adjusted the frequency and listened again.

'Airstrip,' said Maisie, clambering down and squeezing back in among brothers, bags of loo paper and several cardboard boxes.

'Definitely airstrip.'

'Ah that makes sense, so now we know where to start tomorrow. Good job Mais the Daze... now home James and don't spare the horses.'

Pieter and Angus had been busy in camp, and when we arrived the solar lights were on, the candles were lit, the gas cylinders had been rolled into place, jerrycans of diesel had been neatly stored in the workshop and Pieter was drinking warm whisky, roasting spices and chomping at the bit for the arrival of ice and fresh veggies.

'Why did you take so long?' he asked, proffering a perfunctory kiss.

'Lioning,' I replied.

'Anything interesting?'

'Not particularly... just the Santawani girls and babas.'

The smell of Chinese five-spice, dried red chilli, fresh ginger and garlic filled the air, and while the children and I unloaded the car Pieter cried out for ingredients.

'Peppers, anyone found the peppers? And aubergine, I need an aubergine... don't worry Mais I'll chop it large so you can pick it out... onions. Come on guys what are you all doing?'

He was a fastidious cook and got ratty when the rhythm of his preparation was broken.

'All here Maestro,' laughed Travers, lugging the large cooler box full of iced veggies into the mess tent and laying it at Pieter's feet.

'The onions are under lots of crap so you'll have to wait,' I shouted from the back of the car.

It wasn't until after supper that I remembered the mail.

Replete from his heavenly Chinese stir-fry and noodles, Pieter was smoking a cigarette with a glass of whisky balanced on his shoulder. Relaxed. I kissed him on the mouth and then I kissed his eyes.

'Angelest of all angel men – did you pick up the mail from Ensign?'

'I did, it's in the glovebox... don't go... send a child,' he said, pulling me onto his knee. Oakley dragged himself away from the Christmas chocolates, which were rapidly changing state from solid to liquid, and came back from the car with a pile of brown envelopes and emails: some project-related, some from Neecie for the kids, and one for me from Richard Dawkins.

I read it and reeled.

'No,' I shrieked, jumping off Pieter's lap; had I been wearing pearls I would have clutched them.

'What no?' asked Emily anxiously.

'No, no this can't be true...' I gasped.

'What Mum? What's happened?'

'Your book... Oh my giddy aunt.'

Taking a deep breath, I explained that I had sent Richard the first chapters of the children's book.

'Why on earth did you do that?' asked Travers.

'Because I think it's rather good that's why... he's a dear friend and I was too close to be objective... I knew he'd be honest.'

'What did he say?'

'He loves it,' I sobbed, 'he showed it to a literary agent chum, who was having supper with him the night he got the email, serendipity on skates... she loved it too. Listen to this...' I fumbled to find the lines. 'Here it is... "I hope you won't mind but she thinks it would be a good idea if I wrote the foreword: of course I'd be delighted"... *I hope you won't mind*... bless his darling Darwinian socks.'

'What's a foreword?' asked Maisie, but no one replied – we were too busy leaping around the kitchen whooping like baboons.

'What does this mean Mum?' cried Angus, whizzing in circles with Oaks on his back.

'It means a lot of bloody hard work,' I said, tuning the satellite radio looking for music to dance to, 'and there are no guarantees you'll get published but oh boy can you hear that? That is the sound of doors opening my darlings... humungous doors with bloody great knockers.'

The Lion Children was published by Orion in 2001, and doors swung wide.

On Christmas morning, the five stockings hanging in the mess tent were bulging. Oakley examined the sand for sleigh tracks and found them behind the tent (years later Maisie told me she had spied the Coke can Pieter had used and had hidden it from Oakley's sight). After breakfast Pieter and the kids drove to Santawani to collect water (an elephant had dug up the water pipe overnight) and Emily and I prepared the feast. While we were tra-la-la-la-ing a wind drove louring rain clouds directly over camp and the heavens opened.

In a startlingly short time the parking area was a pond, the kitchen was afloat and Ems and I were slipping and sliding across the floor in helpless giggles. Pulling the turkey out for a basting I dropped it and watched it skim gracefully under the kitchen table from where I retrieved it, wiped it down and put it back in the oven.

'Gomoti, Gomoti come in please,' the radio in the mess tent crackled into life.

With the lithesome grace of a newborn giraffe, I skated across the skidpan of spilled fat and stuffing to answer the radio.

'Looks like you guys are having a touch of rain,' Pieter's voice teased, 'we can see it from here.'

'What's up?' I replied, 'I can't chat I'm very important.'

'We have some new lions here.'

'No.'

'Yes,' he replied, 'five, at six palms by the bush where the kudu always lurk.'

'Are you sure they're new?'

'I'll pretend you didn't say that. We've a decision to make... to collar or not to collar. Bring the vet box and the biopsy darts.'

'We're on our way.'

Christmas was just another day for lions, so we feasted late and played the games we always played and laughed until the sky began to lighten.

On Boxing Day Maisie and Pieter huddled in the mess tent – glued to *Titanic* – the boys played volleyball with Stephen, Lettie, Rhoda and their gang of kids, and Emily and I slipped out alone to find the Gomoti pride.

Botswana 1999

*

The lions were not far from camp, asleep on an open flood plain.

'Idiots,' I mumbled while checking their whisker patterns through my binoculars, 'out in the open, no shade. None of them know how to behave.'

Emily was holding the GPS out of the window.

'Shall I read it out now?' she asked when the location had been fixed.

'Give me two secs,' I said, peering through my binoculars into tall grass, 'pick up your head there's a good girl... come on.'

Emily's grey eyes were blue under a clear midday sky. We sat quietly together watching the females sleeping while the cubs flopped about.

'Mum?'

'That's me.'

'Take me through these lions,' she said seriously.

'What do you mean?'

'I mean who are they? I feel such a fool asking when the kids are in the car...' She sounded miserable.

'My darling girl what's up?'

'I feel so hopeless here... I don't know where I am half the time. The kids have to tell me where things go... I didn't know the snake machete lived by the brooms. I didn't even know how to fill the generator last night when Pieter asked me to... And the kids know all the lions by heart... and they all look the bloody same to me,' she howled.

Poor Ems – she had helped raise her siblings: changed their nappies; sung them to sleep; held their heads when they puked; celebrated their victories and comforted them when they were wretched, but now they were bush-wise, wild children, living by their senses, and feeling the wilderness with a rawness even I could not share.

'Bubsy, I had no idea... they love you to bits and back,' I tried to comfort her, 'they need you just as much as ever Ems. They miss you so much when you're not here.'

'I know... I know they... love... me,' Emily hiccuped through her tears, 'but it's not the same... camp is their home... but you're home... Mamma... you're my home... not camp.'

'I'm sorry, I had never thought about how hard it must be for you,' I said, 'I think I know what we need.'

'What?'

'Time back home in England... a real Hollybush Christmas again... like the old days.'

'But Mum, no money, it's so expensive to fly everyone back... and what about the people who are renting Hollybush?'

I roared with laughter.

'We've got a year to sort that out. But let's do that... it would be great for everyone. Neecie would love it... the kids would love it and Oakley's got no memory of his English home... frankly, the home that puts food on our table. Thank fuck for the rent because if we relied on project-funding we'd starve.'

One of the lions got up to pee.

'Which one is that?' Emily whispered.

'Barbera, she's got no teeth... all gums. At kills she gets the entrails and sucks on the intestines like a straw.'

'Wow.'

I pointed to the other lions.

'That thin one there is Gamay... look at her hindquarters when she gets up, all sunken in. She gets the same food the others get but she looks like shit... she's sick for sure.'

'Who's that one.'

'Margaux. She and Grenache... are pregnant... the cubs are due February twelvish... so you'll be gone before they're born which is a pisser.'

'Do you know who the dad is?'

'Inferno and his boys. We'll know for sure who sired what cub when we get the DNA results back.'

I giggled thinking about the surprises that awaited us.

'It's a soap opera out here... lions are loose and flowing with their favours.'

'Will you carry on sampling?'

'Oh, for sure. We're done here... let's go and find the Santawani girls so we know where they are ready for pooping later... oh I love having time with my girl.'

On the way, we chatted about the men in our lives. I had been dying to hear the nitty-gritty about Emily's new man: Jimmy. I knew him and adored him. He'd been at school with Ems and he was a regular feature in Hollybush life, but as far as I knew there had never been a romance. Apparently, that had blossomed recently, when they were reunited after several years, during a merry weekend with friends in Devon.

It was bliss talking freely about our burgeoning sex lives unimpeded by younger ears. I have always talked openly about sex with my children, and being surrounded by mating animals there were no mysteries related to the mechanics. But the intimacies and problems related to being in love and living with a man – those were things I could share with Ems.

'Are you happy, Mum?'

'Blissfully.'

Emily turned to me and spoke with her eyebrows.

'What?' I said defensively.

'Nothing,' she said primly.

'What nothing? Spit it out,' I said.

'It's just I've noticed some tension... nothing dramatic... just not the same ease as last Christmas.'

She was right. Something had shifted and I couldn't put my finger on what it was. Pieter and I were still in love, still finding time for quiet moments on the Gomoti watching the sunset together. I still missed him when he was away for the day, and longed for the precious release when we slid into bed, and breathed in the tenderness of being alone. But as the children and I became more competent in the bush, as my understanding of lions deepened, and my research into endocrinology and the immune system intensified, a dynamic had shifted. I was no longer his student. I was standing on steady feet in the wild, and I was now officially co-principal researcher. Things had changed. And somewhere, in a corner of my heart, lay a truth I didn't want to look at.

'There's a lot going on Ems... he's writing his book and we're working like beavers... not enough funding... keeping up with school work...'

Emily turned her face away. She knew I was deflecting.

'I'm not an easy person to live with Ems,' I said.

'Tell me about it,' she laughed, 'I just want to know you're all right that's all. So I don't worry.'

'I'm fine Em. It's hard for him sometimes... no respite... living in a goldfish bowl.'

She looked at me with steady eyes.

We dropped the subject.

Two years later Emily came to camp with her own cub: Jack sired by Jimmy. In the early mornings, I would lie awake listening for my grandson to stir. Leaving Emily to sleep, I scooped her steaming bundle into my arms and took him up to the kitchen for warm milk and rusks. He smelled of pee and Emily, and I loved him from a new part of my heart: parts that blossomed new for each grandchild. Out came the old Disney tapes and Jack and I went on companionable morning game drives. Every bird, impala or giraffe ignited wriggling laughter and I remembered Oakley's joy – long ago at camp Okuti. In the evenings while supper was cooking, Jack and his eight-year-old uncle bathed in the old tin tub in the kitchen tent and everything was well in our world.

Jack saw many lions through baby eyes.

But he never saw the Gomoti pride.

By the time he was born all the females and their cubs had been poisoned.

39

Comeragh Road, London 2013

'Darling I'm going to a Naomi Wolf lecture on the vag tonight. Fancy coming?' I shouted upstairs to Oakley, 'V.a.g.i.n.a.s. all you need to know.'

'Thanks Mum . . . I'll pass on that. I'm finding my own way.'

I laughed.

I pottered off alone to the Intelligence Squared lecture at the Royal Institution. The neuroscience of sex fascinated me and I had been intrigued by the blurb advertising Wolf's lecture: 'The vagina is much more than a sex organ – it is integral to female well-being, and a catalyst to female creativity, confidence and identity . . . latest neuroscience reveals fascinating new discoveries about the vagina and female well-being.' It surprised me that it needed to be said that the vagina is connected to the brain: of course it is.

Listening to Wolf lecture on her new book, I was interested but detached: until she spoke about my secret and my vagina-pulsed muscle memory. What was that, Naomi? Did I hear that right? A neurologist from Wisconsin had found a statistically relevant correlation between balance problems and past sexual trauma? Losing balance. Fear of falling. I had always laughed about it. Such a silly little anxiety. How funny that I nearly fainted on a Ferris wheel. How ridiculous to be afraid of walking on stepping-stones. Losing my footing. Fear of being pushed. Sometimes my legs stopped working. I couldn't speak about it. My legs and my mouth shut down. It had always been that way. Fear so deep it led to silent blackness. The darkness that drove me under the table. The darkness I had seen in a child's eyes long ago in Sehitwa. The veil of detachment fell away and my vagina connected to my memory.

At the end of her talk, during Q and A, I celebrated Naomi's desire to explore the connections between sex and neuroscience. Understanding its neurology does not destroy the romance and sensuality of our sexuality – any more than understanding the spectrum of visible light destroys the wonder of a rainbow. The science of sex was beautiful to me. Less lovely was my vagina's close relationship with the science of post-traumatic stress.

I bought her book and asked her to sign it.

'Who shall I say?'

'Oakley, sign it for Oakley please.'

Sitting on the Tube on the way home I could feel the shadow of redundant fear that no longer had a place in my life. I focused my mind on lions. The wonder of tiny cubs emerging from dens: we'd seen hundreds and counted them down as they died. Only one lion appeared to mourn her loss. Sancerre... she had called for her cubs for days, maybe she was just sick. She broke away from the pride to live a solitary life. Sancerre... was nurturing. She had three more cubs... they died too. She grew thin and sick and died alone in 2000.

I felt grief mounting inside me: I pushed it down. Don't cry on a train you idiot: lions die, you saw so many lions die, get over it. But Sancerre was my lion... I loved her... the tears are coming: fuck that: think don't feel. Lion vaginas: we would never know what memories they connect to; think about what you do know. Think about what you observed. I miss the lions so much I can't breathe. The lions never loved us. They tolerated us and that was a privilege: the wild stories live inside my head. Secret histories.

We are the sum of all our stories: snippets of memories that resonate through our bodies and seep into our souls. I could feel the tears heaving: I was alone in the blackness, no one could see me now. The children don't know all the stories. It's the little ones that break you. They get into the cracks and make you scream. They come when you don't expect them, and fill you up and make you want to stop.

I had wanted to jump in front of trains. Time out. That's what wanting to die is. Not an end – just time out. Sancerre took time out: she was alone. I was never alone: the children saw everything and what they saw can't be unseen. I wanted to die so much. To be clean again. Unbearable bleakness: you are better now: don't go there, it's over. Think about the lions. Lion mothers. Come back. The smell of London grime leaked back into my senses: you can't smell when you are dreaming. I was back again. Keep steady. List what you know. Lists are calming: data.

Imperfect lion mothers: the reality you never see in sentimental documentaries. Nothing is perfect: good enough is as good as it gets.

Lion fathers: some devoted, cosy dads – Médoc and Inferno were cosy dads. But the females had the power. The classic Lion King fathers lived on the exposed open plains of the Serengeti. But in the Okavango things were different: there were places for females to hide in the secret woodlands, marshes, riverine forests, acacia forests, mopane thickets, and among the crazy mazes formed by dried-out riverbeds. When strange males wandered through their territory canny females took control, and moved their cubs to the hidden places. Hiding. Females hiding. Mothers hiding in tumbledown shacks. Hiding from fear.

'Are you beach-body ready?' 'Are you beach-body ready?'
'Are you beach-body ready?'
'Stop staring at me like I'm some piece of meat... I'm lovin' it.'
Meat... meat...
Don't read that rubbish. Meat. Picked over like rubbish. I'm not rubbish... I'm not rubbish... think. Was I with Travers or Angus when we saw the baby buffalo being eaten? Which child was it? Four sub-adult males took forty-five minutes to kill the calf. You never see that on documentaries... never see the long deaths. The buffalo mother was standing by lowing. The cattle are lowing the baby awakes. Prey eaten alive. Do they go into the black? I hope they go into the black.

Some hunts were masterful... cunning, cooperative... chilling... brilliant. Some were Feydeau farces... pratfalls, double takes and cries of 'It went thataway.' Dolcetta fell over twice on the Mogogelo... we all saw that... I laughed... did I laugh out loud?

The train stopped in a tunnel: a man beside me was reading the *Metro* and sucked in air between his teeth... perhaps the delay irritated him... I looked at the floor. The train was crowded. Each station more people.

The train started again... Stay inside your head... don't read those advertisements again... find the pictures in your head... Inferno's scarred nose. He was so relaxed he would mate right up against the car, making Oakley laugh. Lion sex was never dull... consensual, non-consensual; violence, courtship, patience, dominance, flirting, infidelity, adolescents experimenting, occasional male and female homosexual activity. We learned their ways... I could see them... every animal... every bush I found them under... each sighting... the last time I saw Freixenet she was in Mogogelo pride territory... everything had changed by then... the lions were shifting to new ground... so were we... everything was changing... betrayal... don't think about that... Freixenet's little female cub with a displaced hip, limping along... what had happened to her?... I never knew the end of her story... so many stories torn up.

The train stopped with a jolt and the doors opened... people moving in against the concentration gradient... a woman carrying a small child clambered into the throng. They looked exhausted. I stood up to give them my seat. She looked surprised and smiled. Squeezed among strangers I found my patch of floor and let my body rock with the movement of the train. I had become used to standing in confined spaces pressed up against strangers. Jostling for a foothold, editing out the smells, avoiding people's eyes, missing kindness and tender human connection to avoid the cold, sickening stare of a stranger stripping me naked in his head. In the wild it is essential to be open: in a city it is safer to close down.

When I got home I had a long hot shower.

40

With the Lions: Botswana 2000

Angus was peaceful. Resting his chin on his arm, he gazed out of the open car window watching Cristal being mounted for the fourth time in half an hour.

Médoc growled deeply, fussing and biting her neck as he ejaculated, and she snapped her head around at him and snarled. He dismounted and flopped down a few feet away from her.

Angus raised his chin waiting to see what Cristal would do...
'Yup it's a roll... got that down Mum?'

'One, two, three, four, five, six, seven...' I said, counting the seconds the female lay on her back, inelegantly waving her legs in the air, and recorded it in the data book.

'Why do they roll after some copulations and not others?'

'I dunno Gus. Maybe it's a response to more powerful ejaculations? I have no idea. When Dad and I were trying for you I used to lie on my back with my legs up to let gravity help the little swimmers.'

'Seriously?'

'Yup. Maybe lions do the same.'

It had been a hard track. The signals from Cristal's collar had been bounced around by the trees and it was mid-afternoon by the time we found her in a small clearing in a densely wooded area. Médoc was in possession and his companion Montrachet was resting under a bush. Gus and I knew immediately it was going to be a long session. For only yesterday we had observed Cristal without the males, so this was the beginning of her five-day oestrus during which time she would be mated every fifteen minutes or so – give or take.

'They'll make beautiful babies,' Gus giggled. Among the ragged-eared, scarred, workaday lions in our study Médoc and Cristal were the stand-out chocolate-box beauties. Blonde Cristal was usually joined at the hip to Freixenet, a small, fierce ginger lion, and Médoc mooched around with Montrachet and Mersault; we hadn't seen the latter for a long time.

'Montrachet will move in on her at some point so there'll be no telling paternity for sure,' I reminded Angus.

Like all cats, lions need the stimulus of mating to induce ovulation: currently Cristal was secreting a functional cocktail of oestrogen that was sending Médoc wild with excitement and ripening ova in her ovaries. Ovulation would occur within the next forty-eight hours or so, and by that time Médoc would be shooting blanks: sleepy, patient Montrachet was just biding his time.

'It's so funny the boys always squabble on kills but are really chilled when it comes to sharing a female,' Angus commented, 'I guess selection acted in favour of males who didn't battle over access to girls.'

'Sure, fights can be fatal and dead lions don't make cubs... Okay here we go again,' I said, reaching for the data book.

We spent a companionable afternoon. The bush was settled. A couple of francolin strayed into the clearing pecking for seeds, otherwise only Médoc's brief orgasms disturbed the hum of bees and the rustle of leaves.

By the time the shadows lengthened I had filled four pages with carefully recorded observations. Cristal had barely moved from where we had found her and Montrachet had fallen into a deep sleep – his great head flopped down between his paws. The sun went down behind the trees and the intervals between copulations gradually lengthened. Everyone was tired.

'Okay home time I think, don't you?' I asked, 'they'll still be here in the morning, we won't miss much.'

'Good plan,' agreed Gus, looking around him, 'we came in from over there – look there's our tracks.'

'Dear heart if we try to follow our tracks we'll never get back – we went all over the shop coming in, don't you remember? No, we'll go out due east and eventually hit the South Gate road.'

Glancing at me with approval, Angus packed up the snacks and water bottles that littered the front seats and we set off merrily for a night drive home. The plan was perfect, its execution was not. Three hours, and one puncture, later we were quite spectacularly lost.

'We're useless,' laughed Angus, 'this wouldn't be happening if Pieter or Trav were here.'

'This is so true,' I said briskly, pulling on the brakes, 'I have a plan. Let's radio-track back to the lions and wait till morning. In the light of day we'll find camp easily.'

'Love it,' said my staunch companion, 'we can get lots more data, and I'd feel safer with the lions than stuck in a forest.'

I knew what he meant about feeling safer with the lions. For a treat, a few weeks ago, Oakley and I had made a bed in the back of the car and spent the night by a hippo pool. We had a picnic, ate sweeties and read Sherlock Holmes while ungulates and elephant came down to drink. In time the two Mogogelo pride males emerged from the shadows, and seeking warmth they flopped down on either side of our car, pressed up against the doors like bookends.

'Nothing will come near us tonight, with the boys here,' whispered Oaks.

'Safe as houses,' I replied. The four of us slept soundly.

With the help of telemetry Angus and I made it back to the lions, and as predicted they hadn't moved. Cristal was napping and Médoc was lying restlessly beside her. After a while she got up and Médoc tried to mount her, but was swiftly rebuffed by vicious, lip-curling snarls. Cristal squatted to pee while Médoc circled around her in anticipation. When she finished he buried his nose in the saturated sand, and licked it up with his coarse tongue until his body quivered in an ecstasy. The smell of her sex triggered a tooth-baring, nose-wrinkling grimace that stretched his neck back, draining an elixir of oestrogen into his vomeronasal organ and producing a spike of testosterone that swelled his scrotum and drove him inside her body, where he pounded his power until he ejaculated, emitting a smothered roar bitten deep into her neck. Cristal crawled out from under him and rolled.

The smell of urine must have seeped into Montrachet's dreams, for he awoke aroused, and, striding into the clearing, he greeted his pride mate by rubbing heads and leaning his weight against his body. Médoc leaned into him briefly but turned swiftly to lie close beside Cristal. Montrachet circled them a few times before walking off into the thicket.

'Bless him – he needs a cold shower.'

'Mum?'

'Still here.'

'How many of our lions have FIV?'

Ninety per cent of the study lions we had tested were positive for FIV (feline immunodeficiency virus) and it was worrying.

'Most of the ones we've tested so far ... but they're not "our" lions Gus.'

'You know what I mean. Is it like HIV?'

'It's a lentivirus, so it's a slow virus, and it's a retrovirus that attacks immune cells so yes it's like HIV, but it's been around in lion populations for a very long time.'

'So, they've adapted to it?'

'Some say ... but I'm not so sure FIV infection is without consequence. Look, no one dies of HIV, people die because HIV weakens their immune system, and when it has finally been beaten into submission they get AIDS and die of infections from other pathogens.'

Angus's eyes drooped. He knew this wretched reality... people he knew and loved were living with HIV.

'I think it's the same with the lions Gus. FIV doesn't kill them directly... but sure as hell it weakens their immune system. Think of the cubs we see wasting away, and the adults who look wretchedly thin with no muscle on their hindquarters.'

'Like that boy we saw in lion valley?'

'Exactly... wasting is a symptom, so is gingivitis and diarrhoea – all the things we see... I worry that immunological challenges may be why some females are failing to become pregnant or re-absorbing embryos in early pregnancy.'

'Why?'

'It's early days Gus... I'm still trying to make sense of it. Reading lots of papers on work done with cats, rats, sheep, people... you name it. The links between the immune system and the reproductive system are fascinating. There's a hormone I am riveted by that may help us.'

'More poop?' groaned Gussie.

'Nope, this time piss may hold the answers,' I laughed, 'less smelly.'

I had become fascinated by the power of a versatile peptide hormone called prolactin. The multifunctional little hormone sends chemical messages whizzing across cells, tissues, organs and systems. Ubiquitous in mammalian, piscine, reptilian and avian species, this merry little hormone has been sending out chemical messages for over eight million years.

What riveted me were its interactions between the immune and reproductive systems. It had been shown that infection triggered elevations in extra-pituitary prolactin, thus inhibiting the secretion of reproductive hormones in males and females. It had also been suggested that immunological responses might have resulted in early pregnancy failure in FIV-positive domestic cats.

Field research is plodding work, and finding non-invasive ways to access intimate data was always a challenge. But if we combined intensive observations with data gathered from poop, piss and biopsies we could build a dynamic understanding of lions' internal worlds.

'You're excited about this aren't you Mum.'

'Very, Gus,' I said, 'it will complement the genetic work Pete and Rodrigo are doing on FIV. What a team... now snuggle down, this is going to be a long night.'

Rodrigo Serra was a young Portuguese vet I had head-hunted a few years before. Rod's annual visits to collect blood samples were a high spot in the project calendar: the children and I loved him like family.

I continued my observations, and Gus settled in the back seat wrapped up in a blanket. Pieter often teased me for bringing so much stuff with us every time we went out, but when we left camp we never knew what time we would be back, or what might befall us. Blankets, books and snacks were as essential as water, a wheel spanner and a hi-lift jack.

The stars were vivid in a moonless sky, and a light wind wafted a delicate, nutty fragrance I did not recognize: some night-flowering plant was tempting pollinators in the undergrowth. It was half past one in the morning and the lions were resting between bouts, when Gus murmured sleepily.

'Mum?'

'That's me.'

'Are we the only animals that like sex?'

I pondered for a moment.

'Dolphins have a very happy time.'

'Baboons play with themselves,' added Angus.

'Bonobo chimps are also merry wankers. No, we are not the only species that likes sex. Oops I think they're off again... hold that thought.'

For the last twenty minutes Médoc had been lying flat on the ground, his eyes heavy with fatigue. However, Cristal looked eager for action. She got up and, raising her tail, stood coquettishly in front of Médoc. Impaled by her scent, he hauled himself up, mounted her perfunctorily and flopped back down on his side. She stayed on her haunches, her tail twitching from side to side – a sign that indicated all was not well in the state of Denmark.

'She looks cross Mum, look at her tail.'

For the first time since we had joined them Cristal glared at us and snarled.

I turned on the engine and slowly reversed a few metres. She settled.

'Poor thing,' whispered Angus affectionately, 'night-night, love you Mum,' and, pulling the blanket up around his neck, he rolled over and went back to sleep. The lions dozed and nothing stirred. I continued monitoring until the air chilled: the harbinger of dawn. Gradually charcoal faded into glinting mercury, and night-bleached green quickened, spreading across the bush to reveal Montrachet standing deep inside the thicket: watching.

I waited until he mounted Cristal, then drove home.

As we arrived in camp, Oaks rushed to greet us ashen-faced.

'Where were you? What happened? Pieter is such a bastard he wouldn't go out to find you. I hate him so much.' He flung his arms around me and, bursting into furious tears, punched Angus hard in the stomach.

'Wow what's that for you little beast,' Angus rolled him onto the ground where they tussled in misery and relief like puppies.

Travers stayed sitting under the Kitchen Tree, he was livid.

'We were so worried Mummy,' said Maisie gently, 'I knew you were okay though. But Oaks was desperate.'

'So sorry everyone. We got lost and used up the spare tyre. It was best to stay put,' I replied.

Pieter grinned at me, and raised his eyes to heaven.

'Told you. I knew there was nothing to flap about. I wasn't going to risk taking everyone out on a fool's errand.'

I went into the bucket-shower 'bathroom' to brush my teeth. I felt flat. Pieter was right – it would have been silly to try to find us at night. But all the same... Travers joined me. Relief had thawed him but he still looked serious.

'Mum, you've gotta get better at navigating. We hoped you were just lost but you might have been tipped up by an ellie. Oaks cried all night.'

'Was he with you?'

'Of course. Pieter's hopeless at that sort of stuff. He was right though – trying to find you would have been silly.'

I kept my counsel on that point. Travers and Pieter were becoming a strong unit, and Trav was comforted by pragmatism. They didn't know which lions we were with – they didn't even know what pride territory we were in... it was a sensible decision... but if you are in love?

A pinprick of doubt numbed me for a second. I shook it off.

41

The Royal Institution, London 2012

I had an odd encounter after Naomi Wolf's lecture; at the time I didn't take it very seriously. With a signed copy of *Vagina: A New Biography* tucked under my arm I was squeezing through the mêlée when I felt a tap on my shoulder.

'Hello, excuse me,' said an engaging, dark-haired young woman, 'I wonder if I could ask you about lions?'

During the Q and A with Naomi I had mentioned something about lion sexuality.

'Sure,' I said, 'I'm never happier than when I'm talking about lions. There's not much call for it round here,' I laughed.

'I was fascinated by what you were saying about lion sex, and raising your family with lions. I wonder if you might like to give a small talk at next year's Women of the World festival at the South Bank?'

'Blimey,' I replied, 'that sounds quite daunting. But I'd love to be a woman of the world. Tell me about the festival – I've been away for a long time and I'm afraid I've never heard of it.'

'Oh, it's not been going long – only since 2010, it's been gathering momentum.'

I was glowing. Someone wanted me to talk about lions.

'It would be what we call a WOW bite,' she continued, 'just a short talk – very informal in one of the smaller venues.'

'How great. Any specific aspect? Maternal care? Sex? Lion populations plummeting? Poison? FIV?' I inquired.

'FIV?' She sounded puzzled.

'Feline immunodeficiency virus. Cat AIDS. Domestic cats have it, so do lions.'

'Goodness me I had no idea. How does it affect lions?'

'It's a controversial topic... most researchers say it makes no difference... I argue for some individuals it has a negative impact on reproductive output.'

She glazed over, but nodded politely, and said she would ask the festival director, Jude Kelly, what aspects she thought best. She told me more about the festival, and some of the topics they were going to explore: among them rape.

My heart lurched. For the first time I was feeling a visceral connection between my life in Africa and my life in London.

'I know something about rape. I used to work for Women Against Rape in Botswana,' I took a deep breath, 'also, I would like to talk about what I've learned... from my own rape...' I petered out.

'I'm so sorry,' she said. It was obligatory: poor thing, people never know what to say.

'Oh, I'm fine. Better now,' I said, probably too brightly, 'but I've learned something I would like to share.'

'Oh, I'm sure Jude would be interested. I'll call you. Thank you.'

I was convinced I would never hear from her again.

Anyway, I was busy. It was a happy time. From morning to night the house was bustling with young. Angus had moved in – he was studying for a postgraduate diploma at the London School of Journalism, and at the same time speech-writing for an independent peer in the House of Lords.

As always, Gus found his nesting place, and in the evenings he stretched out on the metal daybed in the sitting room, socks off, vape charged, writing speeches or learning the complexities of libel law. Some evenings, he and I would snuggle in to watch *MasterChef Australia* on Sky Catch Up, and we had no control: episode followed episode. We loved Matt and Gary and dear George, and we lived and breathed the agonies and ecstasies experienced by contestants.

London 2012

We sweated during a pressure test – were deeply concerned by a risky risotto – gasped at a whisper of spun sugar – shivered at the quiver of a perfect panna cotta and wept when a contestant gained an immunity badge. Inspired, Gus and I would wipe away a tear and dash down to the kitchen to do something witty with a scallion and a salmon skin. Safety seeped in. He'd talk about other stuff when he was ready.

To my surprise, I did get a call from Jude Kelly's office, and a date was fixed for our meeting. Jude's office in the South Bank Centre was nondescript: Jude was not. She was tiny but she filled the room with rolled-up-sleeves energy. She reminded me of a black and white honey badger: tenacious, uncompromising, on a mission. We both were.

She was coolly compassionate, and that suited me. She wanted to raise awareness and to encourage women who had been raped to come forward. I was open and honest, and that suited her. I too wanted to raise awareness and I had empirical evidence of the power of choral voices. I told Jude about Post a Letter for Justice Day and how over one hundred thousand women had written to the President. Sacks of mail blocked the presidential hallways – indeed W.A.R. had received a curt phone call on the subject. The means of delivery was deemed poor manners, but the pith of the message was acknowledged with grace. The President heard the stories and within a matter of days meetings had been set up with the Ministry of Health and the Commissioner of Police.

But there were other stories... silent histories... Jude wanted to know more. She wanted my story, and so I told her.

She was a good listener.

42

Maun 2003

Two paths led back to the town house we were staying in. One was isolated and ran along the river, and the other led up onto the more populated main tar road. I chose the one most travelled, and that made all the difference.

I was wearing shoes that day, just little plimsolls from the PEP store, a pair of beige trousers, a new brown belt and a white T-shirt. I was feeling energetic and fierce as I swung along the road after a celebratory meal with friends. Finally, we had been granted a four-year extension on our research permit. Home was safe, and now we could really buckle down and answer questions that were burning in my brain about the impact of FIV on lions. I wanted to start sampling the Mogogelo pride: new pride males had moved in and it was the perfect time to begin collecting data. This time poop and pee. The hormone tests we were going to do on the urine had never been done before in the wild. I was busting to get back to camp and get to work.

I lengthened my stride, the light was fading fast and I wanted to be home before dark. Hearing someone coming up behind me, I turned in greeting.

'Dumela,' I said, smiling.

There were three of them: they jostled me.

'Dumela bo Rre,' I said, wondering why one of them had put a knife to my throat. I looked into their faces and did not understand. They pushed against me, knocking me towards the sand on the side of the road. I was still standing. I wondered why they were doing this. Soon they would be gone and I'd walk on. They pushed me again and I toppled. Dragging me by my feet, they pulled me down a small incline. It was very puzzling. I wondered if broken glass and tin lids would cut me. I realized what was going to happen when I felt them pulling on my trousers.

This is happening to me. There are three of them pinning me to the sand. Where can I go? Be present. Don't forget... remembering is too painful. What they are going to do won't kill you. Stay alive. Where can you go and be present? A few limp stars appeared... I tried to remember the colour of hydrogen. Was it more blue or red? There was green in the spectra. How much? I was clever while they fumbled with my body... I looked at the stars... bar codes in the stars... I tried to remember... each element emanates its own light... I was clever... so clever... don't think about what he's doing... I have been here before... I know this place... what a terrible conformation... I have beaten this before... don't go into the blackness again... you're a grown-up this time... so clever... helium has a colour... I felt hands squeezing my throat until I could barely breathe... and the knife point... it was rounded... I could feel that... dull grey metal... I couldn't remember the colour of helium... I panicked. The stars were too far away to help me. I needed something fresh... something closer... as each man entered me I pushed them out with my babies' heads... I was stronger than the earth... I was so strong... I pushed so hard... my babies' heads cleaned me... one by one... I ejected each man... I was wild with power... I was omnipotent... omnipotence is a dark thick space... I could not breathe... such power. I will not die here in dirty sand among the plastic bags and rusty tin cans... I will see my children again... I will not die here. I could not feel the fear. I could not feel the earth spinning. There were no points of reference.

The last one was the most dangerous. He was whipped up... he spoke to me. 'Kiss me,' he said. I could feel the dirt of him. 'Think of your mother,' I said. He looked shocked. His fingers tightened on my throat. I couldn't breathe. Kiss me. His lips touched mine and I hated me. He squeezed my throat until I heard it crack... I was present... I hated my weakness so much I could taste it. He finished and they began to turn me over and I felt a bursting of rage so powerful I could taste metal... I knew the next thing they would do. I would rather die... I could feel the silent blackness coming towards me... I began to slip deeper into the dark... this time I won't come back. Suddenly they stopped and scuttled away like beetles. I had beaten them. I was too strong for them. I learned later they had been deterred from their task by a brief commotion caused by a car running into a donkey: a common occurrence, no harm done.

I fumbled for my trousers and pulling them up I stumbled onto the road and flagged down a car. It was a small white car drive driven by a Motswana man. His passenger wound down her window.

'I have been raped... please take me to the police,' I said, climbing into the back of their car without an invitation. The woman was embarrassed and so she laughed. I understood her reaction. I was not offended. They dropped me outside the police station. I could feel the dust in my bones. I walked into the station and turned right into reception. I knew the policeman behind the counter.

'I have been raped,' I said; he looked shattered.

'Come Mma Kate,' he said, 'sit down... I will get a car to drive you to the hospital.'

'No,' I said, 'I want to report. I want to give my statement... while I can still remember their faces.'

'No,' he said, 'you must first go to hospital.' He was following the protocols W.A.R. had advised in our workshops.

'I will get a lady officer to drive you,' he said.

I didn't want to go to hospital. I wanted to tell my story. How odd, I thought. I must remember that.

'No need... just someone kind... like you,' I said.

I don't remember the drive to hospital. They took me to Dr Patrick's private hospital... perhaps I asked. It was new.

The reception was marble. Cool under my bare feet. I asked the nurse to call Anne Sandenbergh. Then I asked for Dr Patrick.

'He's not on duty tonight.'

'Please tell him.'

'He's not here tonight, you can see another doctor.'

A man in a white coat appeared beside me.

'Come with me.'

'No thank you, I want Patrick.'

'Don't you want me to examine you?'

What a fucking stupid question. I don't want you near me... I hate you.

'No thank you,' my words were ice. He shrugged and walked away. I turned back to the nurse.

'Tell Patrick, Kate has been raped. He'll come. I'm going to his office now.'

I crawled under his table. I waited. I don't know for how long. It didn't matter. He came, I knew he would. I could see his feet in the doorway. A fragment of fear vibrated. He didn't call my name. He didn't pull on my arm to drag me out. Instead he crawled under the table beside me, and I laid my head on his chest and my first fragment mended. He was black and he was safe and that mattered. He rocked me and I shuddered new tears: from a gash in my life.

He asked me if I wanted the gynaecologist to examine me.

'Only you,' I said.

He was efficient and businesslike, as I knew he would be.

'Is there semen?'

'Yes,' he said, 'you must have put up a fight – there will be bad bruising, but there are no lacerations.'

'I don't remember fighting.'

'I know you hate antibiotics, but really you must. The risk of STDs.'

'I want every antibiotic in Africa pumped into me now.'

He looked at me.

'How do you do it? You women amaze me. How can you find your laughter?'

I didn't know I'd laughed.

He prepared a cocktail of medication and delivered it with precision. Nothing hurt.

'I will have to test you for HIV.'

Every word was kind. I felt it in the shadows.

'Sure.'

'Then we can start you on the AZT.'

'Thanks.'

He drew blood and left the room.

I lay on the examination table and stared at the ceiling. My head was empty.

In time, he returned.

'You're negative.'

'No big surprise there. There were three of them, Patrick. Not great odds I'll stay negative.'

He held out a packet of AZT and looked at his watch.

'Take one now and then one every eight hours, the timing matters. Best to set an alarm. Don't miss a dose. You know how this works, Kate.'

'Yup, inhibits the reverse transcriptase. Yada, yada.' I breathed deeply. Statistically there was a good chance the virus was inside me. I had to choose my worries. I chose to trust in science and let the toxic drug denature the shit out of those enzymes, and any others that got in the way.

'You will need to be tested again in four weeks, then after six months and, just to be one hundred per cent, tested again in a year. It's a twenty-eight-day course – no alcohol while you are on it.'

While I was in the examination room I was safe – protected from the outside – from other people. I had no idea how bad things would be. I was in an iron bubble in which there was no light or transparency, just movement – forward into a new life.

'You can shower now Kate.'

The water was hot – the pressure was strong for Maun. I didn't turn my face up to the rose and try to wash my soul – like they do in the movies. I had grown used to saving water. I soaped the grey Kalahari sand off my skin quickly and efficiently, dispassionately noticing livid fingerprints on my inner thighs.

Back in reception, it was chaos. Pieter was shouting at a policewoman, Anne Sandenbergh was trying to placate him . . . I don't remember much.

But I remember Travers standing in the doorway watching me.

I saw his face stripped back to atavistic rawness.

I saw myself reflected in his eyes – defiled – his mother – his clean place – filthy – unbearable.

He didn't know I had seen him.

He left.

It would be years before we found our way back to each other.

43

Comeragh Road, London 2013

The meeting with Jude Kelly had been well conducted. She was careful and I was clear. We covered a lot of ground. But as I put my key in the front door, my battery drained and I felt exhausted.

'That you Mum?' called Oakley from the kitchen.

'Who else?' I yelped weakly, flopping down onto the sofa.

Oakley came into the sitting room and turned on the telly – Sky Sports – save me.

'You okay? You look terrible.'

'Thanks. Just tired. I had that meeting today. You know the one about the r—ing.' Oakley was eight when I was raped: he hadn't liked saying the whole word.

Checking the results for a match, the boy's face tightened.

'Sorry Mum... that must have been hard. Do you want to talk about it?'

I laughed.

'No, my angel... you're off the hook.'

He laughed too.

'Thank fuck for that. I'm out for supper tonight. Back later.' He left the room to get his coat. Then he came back and kissed me on the top of my head.

'I love you Mum. You know that don't you.'

The front door slammed. Some halfwit was droning on about some

London 2013

godforsaken football stats. The remote control was on the mantelpiece. I was too weary to get up.

The sediment had been stirred and all the dark times were swirling in a clear glass... so clear... I could see it all... I could feel a howl rising... I shut my eyes against it... not now don't look now... don't slip... rest... move forward... one step at a time... don't slip into the slime... remember the good times: they were real too.

44

With the Lions: Botswana 2000

Travers and I couldn't see Médoc. The signal from the receiver was loud, and way off-frequency. We were straining our eyes looking this way and that, even looking up in the trees. Sometimes lions climbed quite high, though we had never seen this boy in a tree. We hadn't seen him for over six months; I was relieved he was still alive. Of the once-magnificent triumvirate, Médoc was the last one standing.

'Where the hell is he?' Travers was usually quick to find the outline of a pair of ears deep in the grass – he was becoming frustrated, 'How far off-frequency are you?'

'As far as I can go,' I replied, 'he might as well be in the car he's so close.'

'Mum, look over there, an ostrich nest.'

'And look there... inside that bush, that's our boy,' I whispered.

I stopped the car, and putting the tracking equipment onto the back seat I sat back to survey the scene. I had never seen anything like it. The ostrich nest was more like a Neolithic settlement than a bird's nest. Six eggs lay in the centre of a sandy circle defined by slightly raised edges. The only sign of the mother was a few scattered feathers rising and falling in currents of warm air.

Médoc was huddled uncomfortably inside a dense hebeclada bush, and beside him lay two cracked eggshells. His golden face was pale, no dried blood darkening his skin. Travers and I scanned the sand for scuffle marks but we saw none. As the lion had approached the mother ostrich must have run away – moulting feathers in her haste.

Sitting in rapt silence, we waited. Médoc was watching us from under the bush – his eyes soft and relaxed. We were close to the nest, on the tipping point of the invisible line drawn between man and animal: an olfactory border through which messages were relayed by pheromones, hormones, diesel fumes, apple shampoo, musk, urine, bacteria-rich breath and sweat. Sensing Médoc's need, I put the car into reverse and pulled back a couple of metres. A few minutes later he emerged from the bush looking worryingly thin. The muscles on his hind legs had wasted, and an Andes of vertebrae rose up beneath the loose skin on his back.

'Oh Mum,' Travers whispered his anguish, 'this doesn't look good.'

Moving slowly and deliberately, the sick lion walked to the nest and lay down directly opposite the car, facing us full on. He was still handsome, though his mane was thinner and the glint of gold was tarnished by dust and poor grooming. Reaching his head forward and opening his jaws wide, he took an egg between his teeth and attempted to crack it. His long canines chipped at the shell as his jaw clamped fast on the creamy oval that could withstand the forces of a three-hundred-pound bird. Twisting his head this way and that, he struggled against the power of an arch until he managed to weaken the structure with a single puncture. From there his task was easy, and spilling its viscous liquid the egg fell apart, releasing a wet fledgling onto velveted paws. Shaking free from the last shackles of shell, the bird looked up and imprinted all its trust onto the face of a lion.

Tipping his head quizzically to one side, Médoc looked at the creature, tapped it tenderly with his paw, and then ate it in one mouthful. Travers and I did not move a muscle: I could hear our hearts beating in the silence. Outside the only sounds were the trill of cicadas and the sweep of a bird's wing in the sky. Médoc watched us for a while, and then stood up to reach for another egg. This time he slumped down, proffering us a sideways view of his long, lean body and black tufted tail. At a leisurely pace he ate the contents of the nest: cracking each shell and slurping on the nutritious fluid while each living morsel rested peacefully on his paws gazing up into his eyes.

'Land Rover 1 Land Rover 1 this is Gomoti – where are you guys?' The voice exploded from the car radio.

Travers hurriedly turned it off but the moment was broken. Médoc looked towards the car and stood up. His tail swished briefly, an indication he was as irritated as we were by the invasion of the peace. He had finished his final snack and the light was fading. Half-heartedly lifting his tail, he sprayed up against a sage bush before moving off towards the west to catch the last remnants of light before the sun went down. He was no longer the king of his domain: night-time was dangerous for a solitary, sickly lion.

I turned on the engine and drove around the area to see if we could find any sign of the female ostrich but there was nothing to see. Loose sand was thin over the surface of the winter-hardened ground and tracks soon blew away.

Travers turned the radio back on and spoke into the receiver.

'Gomoti, Gomoti come in please.'

'This is Gomoti, Trav, shall we start cooking now?' Oakley's voice faded in and out, the signal wasn't good in that area.

'Yes. We'll be back in about forty minutes. Over and out.'

Travers and I were still in a daze. Birth and death with no pain, no cruelty, no violence, no joy and no sorrow: just simply being, and then gone.

'Do you think anyone has seen anything like that before?' he asked.

'At some time in history someone must have, but that is as rare a sighting as I can imagine.'

'We're lucky aren't we Mum.'

'Luckiest people on earth Trav. Relish every second of this my darling one, it won't last for ever.'

'I do.'

We drove on in silence. Time together in the car was always precious. There was no pressure to talk, but the hum of the engine and the calm of the bush liberated trapped thoughts.

'Trav, I've been thinking. We need to think about school. If you were in England now you'd be in secondary school – planning about GCSEs and stuff.'

Travers glanced at me anxiously.

'You're not thinking of going back are you?'

'No way,' I reassured him, 'but we need to think seriously about this next stage. We can't busk it and hope for the best. You need to think about where you want to go to university so I can plan your study. Different countries have different entry criteria.'

He stared ahead, looking out for aardvark holes and other hidden obstacles, as we trundled across a flood plain. 'Do you think I'll ever make it to uni Mum?'

'Darn tootin' you will... if you want to, that is. I won't force any of you to go but I am adamant that all of you will have the necessary credentials and exams... what you do then is up to you.'

'Formal exams Mum... I still read so slowly.'

'You process things differently, that's all. If you look at the grand scheme of things humans have only been reading and writing for seconds; it's a skill our Pleistocene ancestors never acquired.'

Travers looked irritated and reached down between his feet for a water bottle.

'Why does everything always have to be about evolution Mum? It's got nothing to do with bloody Darwin.'

Skipping smartly over the fact that indeed everything was about evolution, and that every gene inside his body was the product of natural selection, I was about to impart words of maternal wisdom when the car came to a shuddering stop – the wheels spinning uselessly in the sand.

Travers leaped out of the car to survey the scene.

'You've driven over a massive log Mum... didn't you see it?'

'Clearly not,' I said crisply.

'We're impaled on the axle. I'll get the hi-lift and lift us up and then you can reverse it. Can you do that?'

'Er yes... thank you very much... I have been reversing for some years now.'

Travers set to work calmly, making no unnecessary movements, for this was the time when the animals changed shift in the crepuscular shadows. I watched my fourteen-year-old working with the relaxed ease he had learned from Pieter. My boy was standing on the other side of childhood. He was in his element. Living in the wild had given him the freedom of responsibility. He was leaving the milky space he shared with his younger siblings, and soon he would start hacking at the umbilical until he was free.

'Okay Mum come out of neutral... clutch down and reverse slowly, okay?'

It was easy. These small problems peppered bush drives, spicing up our lives with tiny victories. The root of our previous conversation was snapped, but I considered it. He had a beautiful mind and it distressed me that he was losing confidence again at school: I had to find a way to rejuvenate it. One thing was for sure: we had to decide between university in America or in the UK to ensure I had time to develop an appropriate programme. I needed to talk to Pieter and to Neecie on the subject. I favoured the Liberal Arts programmes in America, and going to America would mean Trav could spend more time with his dad. But I was scared, homeschooling was a helluva responsibility, and with the children's futures in my hands failure was not an option.

In time we turned onto our track and wending our way slowly through deep sand I could see the lights of home, intermittently glinting far away through the trees. When we arrived, camp was glowing in the light of the hurricane lamps, and I sat for a while watching my people.

Maisie was laying the table, spreading a clean white damask cloth, and lighting the candles; Angus was putting finishing touches to supper; Oakley was curled on the daybed beside the kitchen table reading *Frog and Toad Are Friends*, and Pieter was in the mess tent writing up data on the computer. Travers washed his hands at the sink and shared the news.

'You found Médoc how amazing!' cried Maisie, 'I was scared he was dead.'

'Why didn't you tell me you were looking for Médoc I'd of come,' grizzled Oakley, 'he's my best lion after Inferno.'

'I didn't know we'd pick him up, Oaks,' I said, clambering out of the car, 'I thought I'd died and gone to heaven when I picked up a faint signal.'

'Where was he?' asked Pieter, walking in from the mess tent with a glass of whisky.

'Behind lion valley in a gawd-help-us place. I picked him up from the mound on Baby Jackal Plain – how I got a signal from there I have no idea. It took ages but we found him, and you won't believe what he was eating?'

'Aardvark,' said Gus.

'No.'

'Pangolin?'

'Honey badger,' cried Maisie.

'Don't be daft, lions are scared shitless of honey badgers.'

'You'll never guess,' said Travers.

'Ostrich?' suggested Angus.

'So close. Ostrich eggs,' I said, putting them out of their misery.

'He's sick then,' said Pieter.

'Yup, he looked bloody awful. I think he's another one going to bite the dust. If one more person tells me FIV has no impact on these lions I shall scream. I'm foetid. Do I have time for a shower before supper Gus?'

The no-walking-across-camp-after-dark rule applied to adults too, and clambering back into the car I drove to the reed shower we had constructed beside the bedroom tents. Mercifully, the days of heating water over the fire for bucket showers were over – nowadays our water was heated by a gas burner nailed to a tree. I angled the car to shine the headlights inside, to check all was clear – we had found a female lion drinking out of the drain one evening, and elephant often dropped by for a slurp. Singing loudly, I lathered my hair looking up at the stars; I was as happy as a woman could be.

'Mum we can hear you. If you love us I beg you stop with the singing.'

After supper Pieter made an announcement.

'There's going to be a lion conference in Maun next month, they want us to present our work.'

'Cool,' said Angus.

'Maybe,' replied Pieter dourly, 'these conferences don't often achieve very much. Anyway, I'm going to present the male data, you might as well talk about your repro work,' he said, looking at me.

'I want to talk about the prolactin link... all the...' My words of wisdom were obliterated by the sound of children beating their foreheads on the table.

'Mu-u-u-u-m, don't... hormones are *so* boring,' Maisie spoke for the team.

'Seriously Mum,' said Travers, 'why don't you just present the poop work... you've got the results back, you've got really interesting stuff.'

It was true, the results we got back from the Smithsonian had clearly shown the Santawani females had returned to their regular reproductive cycle within five to six months of giving birth. Nothing pseudo about that. I wanted to repeat the work with another pride and then publish. But far more pressing was the possible negative impact of FIV on reproduction. I was eager to monitor fluctuations in prolactin levels; however, I was too sleepy and happy to argue the intricacies of the endocrine system with the kids.

Pieter lit a cigarette while the children cleared the table.

'Is there any pudding Mum?' asked Oakley.

'Sorry darling, supplies down to their last gasp. I think there's a packet of gingernuts lurking somewhere.'

Oaks wandered into the larder in search of something sweet, and I lay down on the daybed and gazed up at the athletic acacia rat running across the tent poles like a high-wire artist. The pretty little creature always appeared soon after supper. Flattening his soft, pliable body against air resistance, he whizzed around his familiar course along the metal rafters. From time to time he would scurry down one of the tent legs and scuttle across the floor to pick up a nutritious nugget before legging it back to the safety of the roof. The reliable rat was part of the rhythm of our evenings – just as the supper-time visits from the porcupine had been, years ago, at Santawani.

Angus snuggled down beside me to watch the show. He smelled like fresh hay.

'Do you think it's the same rat every night Mummy?'

'Not a clue, but I like to think so,' I said sleepily. Gussie radiated warmth, and my eyes grew heavy. Tired from trundling among the lions all day, I was drifting softly, listening to the sounds of an evening turning in its basket before finally settling down to rest. The clatter of cutlery and scraping of dishes being loaded into the larder, then the thump of the wooden pole being punched down and wedged across the larder door. Bare feet slapping across the sand-gritted plastic groundsheet, then thrumming softly when our huge rug absorbed the vibrations of busy childish feet. Cigarette smoke mingled with distant elephant and the mushroom scent of night-cooled sand. Someone knocked against the daybed as they pulled out the bench before wriggling back down to sit at the table. A book was opened and I caught a waft of musty pages. Soon the rat scampered towards the storeroom to feast upon the dirty dishes. Quiescent stillness. In time, I was roused from my torpor by an insistent roaring from the other side of the river.

'Inferno,' Travers murmured affectionately, 'good boy.'

'Games tonight Mamma?' asked Maisie, 'or are you not in the mood?'

'I'm easy,' I said. 'Happy with whatever, nothing too strenuous, don't want to move.'

Hot candle wax had overpowered the last puffs of tobacco, and rolling over like a bear I hunted down the lingering molecules of ingrained infancy in the nape of Gussie's neck.

'I am E,' said Pieter, he was using his silky voice that night, his warm family voice.

'Are you the father of humanism?' asked Travers.

'No, I am not Erasmus.'

'Did you have a turtle called Skipperdee?'

Pieter paused for a moment to think.

'Ah... no I'm not Eloise. Nice one Mais.'

We played Botticelli until the candles faded.

45

Maun, Botswana 2003

The morning after the attack I made pancakes: twenty for four children. I believe I sang as I whisked the mix. We were in the functional, sterile house in Maun where we had long stay-overs when in town. We were going back to camp later and I was planning the shopping in my head: onions, carrots, butternuts; cabbages, potatoes, sugar, flour, case of long-life milk, ketchup, ice... don't forget the ice... vegetarian sausages, vegetarian schnitzels, cooking oil we are low on that... sugar, have I said that? Cereal... Frosties... do we have Frosties in Maun? Cheerios? What is the cereal they like? It worried me.

'What cillawool do you guys eat?' I called out and swallowed: it was painful.

'Honey Nut Loops and Coco Pops,' said a sleepy voice.

'That's the chap,' I was back on track, 'breakfast is ready.'

The children came in to breakfast in dribs and drabs.

'Mum are you all right?' asked Angus, looking aghast at the crêpe mountain.

'I'm fine.'

'Oh Mum,' he said, his eyes full of pain.

'No really... I'm tickety-boo... let's eat.' Oakley came in next and gave me a morning hug before helping himself to a plate of pancakes and golden syrup. He had a dry nest of hair on the back of his head. I couldn't smell him. I poured myself some Alta Rica instant coffee and sipped on it: hot, tasteless, painful to swallow. How odd. Pieter must have smelled the coffee.

'Morning all,' he said, and I froze. His voice was so loud. He put his arm around me. I readjusted my mind. I had slept beside him – he was safe.

Travers was next, displaced anger spitting out of him like fat from frying eggs.

'Morning,' his voice was rasping and cold. He glanced at me and took his pancakes to the sofa where he jostled for space.

'Budge up Oaks.'

'You budge.'

'Guys,' said Pieter curtly... his voice hurt me it was so loud... so male.

Maisie was the last to arrive. She was soft. She kissed me.

'Mummy,' she said gently. I struggled with something inside my mind. I tried to find my mummy place... I couldn't find it. Think. Be smart. Use your head. Everyone ate so quietly, that wasn't normal. Why was everyone so quiet?

'Look guys,' I said... it must have been forcefully because they all looked up, 'this is not going to make a difference. Three stupid men are not going to make a difference. They were stupid... what they did was just... pointless... a rubbish thing to do. It's not going to make a difference. I won't let them own one more second of my life... not one more moment... do you understand?'

Travers looked me straight in the face.

Defiant.

He knew I was talking bollocks. It made me angry.

'Shit happens. No one is to blame.'

Oakley burst into tears. Why was I shouting at him?

'Darling one, I'm so sorry... I'm not cross with you... I'm not cross with any one of you... I love you.' The words came out of my mouth but they weren't connected to my soul. Someone knocked on the door and Angus opened it. It was the police. Oakley looked at me in confusion.

Botswana 2003

'It's okay... they are here to help.'

'To catch the baddies?'

'Yes... to catch the baddies.'

'What did they do Mamma?' his voice was small. How do you tell your eight-year-old son what men can do?

'Something bad Oaks but look at me... I'm fine.' Oakley looked at me, his eyes widening in fear.

'What's that on your neck Mamma?'

I went into the bathroom and saw the bruises. Purple fingerprints on my neck... how dare they leave marks on me. Fuck 'em.

I heard voices next door. The Scottish paramedic Alison Brown had arrived. Pieter had given the policewoman a cup of coffee, and she was sitting on the sofa with a clipboard on her lap. Too many people. Pieter must have seen that on my face and he asked Travers to take everyone for a walk. I broke into a sweat.

'Take care Trav... don't go far.'

I could feel shame burning up inside me... please go children... don't look at me. It was as if an animal was eating its way through my stomach. It made me feel sick.

I sat down beside Alison and felt the tears coming.

'Kiss, Mamma?' said Oaks. He kissed me once, then twice and then again. 'Say I love you, Mamma,' he said.

'I love you,' I said.

It would become a ritual.

Words felt like splinters in my throat. As they left, Travers let the door bang. I didn't want them to go but I wanted them far away... what did I want?

'Alison I've got to tell you something,' I needed to tell Pieter too but obliquely.

'Anything.'

'You will hate me when I tell you.'

'Never.'

'You will... you will.'

How could anyone not hate me for this?

'Only tell me what you want to Kate.'

'I want to...'

I can't stay stuck. I must move forward. Own up. I was afraid of the tears that would come. Were they like the tears that would kill me? Were they like the tears that had been stuck in me for years... the black tears I haven't cried. Think. These belong to yesterday. These are fresh.

'I let one of them kiss me,' the words fell out of my mouth in a gathering roar. I hid my face. What a way to lose the respect I had earned over the years in Maun. Only Pieter kissed me on the mouth.

'Of course, you did... you did everything you could to stay alive,' Alison's voice was calm and steady. I couldn't look at Pieter. 'You did everything you could so you could have breakfast together just like you did this morning.'

'Why did that feel more intimate than what they were doing?' I asked.

'I don't know, Kate... perhaps because you couldn't disassociate.'

Good point Alison I'll file that away for later. I couldn't let a new thought in. There wasn't room in my head. All my thoughts were jostling for position. They bumped into each other, and when they connected it hurt. Prioritize.

The policewoman finished her coffee and put the empty mug down on the floor. I had forgotten she was there. She pulled out a pen and wrote something on her clipboard. She asked me questions. Where was I when it happened? Why was I walking? What? Why was I walking? I don't understand the question. I can't remember all her questions. She did a good job: kind, businesslike, and professional. She made me feel safe... remember that... tell Anne Sandenbergh... so important to make the victim feel safe. I went cold inside. I was the victim now, but that was not my word. That would *never* be my word.

'Kate we've got to go now sweetheart,' Pieter was kneeling down beside me.

'What?'

'We've got to go now... this officer needs us to meet with CID officers so we can find the scene.'

'The scene?'

'You said you passed Sedia, can you remember exactly where it happened?... she needs to know.'

I shook my head. Passed Sedia Hotel... on the left... there was a bush. Perhaps it didn't happen. That would be nice.

'Don't worry we'll find it.'

Pieter took me in our car. The white Land Rover with Lion Research written on the side. The wildlife department insisted that researchers mark their vehicles because unlike tourists we were allowed to go into protected areas. I worried about Inferno, he had a nasty bite wound, it was beginning to abscess. We never intervened when lions were wounded but it was hard to watch this great creature limping, trying to keep up with Cristal, Freixenet and the cubs. They had three now, Cristal had managed finally to keep one of hers alive, we had named him Roederer (his brother Louis had not made it). Freixenet's boys, Riscal and Rioja, were three months younger. It was odd how clear the lions were in my head.

Pieter turned right onto the road and I could see Sedia in the distance. I felt cold inside. Don't make this a thing... you're going to have to pass this place again and again on the way in and out of town. It's just a place. Perhaps it didn't happen that would be nice. Have I just thought that?

Pieter pulled up beside the police car that was waiting on the side of the road. There must have been introductions, but I don't remember them nor do I remember how many policemen there were. Pieter turned off the engine and paused before he got out. He gripped the steering wheel. He did not look at me. He got out. I sat and watched him shake hands with the policemen. He always slightly embraced the person he was greeting with a light touch on the shoulder... very genial and relaxed... very irritating. My legs were not working properly. Pieter opened the passenger door and reached in for me. I stood on the sand, leaning against the car to keep steady. The sand was grey and dirty.

'There is something I must say,' he said.

I turned to ice. I knew what it was.

'I must say it and then I won't say it again. Ever.'

Don't say it Pieter. Please. Not now. Don't say it.

'I am angry. Very angry.'

'With me?'

'Yes.'

There, it's out now. Do you feel better? I took his anger and sealed it in a box inside my head. Those words should not have been spoken. Not here. Not now. Not ever. Think Kate, think. How can you make this safe? He cares, that's why he's angry. This is the anger you feel when a child runs across a road without holding your hand – you are cross and relieved – it's that kind of anger. That's a loving anger. That's safe.

We walked along the side of the road looking for tracks, just as we did with the lions. Pieter found my tracks, my story in the sand, he saw the place I had been jostled. My tracks joined by one, two, three pairs of feet. It did happen. What a pisser. Where did they come from? They must have crossed the road before they came up behind me.

'Drag marks here,' said Pieter. Drag marks in the sand like the ones the lions make when they drag a carcass. The drag marks took me up a slight incline and then down into a dip. I had just missed a rather nasty bit of broken glass. That was lucky. Someone found a shoe.

'You must have struggled here,' Pieter's eyes were scanning the sand intently as he walked on. Then he stopped. He stood still for a second and then he looked up.

'This is where it happened,' he said, and the policemen joined him. They collected the other shoe, my knickers and a condom. One of them had used a condom. How thoughtful.

'What were you wearing?' asked a policeman. I assumed to make sure they had collected all the evidence. And then it hit me. I was wearing a new belt... it had a nice buckle. I had bought it that week and I was wearing the watch the children had given me for my birthday. It was blue. And a bangle. I hadn't noticed it had gone from my wrist. We searched but could not find anything. They had stolen my belt and my watch and my bangle. How had they had the time? Rage fermented in me. I felt hot like a midden heap. I was rubbish in their hands to be picked through like a garbage tip.

'We're done here,' my mouth twisted in anger and I wanted to be sick. Pieter looked after me well. He took me away and he was very kind. He held me while I cried, and kept his promise.

My anger stripped me of my energy. I slept a fitful sleep and Pieter told the children we wouldn't be going home today. I woke with the smell of skin in my nose. A powerful acidic charcoal smell, it smelled rank... no, that's not right. I rubbed my nose against my pillow to wipe away the smell but it wouldn't go. It filled my head with panic and I gagged. I ran a bath.

'Mamma,' Maisie called to me, 'look at this.'

My friend Mel Oake had dropped round a basket of handmade soap and a bunch of white lilies. I had never seen white lilies in Maun. Where had she found them? So clean. I buried my nose in them and breathed deeply. Faint smell. Tea. Earl Grey. England. I didn't want to fear the smell of skin and woodsmoke and from that day I did not. Another box ticked.

Taking my new soap, I went back into the bathroom and took off my clothes. I shuddered. My inner thighs were now deep purple, Dr Patrick had told me I must have resisted. I only remember fighting in my head. My vagina connected to my brain.

Maisie came to keep me company while I bathed. I tried to hide my legs under the bubbles but she saw. She had been fourteen for less than a month when she saw what men can do to women, and I was too fragmented to save her. The tendrils of empathy that connected me to my children had been cut. I was not a mother any more. I was barely human. It was not the rape that frightened me. It was seeing face to face what one human can do to another. The shock was savage. Debased by my own humanity. How do you climb back from there?

While I was on AZT I existed on the threshold of life before and life after. The drug was disempowering the enzymes that would enable HIV to replicate inside my body, and I was careful not to drink anything that might inhibit the actions of my anti-retroviral cocktail.

On the outside, I was in familial space, but internally I was living in an alien landscape. Years of living in the wilderness had fine-tuned my senses and my reactions to potential or actual danger were swift, focused and unhysterical. But after the attack my response to surprise was shattering.

One afternoon, I was happily cooking lunch after a productive school session. The children were playful and teasing and Angus came up behind me and put his hands around my neck and fear broke me into pieces. I ran into the pantry and huddled on the floor by the freezer gibbering; poor Gussie was devastated and tried to comfort me but he was too scary. Maisie was the only one I could bear to let in, and shooing the boys away she led me gently to the kitchen table where I sobbed my heart out.

'I'm so sorry boy. It's not you... it's not you my darlings... I don't know what's the matter with me.'

And really I didn't. I no longer felt like me. The wellings of love that had fuelled my days had been replaced by eruptions of fear and trembling shadows of deep rage.

Soon after the attack I had called Emily. But I didn't check to see if she had anyone with her. I told her and broke her with grief and she had no one there to hold her. My girl who had never let me down: left alone. I was walking on a wire and no one else mattered. Just don't fall. Apparently two other women had been raped that week. The police couldn't be sure it was the same gang. But the description of the knife was the same. I remained detached.

I called Lalla Dawkins. I don't know why. Our conversation was brief. Half an hour later she rang back.

'Katy, I'll be with you tomorrow. Richard has some air miles and he's booked the flight. Arrive Maun 3.30 p.m.'

I slipped off the wire into a safety net.

I don't remember the logistics. I suppose Pieter must have been in camp with the kids because I was alone at the airport when Lalla arrived. Putting her luggage in the back of the car, she took in the bruises on my neck and arms.

We drove out of town past Shorobe and onto the calcrete road. A car passed us and we choked on its dust.

'Katy do you want me to cry or not? I can cry. I want to a lot.'

'Oh laugh please Lalla, for fuck's sake, let's laugh a lot.'

'Fine. I was just checking. How are the children?'

'I don't know, miserable, angry. Frightened. There was a town meeting. Lots of testosterone... sweet really... all the men in town rallied and gathered at Audi Camp planning how to catch the baddies. I think they are putting posters up... not sure. Trav and Gus were there.'

'Maisie?'

'No, not Maisie. She was furious not to be included. Hurt. Too much for me.'

'Do you care if they catch them?' she asked.

'Couldn't give a shit. Seriously least of my worries. I'm not looking for redemption in prosecution. If I mind about that and they don't catch them then I'm done for.'

'Very sensible.'

'Well you know me... sensible is my middle name.'

'Richard is shattered, but of course doesn't know what to say. He sends masses of love.'

'Bless, he's in good company, no one knows what to say.'

'I assume you are on AZT. Are you worried about HIV?' I loved her for being matter of fact. So many people had avoided the subject.

'Nope, I have total trust in the drugs, and was on them within hours. One of the good things about understanding the science is that it cancels out unnecessary anxiety. I have suddenly become rather good at departmentalization – a new skill.'

'So raping and pillaging has its benefits... bloody marvellous,' we roared with laughter and turned off the road onto the track leading to the buffalo fence.

A few days after Lalla's arrival in camp, I unrolled one of the tent flaps in the mess tent and a tiny pouch mouse tumbled onto the sand. She died instantly leaving behind three babies. They were no bigger than the nail of my little finger. We named one of the minuscule creatures Iorek Byrnison in honour of Philip Pullman's armoured bear. Pieter laughed uproariously when I said I was going to hand-rear the mouse pups.

'You're insane, what will you feed them?'

'Watered-down milk.'

'Ultra Mel, long-life cow's milk ideal for creatures the size of atoms, good luck.'

The mouse pups were so small they could only take one drop at a time, and they had to be fed at regular intervals. During the day, the children helped using a pipette. At night Lalla and I took over. The mice were wrapped in cotton wool and settled down in a matchbox on my bedside table. Before going to sleep, in a bed next to Pieter and me, Lalla set the alarm.

'What time is pill o'clock, Katy?' I had to take a dose of AZT at 2.30 a.m. and she knew it was important I took each dose at regulated intervals.

'You girls are not thinking of waking for those bloody mice are you?' said Pieter, sitting up in bed reading.

'Indeed we are Dr Kat,' said Lalla cheerfully, 'and I'll thank you to keep your uncharitable thoughts to yourself.'

While they were there Lalla and the mice cleansed my nights of darkness. Night-time was hard: trauma makes fools of us all. Just when you need sleep the most, your body pumps fear into your veins and paints visions behind your eyelids. Outside in the bush nocturnal animals went quietly about their business. Jackal and hyena made their presence felt, and of course the lions. Even in my darkest nights I never feared the lions.

During the numbing nights squeaks woke us, and after fumbling to light a candle, Lalla and I would feed the mice and whisper good words. Those nights were the milky essence of female companionship and I could feel parts of me mending: parts so deeply buried I had not even known they were broken.

They say rape is nothing to do with sex and all about violence. I'm not so sure. The fear of death is real, it rips your survival instinct from its resting place, but rape takes place in your vagina – how can that be disassociated from sex – from childbirth – from love – from the soul of womanhood? I remember all my love-making, I remember each childbirth, I can feel each menstruation: every nerve ending relays a story. Did I feel the story told by three strangers inside my body? At the time, no. Fear of death anaesthetized me. But the story was told and absorbed into my history. It began leaking into every crevice of my landscape, hiding inside rocks, expanding in the freeze until later incandescent rage shattered me to shards.

One morning, I put the mice down on the table while I got dressed and a gecko slid down the tent wall and ate them in one gulp. I didn't cry: such is life in the wild.

To begin with I was vulnerable, easy to nurture, but as time passed, open, transparent, colourful me began cracking and twisting like stained glass in a fire. Lalla noticed. It was her last afternoon and we were alone with the lions.

'Don't start drinking, Katy; not while you are so raw. It's not good for you and it's not good for the children. At the best of times too much red wine can bring out your demons.'

'So now you fear Godzilla may be released?' I laughed.

The sun was low in the sky. Translucent amber light, vividly differentiating the shades of green in the grasses and shrubs, etching the shadows of the tree line against a yellowing sky.

'I'm proud of you Katy; you're strong and clear and you've done well these last few weeks. But you've broken... you know that. No matter how many plasters you put on, those wounds will pustulate. You're holding at bay going bonkers, and doing a bloody good job. But if you drink when you stop the medication you'll lose control.'

'Do you know what Maya Angelou says?' I replied, 'she says bitterness is like cancer... it eats upon the host. But anger is a fire that burns all clean.'

'Yes well, that's bollocks. Your anger can be messy and destructive. I've seen it in action once or twice, Katy, and it's not a pretty sight.'

One of the lions got up to pee, inspiring the entire pride to empty their bladders, and for the next half-hour it was action stations. At that time, I was testing to see if we could collect enough regular pee samples to generate statistically relevant data. If we could get viable samples, our collaborators at the Necker Institute in Paris would set about developing a field-testing kit for us.

The pee had to be collected seconds after delivery before it evaporated or was absorbed into blotting-paper-dry sand. As a female finished squatting I drove over and moved her on before leaning out of the car and grabbing a handful of frothing sand in a plastic bag. This was then labelled while I waited for the next sample. Back in camp the saturated sand would be centrifuged to extract the liquid. Lalla was a supportive companion and we worked calmly together. By the time we had finished, the sun had set and the world was shades of grey.

'You're lucky to be here... this place is healing,' Lalla said, 'I don't want to go.'

I didn't want her to go either. She had been our linchpin. Incapable of flummery she got directly to the point, and understood all our needs. But I wondered if she was right about the wilderness being healing: it seemed a romantic notion. To me the wilderness was a tumult of questions; the more I understood the land and its occupants the less I knew. Its beauty filled my soul: a lilac-breasted roller poised on a swaying reed, a herd of tremulous impala browsing in golden light, lions lying in a field of flowers. But I knew the terror of the wild. Even before the attacks I had trembled under canvas while tree-ripping storms raged through camp. From time to time I had been consumed by sudden daylight panic when the bush felt unsettled, lurking and dangerous for reasons beyond my senses' capacity to rationalize: primal fear. Living in the bush had honed my senses to a fine point. But my heart was blunted.

We drove on in silence and I reached for her hand.

'I will never forget our night feeds with Iorek Byrnison. That was a high spot, Katy,' she said.

'You have been my high spot, Lal. I think you may have saved me.'

'No one can do that for you Katy.'

In the days that followed Lalla's departure danger had a taste. My wild body was erupting spikes of adrenaline and corticosteroids, and my mouth was metallic and crushing. But I was not the only cruel one.

Someone said something I shall never forget.

'You're so angry, Kate... no one can help you while you are so angry.'

Perhaps I was shocked because the words were spoken by a woman. Apparently, she needed me to be more appealing before she could part with her sympathy. But grief is ugly, smelly, feeble and barbarous; grief has no trust and allows no whimpering. My children knew that. They were not afraid of sorrow. They were afraid of whisky.

When I finished my course of AZT I started writing poetry in the afternoon after school. Poetry powered by a glass of civilized chilled white wine at lunchtime. The poetry trap ensnared me for a long time. A glass became a bottle. It let words creep up through the cracks and release the pressure that was building inside. Crisp, citrus, soundless words: the unspeakable on a page.

I had an insatiable desire to be alone, and when I sat at the computer in the mess tent I felt shielded and invisible. I lived in the middle of nowhere, no Internet, no telephone, no electricity, but I was never alone. In the afternoons I heard the Land Rover chugging into life and Pieter calling across camp.

'Lioning... anyone coming?... Be quick I'm not waiting.'

A child would answer and then another and I would hold my breath... go... go... my ears strained as I heard running and the tap turned on to fill a water bottle... a short squabble... don't change your mind... go... go... a car door slammed and then another and then the car would move away and wend its way through the palm scrub... the tone of the engine deepening as it slowed down at the river... turn right at the river... my muscles began to relax as the higher pitch of the speeding engine told me they were on their way to the Moremi, and slowly the sound of the engine would evaporate into the air and I would feel peace. But it would be short-lived.

'Mum do we have any Ouma rusks left?'

A child had stayed behind to keep me safe.

'In the pantry.'

'Not those ones, they've got raisins, I hate them, do we have any buttermilk?'

I could feel my soul creak under the strain.

'Dunno... use your eyes.'

The presence of a child in my alone space was unendurable... don't make me be a mother... I can't be a mother.

46

Comeragh Road, London 2010

Oakley and I never talked about the night I threw him out. It was unlike me. To a fault I like things out in the open, but for now that night stays in the shadows. I don't know what triggered my rage. Of course, being drunk didn't help, but in what universe does a mother throw her blameless sixteen-year-old son out into the street? I make nests – I don't destroy them. There was no lion attacking me. There was no reasonable excuse to evict my child from the place in which he felt safe. If you are hoping for a pearl of wisdom here I fear you will be disappointed. I have none. Maybe that's what rock bottom is? Maybe rock bottom is the place where there are no excuses?

The children trusted me when I said I would stop drinking. But it was fragile. I saw that in Travers's eyes one Christmas. I was preparing food and drinking a glass of golden non-alcoholic ginger wine: I turned to see him standing in the doorway, panic flooded his brown eyes.

'Darling, it's non-al!' I cried, 'sweet thing . . . it's fine.'

He laughed and lied.

'Oh I know that Mum, I wasn't worried.'

My boy in the doorway.

One May morning a heavy thunder of feet up the stairs heralded news. 'Mu-u-u-u-u-um, Mu-u-u-um,' Oakley called, before bursting into my bedroom, 'it's here, the letter from UCSB.'

He was shaking.

'It looks thick... that's a good sign.'

'Don't jinx it Mum,' his nostrils were flaring, 'OK here goes... deep breath.'

He opened the letter; I wept, he air-punched and we both telephoned all family members to celebrate. Oh, the relief. Job done. He'd got into four other colleges but this was his dream choice.

When the air settled he snuggled in beside me.

'We did it Mamma.'

'You did it Oaks... against some odds... on your own merit.'

'Ha ha, in your face all those who said it couldn't be done,' he laughed.

While his friends in London had been doing their GCSEs Oaks had been free-wheeling homeschool – and apparently some parents had been thoroughly disapproving. What would become of this itinerant child raised in the wilderness by an irresponsible mother? Apart from Emily, who went to school in England, all the children had opted out of the formal GCSE programme, and I believe this enhanced their development.

Teenagers undergo tumultuous change that is physically and emotionally exhausting. They are navigating a new internal hormonal and neurological environment, and looking at the world through washed eyes. They are quite literally tidying up neurological clutter, which has accumulated in their brains over the years, and carving new pathways. This is fascinating, bewildering, life-enhancing and challenging. It is the time in their lives when they need variety, stimulation, the freedom to explore fresh perspectives, and sleep. Liberated from the pressure of two years preparing for ten turgid exams, the children took their first formal exams as well-read, well-informed, clear-headed souls energized by a defined purpose.

'Mum?' Oakley was flicking through the bumf the college had sent, his face had turned chalky white. 'Have you seen this?'

'What?'

'The fees that's what. I had no idea... it's not just the tuition fees... have you seen this list... books... accommodation... health insurance... student visas... oh my God!'

'I have been here before. Your mother is not a total doofus. Now you're in I'll make a plan.'

'How?' he yelped. Reality hit him, and I was no longer the wonder woman who pulled rabbits out of hats – I was just plain Mum, propped up in bed without her first cup of coffee.

I hadn't the faintest idea how, but I knew something would turn up. That night Angus and Oaks celebrated with various fermented liquids, and, confident that all would be well, I sank a few bracing tonic waters with ice and slice.

Three days later I got a phone call from a Russian woman, and a glorious new vista opened out. I had met Maria briefly, in a flat off the Cromwell Road, while I was tutoring a shiny Russian child. I had liked Maria on sight: she had clever eyes, a sharp wit and a wry smile. She gave little away and I had no idea what she thought of me... indeed to be frank it didn't matter much to me in those days. Now I mind very much because over the last seven years I have learned to love and respect her as a friend and colleague.

'Kate, we met some time ago, when you were teaching Sonia, do you remember?'

'Indeed I do, how nice to hear from you, how can I help you?'

'Am I right in thinking you have taught children who don't speak any English?'

Oh goodness yes... Shaks and Posta on the croc farm... Jumbalani and Tebogo in Jo'burg, and on my farm in the Eastern Cape I taught boys in the valley who spoke only Xhosa. Magical days: we communicated by the universal languages of maths, music and Nature. Too much information, Kate... keep it simple.

'Yes,' I said in a businesslike tone.

'Good,' from her tone I gathered I had ticked a box, 'because I have a seven-year-old boy I'd like you to work with, and he doesn't speak a word of English. Let me explain: I run an educational consultancy for Russian families who want their children to be educated at top schools in the UK. This boy is nowhere near ready to apply, but I remember you homeschooled your children successfully, and thought perhaps you'd homeschool Yan.'

'Seven,' I beamed, 'what a brilliant age to start, yes for sure I'd love to give it a go. What sort of timescale are you thinking?'

'Mum and dad want him to have intensive schooling nine to five, five days a week . . . full immersion.'

'Wow, poor little soul. I won't teach him formally eight hours a day . . . I'd break him,' I laughed, 'but we can go on outings and play games in the afternoon to make life bearable for him.'

'Exactly,' another box ticked, 'I remember you saying that children learn best through play.'

I had no recollection of delivering that pearl, but if I had, my infinite wisdom was undeniable.

'Yan's mother is moving to London, if you can do this she will find a flat near you.'

Wow, this was serious. Hope welled up inside me and I began to feel rather sick.

'I have some other students but I can do some juggling. Yes, I'm happy to commit. But in all honesty, I can't say how long it will take.'

'No one expects that. Let's see where he is after ten weeks, a full term.'

Oh my God . . . dollar signs began to spin in my eyes. My knees buckled.

'That sounds reasonable,' I said crisply and professionally.

'What will you charge?'

My heart was pounding so hard I was concerned I might pass out.

'Well, I need to think about that. It will mean buying lots of educational resources, paying for outings, food, quite a few things on top of the tuition itself,' I responded efficiently.

'Yes of course, please build all that into your fees. Russian parents like clarity.'

'Okay,' I said, and, leaning up against the kitchen sink for support, I began counting on my fingers: rent, college fees, flights to the USA and general living expenses... I gave her a figure. I held my breath... don't be silly... this can't be.

'Fine,' she said, 'that sounds reasonable.'

I took a deep breath.

'Of course, that has to be paid upfront,' I said, 'like any school.'

'Of course, I will get back to you this afternoon but I'm pretty sure the parents will go with this.'

And that is how Oakley's first term was paid for.

For the next five years Comeragh Road bustled with a joyous stream of enchanting Russian children whom I nurtured and taught, and from whom I learned much. Some were daytime students, and others came to live with me like members of the family. As my children had, the young Russians explored the world energized by their curiosity.

Through instinct and experience, I learned quickly each child's interests and foibles, and I spent productive hours tucked up in bed at night conjuring up ways to build, or sustain, confidence, and to make the next day fun. The children learned through play, experimentation and stories. Some had to be prepared for school entrance exams, but the pressure of formal lessons was alleviated by baking cakes, gardening, playing games and going on outings where they could roam freely. Bit by bit they made connections between disparate topics: they found the poetry in photosynthesis, and the science in baking, and soon classroom and outside world were indivisible. They all became fluent, and got into good schools, and there was comfort in knowing that the lessons I had learned from Louisa M. Alcott continued to energize the cycle of education in my household. But there was an additional wonder – a new enrichment: I had full access to the Internet.

Teaching under a tree was romantic, but I am no Luddite, and I relish the generosity of cyberspace. Looking up into the African night sky and finding your way home is wonderful, but so is gazing at a screen on the Crab Nebula (a star nursery) with a child who previously had no idea he was made of stardust. Day by day my mind was expanded by fresh insights, and the children were witness to my passion for learning and my insatiable curiosity. Learning about the universe, and how it works, was a shared delight. The day gravitational waves were detected I nearly exploded with excitement, and oh what fun it was to build the LIGO detector out of old loo rolls, silver foil and a mirror prised from a make-up kit. The child I was teaching had no idea what a gravitational wave was when it was at home, but he knew something wonderful had happened, and seeds were sown that would flourish later.

I loved each child who came into my life: some brave, some timorous, some stultified by the fear of making a mistake, some lively and humorous, some stoically serious, some staunchly rebellious and gloriously naughty: all of them brought joy.

Happy Plumfield days returned.

I was me again. The me I used to be.

47

Gomoti Camp, Botswana 2003

Everyone's life was smeared by the attacks. Travers was the first 'lion child' to graduate from under our tree, but he only had a few weeks of unmitigated joy before his world turned ugly. He had applied to several excellent colleges, but it was his father who had suggested the University of California Santa Barbara.

'Kate, I'm down the road in LA, it's crazy not to go for it, and it's a great school.'

We were on the cusp of the deadline and Neecie called the admissions department to warn them that an application was winging its way via DHL: it arrived just thirty minutes before the official cut-off.

Relieved from the pressure of SAT exams and the gruelling application process, Travers spent time with friends, and I was liberated to focus my worries on our research permit application – to which we still had no response. Bush life is beautiful but the wonder of a leopard up a tree does not quell the primal anxiety a mother feels when her family might lose the roof over its head: albeit a canvas one. Added to that, new males were roaring around the Mogogelo, and the pride was as unsettled as I was.

We didn't expect to hear from any school for several months so picture my amazement when, only a few weeks later, I found a fax waiting for me at Ensign Office Services in Maun: Please contact the admissions officer CCS, UCSB, immediately.

'Hello,' I said, 'I had a message to call you. I'm so sorry, what have we missed out?' I could think of no reason for them to be in touch, other than the application was incomplete.

'Hi, it's Leslie Campbell here: we don't have his CCS application.'

'What's that?' I replied.

'We have to have a formal application, you see, if we are to accept him.'

'I'm really sorry but I think there must be a mistake, he applied to UCSB not CCS. I don't know anything about a CCS.'

I could hear her laughing.

'The College of Creative Studies is part of UCSB... it's very special here... basically it's for gifted undergraduates.'

I made a seal-like awping sound, but I still didn't understand.

'We want him, but we need him to apply.'

'Are you saying he's got a place at UCSB?'

'Oh yes, for sure,' she said patiently, 'but we want him at CCS.'

'Oh my God,' I yelled, 'are you serious?'

I thought I might burst with joy.

Down the other end of the line I could hear Leslie Campbell laughing.

'We'd love him here,' she cried, 'it was a great application.'

'Dear heart, I want to kiss you,' I sobbed down the line, 'and I promise faithfully to fill in the form and fax it to you pronto but first I must find Trav and tell him, I can't hold on a second longer.'

'Of course, no problem, but fax it to me in the next few hours.'

Oakley was with me, and we whizzed around town like the Road Runner on speed, finally finding Travers ambling down the main road on his way to roller-blading.

'Trav,' I shrieked, hanging out of the window.

'Traverrrrrs,' yelled Oakley, hanging out of his window, 'sto-o-o-o-o-o-op!'. Oakley had to be restrained from exiting a moving vehicle in his excitement.

'You've got in,' I panted, '... into UCSB and some smart place want you... too...'

'What?'

'You're in, Trav... my darlingest boy... you've made it.' That was that.

I burst into tears, Oakley nearly exploded with pride and Travers was in shock.

The next few weeks were euphoric. Our joy culminated one day in March, when finally we got a four-year extension on our research permit. Hours later I was raped.

Travers didn't take time out to travel: he stayed to look after his siblings... and me. From the beginning Travers knew I was on a road to nowhere. He tried to navigate me onto a better path. I didn't listen. I was clinging to a crumbling rock-face: resting all my weight on a tuft of grass. After Lalla left, practical, empathic Travers took charge. Without telling me he rang a friend of mine in Cape Town and arranged for me to stay with her. He found a counsellor who specialized in rape, and booked an appointment for me to see her. Travers booked my flight to Cape Town and handed me the ticket.

'Mum you need help, please will you do this for me?'

'Trav I'm fine... I don't want to leave you all.'

'But you need to, Mum.'

How did he know that? I didn't know that. How did a seventeen-year-old boy know so much?

'Mandi will meet you at the airport and take you home. There will be smellies in her bathroom Mum, all the things you love. Someone to look after you. It will be easy for a while... you need something easy, Mum. Something safe.'

I packed and we drove to the airport, and I kissed my family goodbye. I so nearly made it to safety. I walked through immigration control onto the airstrip. The fat blue and white Air Botswana plane was waiting for me; passengers were already mounting its stairs. The tarmac was hot and my bare feet began to burn. A heat haze rose up around the plane. The plane that would crash. I could hear splintering glass and my ears filled with black water as the fear mounted inside me. My limbs followed the zigzag rhythm of the heat haze – my bones would not carry my weight. I was losing balance. I looked up and saw the children waving at me from our familiar vantage point upstairs in the airport. My babies... don't take me away from my babies. The tarmac turned into the blackness... the blackness that always silenced me in fear... I was so afraid I thought I might die if I made a sound... my hands felt light as I floated away.

Pieter came running onto the tarmac and took me in his arms.

'It's okay sweetheart you don't have to go. It's okay.'

I loved him so much, the heat from his body warmed me and the safety of his arms took away my fear.

We drove home. Travers slumped in the back of the car, leaning his head against the window, eyes closed, listening to his mother talking rubbish.

'Think of the women in Maun who have been raped – do they run away to the glamour of Cape Town? Maun is my home and I'm not going to let three men take me away from my home. I'm happy in camp... I love my peeps... I'm fine if I'm with all of you. My healing darlings – just the smell of you makes me happy.' Oh, how I prattled on.

Months later, I was hating my blameless, beautiful children. Powered by alcohol I became a burning-glass.

'I don't care,' I screamed.

'You don't care you've been raped?' said Pieter.

'No, I don't,' I yelled. The campfire was spitting.

'You don't care that the worst thing that can happen to a woman has happened to you.'

'Oh, and you would know about that would you... you're the expert on the worst thing that can happen to women?'

'Jesus, you can be ridiculous. Just listen to yourself.'

'I'll tell you the worst thing that can happen to women. The worst thing is having your cunt cut to shreds, and all the lies about the bastard joys of childbirth. That's the worst thing... that's the shock... the ultimate betrayal... a bit of raping and pillaging is nothing compared to childbirth.'

'I can't talk to you when you're like this,' he said grandly, getting up to put another log on the fire.

'It's what men do,' I spat the words.

Pieter looked at me and his eyes were cold.

'I see,' he said calmly, 'it's what we do is it? All men.'

I felt deflated. My thoughts were slipping like silk, and I couldn't find traction. I was sitting on the elephant skull and my bum was going numb. I felt around in the sand beside me and found the whisky bottle. I poured another glass.

'That's a good idea,' he said smugly.

The whisky was warm. Bells. We had run out of ice.

'Think of the women, Pieter,' I was calmer now, 'every day walking to collect wood or water or just coming back from work. Men just helping themselves. It's what they do.'

'Sweetheart, not all men. It may seem like that now but...'

'But what? What? Who do you think does it? Monsters... baddies... mad people? They were ordinary people, Pieter... *ordinary*... who for some reason felt entitled to my body... that's all. Get over it. I have.'

Liar. You're a liar Kate. The worst kind of lies are the ones we tell ourselves. Who said that... someone familiar? Think of the women in war zones and refugee camps who walk miles to get wood knowing what may happen. Knowing they may be pinned to the ground... think of the women who walk back bleeding from the brutality and stir their fires and cook food for their children and never cry. You are part of that sisterhood now. You're a real woman now Kate. Can you be a real woman?

'I'm going to bed. You need some sleep. Are you coming?' He stroked my hair as he walked past. It felt like an echo.

I could feel a wave of nausea. I walked into the kitchen and poured a glass of water from the tap. I cleared away the unfinished game of Cranium the children had left scattered on the table when they had flounced off to bed. Why had they gone? Something I said? Can't remember. I hated the children. I hated the guilt they made me feel. I had lost my moral compass, so what, I didn't need it any more. Did I still have it when Emily came? I can't remember. Was she here before or after Lalla? How many days was she here? Why can't I remember?

I sat on the sand beside the embers of the fire and felt nothing. There were no stars that night because the moon was full. It was one-thirty in the morning and it was as light as day. Tough to be an impala on such a night. I heard something moving, and looking up I saw a hyena lolloping across the volleyball court Travers had made out of river sand. I smiled. It was typical of Trav to have set such a project and seen it through. It had taken days of digging out creamy, soft sand from the dry riverbed and hauling countless loads back to camp. Travers wanted a full-sized court defined by white sand and he had put his back into it. The others followed his lead, and I had watched my sweaty children working together and I had loved them. Had I really hated them tonight? Poison.

The hyena was a few metres away and it stopped to look at me.

'Fuck off,' I shouted. I was bored by wildlife – seen one hyena, seen 'em all. The creature stared at me for a moment, and trotted away. I was fearless.

'Mummy,' I heard Angus before I saw him walking up the path – the one he'd helped me make with dried elephant shit – bordered by sun-bleached giraffe femurs.

'Are you okay Mum? Did you see the hyena?'

'Yes.'

'Oh Mum,' his voice was thick with disappointment. He sat beside me in the sand. He was wearing an old jersey and boxer shorts – the hem had been nibbled by rats.

'Mummy don't stay up here alone... not like this...'

'Jesus Gus, I just want some space that's all.'

'But not like this. That was dangerous,' his voice was tender and I felt a roaring of anger building up inside me. A hot mountain of pus was emerging from my throat. Lying in bed, Gus must have heard something and been worried. He must have watched me. Stop watching me. Leave me alone.

He had hair on his legs now... my big boys were men now. So young. My anger crystallized into cruelty.

'I don't love you,' I said. I looked at him fully in the face and said it again.

'I don't love you. It's important you know that.'

'It's all right Mum... I believe you,' he spoke as if he was talking to a child, and suddenly I was too tired to carry my anger, and so I dropped it. I felt bereft.

Angus's blue eyes were heavy. His skin was winter-dry. He got up and walked past the trampoline towards the solar panels. He turned them to the east so they would catch the first rays of the sun. He came back to the fire and stood opposite me.

'Let's go to bed now Mum... we've got school in the morning.'

A pain cracked the front of my skull... don't tell me what to do. I breathed through my mouth and smelled whisky.

As I got up I stumbled and caught my foot in my flimsy cotton skirt. I heard it rip. It made me sad. I liked my pretty things.

As we walked towards our tents I noticed our path was wearing away in patches.

'Ellie poop collection tomorrow Gus... just a bit for along the edges.'

He didn't reply. I watched him unzip his tent and go in. I heard Travers whisper something. Judged. Concern was claustrophobic. Controlling. I wanted to tear down trees with my bare hands until my bones bled. Go to bed Kate.

The zip on our tent was broken. A year or two ago I had grown tired of our dark *Out of Africa* Meru tent. On a whim, I had bought a second-hand green and white marquee from my

American missionary friends. It was a joyous circus tent with a central pole, huge and airy, and beside our double bed there was plenty of room for the single bed: where Lalla had slept, and where Oakley slept when the others were in town. I tied the door flaps together with a canvas strap and pushed the wicker basket against it. It would not stop anything from coming in, but it would at least make a warning noise.

Pieter was fast asleep, and he didn't stir as I undressed. His glasses were on his book on the bedside table. He was reading *The Pursuit of Love* and adoring Uncle Matthew. He had fallen asleep with the light on, most of the power was used up and the light was barely visible. I leaned over and switched it off. The skin on his back was smooth and I kissed his shoulder.

'Is that you?' he murmured.

'Yes.'

'Good.' He went back to sleep.

I lay back on my pillow and I missed Lalla.

I looked back on my AZT months. Halcyon days.

I needed Lalla's guidance. My path was crazy. As crazy as she knew it would be. I remembered the night I had been rigid with fear and reached out for her hand. I'd held Pieter's too and between them I felt safe.

I hadn't shaken the sand off my feet before I got into bed and the grit was uncomfortable. I was cold and rolled over towards Pieter. I was feeling too sick for sex but the idea was nice. We had made love soon after the rapes and he was very tender. We both reclaimed my body that night. No, reclaim is the wrong word. My body was always my body. Mine to give in love. I had loved him that night with an open heart, and he healed the scratch on my soul with his body.

Sleep now. Sleep. *Othello* first class tomorrow: reputation, reputation, reputation.

The rhythm of days remained familiar but discordant.

The weeks dragged on and I became more powerful. I was inviolate.

Digging. Digging up the dirt that was in me. Dig out the black truth – the whole truth and nothing but the truth. Whisky was my spade. And night after night I stabbed wildly in any direction until I made contact with my darkness. Night after night I spread my mind-muck across the kitchen table, across our camp, across the children's beds. Night after night they lay in bed fearful that I was going to tip over the edge. I threw plates; I drove my car into a tree; one night I roared my car into Maisie's tent and frightened her so much she drove into town to get away.

'Make it stop, Travers.'

'I can't, Oakley.'

In the mornings I was bright and cheerful.

'Pancakes darlings, or schnitzels?'

'Are you all right Mum?'

'I'm fine my angel – why do you ask?'

'What happened last night?'

'Oh nothing, Pieter and I had a tiff that's all. Now who's going to set the table?'

Morning after morning, my children's weary hearts were worn down by denial. I didn't see them blinking under the strain – trying to forget the night before – while listening to me reading in class. Trying to hold on to the mother they knew. The mother who made learning fun, the mother whose arms were always open for cuddles and hugs. The mother whose laugh came easily. The mother who smelled of Yves Saint Laurent Y and safety – before she smelled of stale whisky and fear.

I looked the same on the outside, still clean and dressed in fresh T-shirts and floaty skirts, but my internal landscape was one in which Salvador Dalí would have felt cosy. Familiar sights, sounds, memories and feelings were all twisted out of perspective; disproportionate mundane objects clustered in a cluttered terrain – with an occasional anachronistic detail thrown in just to keep me on my toes. I was fascinated by my destructive liberation. I was the centre of my world – selfish – isolated – defensive.

I had no idea that I was ill.

School was a lifeline... a precious oasis. While teaching, something deep inside me stirred and tried to stretch. Maybe in tiny incremental steps, those days played a part in my healing. But mainly I doused any feelings I had with alcohol and kept my internal fire raging. My anger was never directed on the men who raped me. Towards them I remained sanguine, noncommittal: a trifle bored. I directed my rages onto the children and Pieter and anyone who came in close proximity. I stopped drinking my lunchtime wine: the wine that had released poetry and sloppy tears. What control. Not drinking in the day proved that I didn't have a problem. My mendacity gave me permission to drink uncontrollably after the witching cocktail hour.

One night a new demon was released. I hit Pieter, accidentally cutting his head open. My phoenix conscience rose up, fanning my guilt into frenzy. Nurturing Pieter and pressing pressure bandages onto the wound, I felt a new fear. I was no better than the men who had raped me. I should be snuffed out. That was the first time I took an overdose.

It made Pieter very angry.

'How many pills did you take?'

'All of them.'

'Why does everything always have to be about you?' he said, pouring me the first of many cups of strong black coffee. He made me walk all night. In the morning, we drove to Maun. An elephant charged us on the way. I didn't care.

I told Alison Brown what I had done. I needed help. I agreed to have twice-weekly counselling at Women Against Rape. I started that day. The counsellor said he would only treat me if I went to the doctor to get antidepressants. I was obedient.

I had dug up the dirt and seen me for what I was – rotten – dangerous – unworthy. While I had therapy, we moved to town to make life simpler. How I longed for time out – stop – please – just for a moment. But days followed days. My children's futures depended on me.

Angus was preparing for his SATs and writing his college applications for UCSB, Duke and Stanford. Keep steady. You can do this.

I bought a box file and he made colour-coded notes:
Council of Trent 1545–1563
Differences between Luther, Zwingli, Calvin
Point Slope equation $y - y_1 = m(x - x_1)$
Mother is to trust as lion is to antelope.

Therapy was exhausting and fruitless. I found no comfort there. The cracks in my romantic relationship with Pieter were revealed and I was advised to leave him. I felt as if I was floating on a raft in an ocean, occasionally bumping into a pod of whales that tipped me up and played with me like a rag doll for a few moments before swimming away. I stayed with Pieter. Detached – shrivelled. I spent the weekends with the lions.

We were living in paradise, but Nature has no cure for human brutality. I formed a new connection with the wilderness: pragmatic – unromantic – dangerously fearless.

One night, after another fight, I ran into the bush. It was dark. The monochrome was bleak. I was barefoot. I heard Pieter calling me. I walked into the scrub between camp and the river. In time, I lay down under a bush. The night was very quiet. In the distance, I heard the broken zip in our tent being pulled up and the slight billow of the tent walls as Pieter pushed through the narrow entrance. A few seconds later I heard the zip being pulled down. He had gone to bed. I smelled elephant, but far, perhaps drinking downstream.

I was cold and I curled up like a pangolin. I heard tiny scurrying movements quite close – probably an acacia rat. I liked sharing the night with him. I liked the rawness of lying on the sand in the dark. A feeling moved inside my womb and grew into something like thwarted joy. I wondered what had stirred that rust and then I understood. It was an atavistic connection, nothing more and nothing less. I was simply doing what my Pleistocene sisters had done: for millennia females had found a bush and curled around their babies while they slept. Why could I feel the link in that abstract chain and not feel the umbilical connection to my children? A warning beat against my breastbone and my hair rose. Something was moving closer – smaller than an elephant, bigger than a rat. It had no smell.

I'm post-reproductive, eat me if you want to. I went to sleep.

48

The South Bank Centre, London 2013

The South Bank Centre's main foyer thrummed to the rhythms of language, an occasional word or phrase cresting a wave before sinking back into unintelligible murmur. Drinking a cup of rather nasty black coffee I watched people flowing like harvester ants on a mission: chaotically organized, jostling and dispersing. In twenty minutes some them would be listening to my story, yet I was surprisingly relaxed and disengaged from fear. I had committed to giving the talk for a reason, so there was no point in allowing anxiety in.

Walking upstairs my head was clear; my thoughts were gathered; my heart was steady; only my legs were unsure. Fear of falling was a natural part of my life, it didn't bother me.

Jude sat on the dais with me and the other speakers. She introduced us one by one. Each of us had a different story, and a perspective we chose to share because we cared. The audience was hushed, respectful: a little awkward. I felt sorry for them. It must have been hard, leaning forward, wanting to understand something that most people shied away from. My talk was last:

'Hello. Thank you for listening today, I know it can't be easy. I will do my best to be direct. I'm not going to go into details – the mechanics of rape are what they are. I was raped at knifepoint on the side of the road by three men in Botswana. I was lucky because I was well cared for by the police and the hospital. I was given kindness and immediate medical assistance. Not to seem over-dramatic, but this was life-saving. In Botswana statistically one in three people are infected with HIV/AIDS – not great odds for me. I was lucky to be in Botswana where antiretroviral treatment is freely available and routinely offered to women who have been raped. I'm not telling that part of my story for the first time. A week after it happened I wrote an article for the local paper: in a small African town it was front-page news. I spoke out because I wanted to break the taboo of silence and to encourage other women to come forward. It's a universal crime, and universally it is shrouded in shame and fear. That has to stop. It seems that whether women live in developing or developed countries, they are still facing the same battles.

'Yesterday, in this room, I listened to Martin Hewitt, the Assistant Commissioner of the Met Police, talk with compassion and frustration about the challenges women meet here in the UK when they report a rape. Indeed, the challenges are so great that many choose not to report. I was horrified to learn that in 2013 things are no better than when I left England in 1994. The ratio of reports to successful prosecutions made my blood boil. But I was also heartened because Commissioner Hewitt cares. He's an active listener and that's what we need. Stories need to be heard and action taken. I have empirical evidence that active listening works.

'Ironically, it was HIV/AIDS that brought the needs of women suffering domestic violence or rape into sharp focus. Botswana took its responsibilities seriously and though I'm not pretending things were perfect – far from it – people in government were listening and trying to do their best. In the mid-1990s, I worked for an NGO called Women Against Rape. I won't drone on and give you all the background but it was the women and children who implemented the change by telling their stories in clinics, at schools, sitting under trees or in broken-down huts. With support from W.A.R. we saw women struggling to overcome shame, fear of reprisal, embarrassment, guilt, anger, revulsion and the myriad of confused emotions that are stirred up by this universal crime. They spoke up. We heard them, we took action, but more importantly the government took action.

'We asked for a meeting with Botswana's Commissioner of Police to advocate for women and children. He listened to us, questioned us, asked for our recommendations, and pondered. Then with no prevarication he agreed to our requests. There and then he gave us permission to implement a countrywide programme of workshops for local police, aimed at improving and unifying procedures when rape was reported. We needed to ensure women got prompt access to AZT. I saw this in action. I reported my rapes to one of the policemen I had trained.

'I don't want to sound like Pollyanna. I'm not looking at this through rose-tinted spectacles. Not for one second am I "glad" it happened to me. There is still much to be done in Botswana, and clearly this is also true here in the UK. But I am telling you that I have seen for myself how things can be improved by sharing stories and by active listening.

'The chapter in my story I want to tell you today is not easy: it's not even my story to tell. I'm here today to speak out for victims of rape we rarely hear about.

'Rape doesn't just happen to one person. It happens to the family too and it nearly broke mine. I learned about the secondary victims of rape because my children were. Secondary victims need to be acknowledged and given advocacy. Living with someone who has Post-traumatic Stress Disorder is bewildering, challenging, dangerous and harmful.

'I'm not ashamed that I was raped but I am desolate that while I was healing I hurt my children. It's no fun standing here sharing this part of my story, but if we peel back the layers of secrecy that shroud sexual violence we'll reach a deeper understanding, and thus be able to provide appropriate support for silent secondary victims.

'Healing is a messy, Sisyphean process – it's not like it is in the movies. I'm not going to tell you how I healed because everyone does that differently, in her own way, in her own time. Healing is about taking back control and I would never dream of imposing or advising any system, pedagogy, therapy or magic pathway to a woman – or a man – who has been raped. Everyone needs to find their own route back and not be judged by how long it takes them. But I was ill – for a long time – without knowing it. I carried on with my life, picked up the pieces, did all the things I used to do; but with Post-traumatic Stress Disorder – and drinking like a fish. Not a good combo. It's true I was living in the African bush under extreme conditions, but the heart of my story is not unusual. Families who welcome back army veterans understand all too well the pain of living with a loved one who has PTSD.

'A while ago I saw an episode of *Homeland*, I think many of you will have seen it. But for those who haven't here it is in a nutshell: a war veteran returns home, radicalized and suffering from PTSD. He's welcomed back into the bosom of his family and he wrecks it. His wife gives a speech at some posh meeting and says simply: "The vets get the help, but who is there for the family?" I remember fist-punching the air when I heard that. It's the family who deal with the midnight terrors, the rages, the erratic behaviour and the violence; all the while loving the person who is brutalizing them. I knew it was true because my children had to deal with that: my wildness, my drinking, my cruelty, my violence.

'The poison of the rapes contaminated me and spilled out into my kids. And there was no one there for them. They just had each other to cling to. They were eight, fourteen, fifteen, seventeen and twenty-three when it happened. All at different stages of their lives, all needy in different ways, all loving and deeply concerned, all emotionally intelligent, kind humans who lost the mother they trusted for years. The person who had been their rock crumbled and they tried to put me together again. Simply put – it took longer than they could bear.'

I heard a man breathe in sharply, he was sitting in the third row, and I can picture him now. He looked at me and his eyes told me he understood. He was kind, and brave enough to look at a raw reality. He gave me the courage I needed to carry on:

'My kids loved the person who was hurting them and that is harmful at a profound level. My job is to heal them but not to do so in silence. Or in shame. AA and NA have programmes for families and partners. We need to provide similar support for the families of the victims of sexual crime. Rape takes minutes but it takes years to heal. How many? There is no definitive answer.

'We can be quite brutally prescriptive with each other's pain. We designate timescales for recovery from divorce: three years. We prescribe five stages of grief: denial, anger, bargaining, depression and acceptance. Boom! – sorted. But healing cannot be fitted to a curve: it's not a neatly balanced equation. It's chaotic, muddled, ugly, visionary, enriching, disempowering, bleak and painful. Healing is neither linear nor progressive. It happens in quantum time frames, each isolated from the others. And that is what makes it so hard to live with someone who is healing. My loving kids celebrated tiny steps, felt relieved when we had good days, were comforted by moments when I seemed to be the mother they knew and understood, and then something would trigger me and everything would go tits up again.

'For me the hardest part has been getting better. When empathy returns you can see the harm you have done. That's why I'm here. Not to talk about the harm that was done to me. But to talk about its knock-on effects. The ripples in the stream.

'I love my children as deeply as it's possible to love. Indeed, I loved them before I met them. If anyone had told me I could be disconnected from my children I would have laughed in their face: nothing on earth could do that. But three strangers ripped me from my family in less than twenty minutes.

'Rape is a violation: for me it did not touch my sexuality: that may seem odd to some of you but I am being honest and telling you my story. For me the violation was the loss of empathy. I lost my root. And I couldn't feel. That made me dangerous to my children. I broke their hearts. And it is a testament to how massive their hearts are that I am here today and able to tell you we are on the mend. I am safe again and strong.

'Being raped did not make me a better person – let me be clear on that. Being raped did nothing but harm; but recovering has enriched my humanity.

'The secondary victims of rape are everywhere: in refugee centres, in forests in the Congo; in war-torn countries, and somewhere on your road; in your classrooms, in your office, maybe sitting next to you on the bus. They need our help. When a rape is reported we must put systems in place to support the families, partners and carers. They are the ones who pick up the pieces and currently they are doing it in isolation. AA and NA give support to families so the model is there: we just need to acknowledge the problem and take action.

'I want to end with something one of my children said to me: "Mum, I wish it hadn't happened to you. I wish it hadn't happened to us. But getting through it made me who I am today: and I like who I am."

I like who he is too.'

The room was silent. I felt no animosity, no judgement. Yet, despite assurances from all three speakers that we were happy to take questions, at the last moment Jude had made an executive decision: for our protection. No questions, no filming, our messages would go no further than that room.

Stripped of my voice, I had told my story into a void.

I had reached more people sitting under trees in Botswana. I was a pointless woman of the world.

The audience shuffled out, and standing limply on the dais I watched them politely jostling in the doorway, checking their programmes for the next venue. Jude Kelly thanked me and the other participants and bustled off to attend to other matters. My legs began to shake. I hadn't expected to respond so viscerally: to feel so empty. Someone was standing by the door looking into the room. Someone familiar was smiling at me: my young cousin.

'Vikki?' I squeaked.

'You didn't think I'd let you do this alone did you?' she said, walking towards me to give me a hug. Well yes actually, I had expected to do it alone.

'My darling girl how did you know? I'm in bits.'

'Twit,' she said affectionately, 'I am Emily's proxy... she's gutted... she wanted to be here... but an OFSTED visit scuppered her plans... so she called me.'

Emily was a primary-school teacher and OFSTED had offered only scant warning of a visit.

Vikki looked so like her mother, the same smile, the same kind eyes. I slipped back into childhood, remembering the safety of my older cousin. I was a stormy child and my cousin calmed my turbulent ways: she loved me with a steady hand and I adored her.

'Right, lunch I think, don't you?' she said, 'you did well but bugger me, eh.'

'With a brick sideways.'

'You've always had a way with words,' she laughed, steering me out of the door and down the stairs.

We walked over the bridge towards Embankment Tube station. I could see St Paul's in the distance, a dogged reminder that unpredictable destruction opens the path for a new vision. In 1666 a few sparks, whipped into life by turbulent winds, gave rise to a conflagration that energized new ideas and changed the face of London for ever. I stopped for a moment to watch the Thames flowing beneath me. Obedient molecules moving from high energy to low energy, yet stirred by Nature's intrinsic anarchy into swirling eddies, sucking vortex and smothering undertow. Life-enhancing rivers were chaos in action: disconnected, amoral, with no purpose: driven by natural laws that allow randomness and disorder.

'It's odd isn't it,' I said, 'how we depend on turbulent power... we harness it... redirect it... use it to keep us safe... yet we fear chaos.'

Vikki reached for my hand and we stared into the water together. She knew the pain of randomness. As a sister in a paediatric ICU her days were spent nursing sick babies and children, who by some quirk of fate had become ill or had an accident.

'Nature is not kind,' she said, 'I guess that's why we need to be... to make up for the unfairness of it all.'

'How do you cope with so much grief Vikki, so much pain? Kids with cancer for fuck's sake.'

'The job keeps you focused: the tasks, the routines, the knowledge you accrue every day keeps you alert. But I don't "cope" with the pain – I feel it too... I couldn't do my job if I didn't empathize.'

She was so young, in her late twenties, and yet she was already grounded. I marvelled how she had held her balance amid the extremes of joy and grief she experienced.

We walked on. She led the way through side streets towards Covent Garden, and before we reached the covered piazza we stopped outside a crisply elegant bistro: white tablecloths, thin-stemmed wine glasses, slim-hipped waiters in black aprons, bread in rustic paper bags.

'Okay?' she asked.

'Looks great,' I replied.

We ordered our food. I don't remember what we ate. I remember Vikki's warmth.

'What was the point Vikki?' I said, chomping on crusty French bread and sipping water.

'You may have helped someone... you were so honest Kate.'

'Yeah, I told a roomful of people what a twat I was to my kids... and then they left. So helpful, so frigging life-enhancing.'

'What were you expecting?' she asked.

'Connection, something purposeful... proactive... YouTube coverage, questions from the audience... anything rather than nothing.'

Vikki topped up my glass from a pretty cobalt-blue bottle of sparkling water.

'Not too much, I'd better be careful,' I laughed.

'How long has it been now?'

'Since I had a drink? I don't know... years. I'm rubbish at chronology, I can't even remember the dates of Gus's and Maisie's birthdays – I know the months but never the days... one is the ninth and the other the tenth... I always have to ask Ems or Cindy.'

Cindy and Neecie had been together for years, and I adored her. We're family.

'I suppose they didn't want to put the talk on YouTube to protect you from trolls,' Vikki continued. And I exploded.

'Exactly... let's hear it for the trolls – let's keep quiet for fear we arouse their idiot wrath.'

The waiter arrived with our food and I simmered down to a constant bubble while he placed our plates on the table.

'Thank you,' I said politely, waiting for him to leave before continuing. 'Look I'm sure you're right... Jude had our best interests at heart, but she sold me another plan. She asked me to talk about something I care deeply about and then she shut down any feedback. I know she did it to protect... but does she think I haven't heard all manner of utter bollocks said to me about rape? There's nothing I don't know about victim-blaming. I've been "trolled" ever since it happened – by idiots, clever people, friends, strangers, you name it, all the classics: What was I wearing? Did I fight back? One of my personal favourites is... Why were you walking? Duh... because I'm bipedal.'

Vikki laughed: 'I've spoken to you sharply about walking, Kate.'

I giggled and tucked into my food.

'You know what, Vikks?' I said after a while, 'I sort of understand why even some women are blamers... it's a form of protection really.'

'How come?'

'No one wants to be raped, no one wants to acknowledge it can happen to anyone, at any time, anywhere... so it's easier to find fault. She was walking... she was wearing a crop top... she was drunk... she was on roller skates or dancing the tarantella in a pink nightie... peeps will find any excuse they can to lay blame because then they can tell themselves they'd never do that... and so they stay safe! It's human... I get it.'

'Does it hurt?'

'My feelings? No... not any more.'

I relaxed in her easy companionship, and we chatted about family and reminisced about the holiday she had spent in camp when Oakley turned six.

'God that was fun... we built him a roller-blading rink under the tree... out of old planks... I'll never forget his face when he saw it. Do you miss it Kate?'

'With all my heart. It was home.'

'Is anyone in your camp now?'

'No. It's dismantled... gone back to the wilderness. Maybe the tree is still standing with our little plaque.'

'Plaque?'

'Just a bit of tin with our number on it from a census long ago.'

Our camelthorn: while I was sitting in a restaurant in Covent Garden an elephant might be standing in its shade, reaching up into the branches and chomping on elephant Smarties.

'Have you been back?' she asked.

'No.'

I don't think I could bear the pain.

'Will you?'

'Maybe... one day.'

No. Never.

Looking into Vikki's gentle eyes I wanted to cry, but I didn't. The gnawing homesickness for Botswana was pointless: the life we had led was over, and could never be recreated.

'You know the saying, "It takes a village..."?' I said, 'well, my kids were raised by a country. Botswana shaped them... empowered them.'

'You had something to do with that too Kate,' Vikki's tone was serious, 'they know what you did for them. It was an incredible life out there. Whatever happened later doesn't negate that. You love them unconditionally and they love you too.'

I looked at her frank, open face, and felt the warmth of her mother shining out of her. Unconditional love was undeniably her truth, but was it everyone's?

I think unconditional love is a false construct: love's ebbs and flows are profoundly impacted by external and internal conditions: in times of emotional drought love wilts, emotional storms can snuff love out, emotional fires can choke and burn love to a crisp, depression smothers love, trauma fragments love into disconnected shards and fear numbs love. Like all senses and emotions love is responsive to its environment.

'They love me deeply Vikki but I took them to the edge of their endurance. When loving me became dangerous they stopped ... for a while.'

'Survival instinct?'

'Sure,' I replied, 'at different times for different reasons ... they took time out.'

'That must have been a bit like hell for them, I can't imagine for a moment not loving my mother,' Vikki said, and I rolled about laughing.

'Dearest child of my dreams I can't imagine anyone on the planet not loving your Mamma.'

But Vikki didn't laugh: she looked shattered.

'Kate, they had the good times too. All those years. That's what they'll build on ... not the bad years.'

I wasn't sure she was right. The bad times teach us too.

49

Gomoti Camp, 2003

Five months after the attack I was having my morning shower when I heard Pieter calling to me from the kitchen tent. I walked up the sand path drying my hair on a towel. The children were waiting there. Everyone look angry.

'You went out into the bush again at night,' he said.

'No, I didn't.'

'Don't lie to me Kate. I saw your tracks.'

'I slept in the mess tent last night.'

'Mum that's so dangerous,' said Maisie.

'Oh for Christ's sake.'

'Mum anything could've come in.'

'Well, it didn't so let's all relax shall we,' I snapped.

'Christ, you must have been drunk. You don't even remember walking into the palm scrub.' Pieter was oozing self-righteous virtue. I felt tears in the back of my eyes.

'Fuck you.'

'Nice. Nice language, Kate.' I hated the way Pieter said my name.

'Mum, we are only trying to look after you.'

'Just come and look, will you.' Pieter strode out onto the wide sand path that led up to the generator. He had such an easy gait. I still loved the way he moved. He disappeared into the thick palm scrub.

'Here,' he called, 'come and see your tracks. They go right out towards the cut line. Look.'

The children and I followed the tracks and they led all around the back of the camp before turning away towards Moremi. They were my plimsoll tracks. The imprint of my Cinderella foot fitted perfectly inside. I was scared.

'Pieter, I didn't walk here last night. Seriously I didn't.'

Pieter looked worried. The children looked angry.

'Mum – it's in front of you in black and white. Oh, anyway I don't care any more. This is just getting ridiculous,' Travers walked away. I could see the pain in his eyes.

'I really and truly didn't walk here. I was writing last night. I was drinking hot Milo. I didn't get drunk last night.'

'Well alleluia! Let's write to the President shall we. Kate didn't get drunk last night. Remember that date kids.' Pieter was on a roll.

The rest of the children gave me withering looks and wandered away.

'I didn't walk there,' my voice was cracking with unprotected tears. I wasn't angry.

'Well the evidence says otherwise.'

'Clearly, and I don't understand it.'

He heard my fear and became kinder.

'Do you think we should go back to town? Give the therapy another go.'

'I don't know. I've been getting better. Things have been clearing. Come and see what I wrote last night. I think it's good. I didn't walk last night, Pieter. I really truly, truly didn't.'

He looked very worried.

'If you don't remember, Kate, it means you are still ill. You're not getting better, sweetheart.'

'But I am. I can feel it.'

He sighed.

'Let's go and find the lions,' his voice was gentle, 'just us this morning.' He put his arm round me and I rested my head on his shoulder. It felt like the old days.

'I love you,' I said, and fleetingly I meant it.

The Land Rover rumbled soothingly as Pieter drove slowly along the river path scanning the sand for lion tracks. I rested my grubby, sand-ingrained feet on the dashboard. Pollen carried in a breeze made me sneeze.

'Bless you,' Pieter briefly stroked my hair, 'this is nice,' he said, 'just the two of us.'

I watched his hands on the steering wheel: graceful, long fingers, his thumbs extended, relaxed. I took his left hand from the wheel and staring straight ahead I rested his fingers against my lips. They smelled of tobacco. I pressed his hand against my cheek. It felt cool. I was present. For a moment I felt like the old Kate.

'You know what?' I said.

'What?'

'You never kept your promise.'

'What promise?'

'That we would make love in the open among the flowers on Bring's Plain. Do you remember?' I laughed.

'Ah yes. I remember. That was a long time ago. Well, it's entirely your fault... you had far too many children. They are everywhere like a rash.'

'Bastards,' I giggled.

He drove the car up onto a discarded termite mound to get some elevation for tracking.

'Do you really need all of them?' he called down – the old joke – as he climbed easily up onto the roof, and I passed the tracking equipment up to him through the window.

Resting my head on the back of the seat I listened for the beeping sound sent out by a lion's radio collar. I could hear Pieter shifting his weight on the roof rack as he adjusted his position, moving the aerial slowly through 365 degrees; tipping the aerial this way and that. The air was dry – a good day for tracking.

'Anything?' I called up after a while.

'Nothing so far.'

The animals must have drunk earlier, there was nothing around that morning, just harvester ants lugging tinder-dry grass stems five times their body length towards a hole in the ground. I heard a car coming from our camp.

'Damn,' said Pieter, stepping lightly on the bonnet as he climbed down from the roof, 'better see who it is before moving on.'

He lit a cigarette. He smoked elegantly. I liked watching him.

A tourist safari truck from Starlings Camp drove up beside us but there were no clients in the back.

'Dumela Rra,' I said to the guide. I knew him well – I had looked after his wife when she had malaria last rainy season.

'Dumela Mma. We have a problem. I went to look for you. One of our girls is missing. I told your children.'

'What girl?'

'She is new – a new tent girl. She had a fight and ran away last night. She has not come back.'

'Whom did she fight with?' I asked.

He looked shamefaced.

'With you?'

'No.'

It was the end of the month. That was when the men got drunk.

Like clockwork the bottle stores emptied of cheap beer and the ramshackle bars spat out their paralytic patrons into the darkness. But usually that happened in town.

'I know where she is,' Pieter's voice seemed cold, 'follow me.'

We drove back along the river and, turning onto the track that led home, Pieter looked at me.

'You didn't go out last night Kate. They weren't your tracks.'

I felt faint with relief.

'PEP store plimsolls size five. For heaven's sake,' he looked relieved but faintly irritated – perhaps I wasn't as unbalanced as he thought.

It was Maisie who found the runaway: she followed her tracks into the palm scrub and found the woman walking, and crying angry tears.

At fourteen Maisie knew what to do.

50

Comeragh Road, London 2014

I knew it would happen. I had begun preparing myself for it a few years ago on the patio – ferociously cutting back ivy, pulling out stinking bob weed and planting a flurry of sweet william and cherry tomatoes. But when it happened it was scary: there was no room for error.

'Mum? It's me,' Travers was calling from America. He sounded distressed.

'Trav? What's happened?'

'Mum, my car ... it was broken into.'

'I'm sorry darling.'

'I didn't know what to do.'

My stomach tightened into a knot. Travers always knew what to do.

'Mummy.'

'I'm here.'

'I don't know what's happening ... I can't stop crying.'

Travers was married now, to his college sweetheart, Jenny. If I could have created a woman for Travers it would have been her. I first met her when she came to camp one summer holiday, and she settled into bush life like an old-timer. She was unflustered by flying bugs and the long-drop loo. She was sensible around the lions, and merciless on the volleyball court. She played our family games at night with ferocity and never bored us on the topic of the itchiness of her mosquito bites.

She was brave, smart and kind. I adored her. Maisie glowered at her. Jenny was taking away a brother, and that was just not acceptable.

But I have never loved Jenny more than when she sent Travers home to me when he didn't know how to stop crying. There was no tussle – no competition between wife and mother – just accurate loving. He had been carrying a heavy load for years and finally the bag had burst, and she knew I was more familiar with its contents. So, confused and wretched, Travers took time off work and got on a plane to London. I cancelled all my classes, put clean sheets on his bed and waited.

Trav was taking action. At seventeen he had taken responsibility for me and booked me into therapy. I wondered – if I had taken action and got on the plane to Cape Town could I have saved us? . . . Don't faff around . . . deal with what is, not what might have been . . . this is not your story . . . your boy is unravelling now . . . keep steady and don't make a mistake. If he's safe enough to break – he's strong enough to heal. He will be raw – one wrong word will hurt him. Don't fuck this up.

I went for a thinking walk, but not alone. I called my dearest friend from Maun, and she poured herself a cup of something hot and healthy, and, sitting in her garden overlooking the Golden Valley on the border of Wales, Bryony Longdon talked wisely over the phone. In many ways, the situation was clear.

One: Travers was dealing with years of hurt, fear and rage. His story was not my story. His hurt was not my hurt. The family Gordian knot had individual threads and I had to make sure I followed his and didn't drop it or get it muddled with someone else's.

Two: my behaviour had taken him to the edge of his endurance and he had walked away. That was sensible of him but . . . and this was the tough part . . . I knew why I had behaved as I had and I had forgiven it. I had to hold on to that in my heart and keep my mouth shut. One whiff of self-justification would obfuscate his journey. My forgiveness was private. My task was to give him the freedom to be angry and to acknowledge the hurt I had inflicted. Keep it simple.

Three: the shadow of my pain was rising up again: this was going to stir the obsolete back up to the surface. I must brush those feelings away as I would brush away a fly drinking from my sweat. I can do that. Keep it simple.

And there was a fourth task: Travers was honourable. His healing had been hampered by his kindness and his compassion. He would never say some of the things he needed to say directly to me because he loved me, and would not want to stir up old wounds: he was protecting me and in doing so hurting himself. So, I booked him into a therapist who specialized in Post-traumatic Stress Disorder and baked a chocolate fudge cake. My function was to be Mum... to be the safe place he had lost. Less than twenty-four hours later I opened the door and there he was. His brown eyes huge, innocent, faintly surprised: an expression he had worn as a small person. We hugged.

Life is not the movies: we didn't skate hand-in-hand and twirl our troubles away, we didn't swing down Bond Street trying on outfits laughing hilariously, nor did we flounder in a Woody Allen anxiety fest. We pottered.

He dozed on the sofa in front of Sky Sport, and he ate Mum food. He told me his story and I listened. We talked family nonsense, laughed and did the washing-up. We had the moments he needed, gently, often just before bedtime, like in the old days. He liked the therapist: but ever mindful of cash he had tried to stop me booking him a taxi to bring him home.

'It's bonkers Mum, I'll catch a Tube.'

'So not, actually,' I said adamantly.

'But you can't afford to splash out.'

'Trust me I can,' I laughed, but it wasn't funny. I knew how exposed he would feel after a session, and sitting in the sunlight in the back of a London taxi was better than jostling in a crowd under the ground.

While he was home we lived to his rhythm. Travers moved incrementally: one step at a time. I had no romantic notion that I could 'make it all better' with magic kisses and a maternal laying-on of hands. Those days were over. But I was safe to be around again, and he needed to feel that comfort.

One evening over supper we were reminiscing about schooldays, and how he had sweated for hours in his tent practising countless SAT tests to raise his scores.

'I was a hopeless case, Mum,' he laughed.

'It's a miracle you can read the instructions on a can my darling.'

After graduating from UCSB, our dyslexic hero had gone on to get an MSc in conservation biology from Oxford.

'The miracle is we all got into uni,' he said, 'I still can't believe we did it.'

'I still can't believe who rocked up in camp that morning... now that really was a miracle,' I said, remembering us melting in the mess tent late one morning, so engrossed in Plato's *Apology* that at first we didn't notice the self-drive truck chugging into camp.

A bunch of bedraggled, discombobulated tourists had lost their way, and we invited them in for cold drinks. Soon a tumble of courteous but bemused Americans were stretching their legs in the kitchen asking the usual questions in no particular order: Who were we? What were we doing here? Did we live here year-round? Where were the lions? Where did the children go to school?

One woman had gravitated towards the mess tent, intrigued by our library.

'This is an eclectic bunch of books, not what I was expecting to see out here. Frankly this whole set-up is pretty surprising,' she laughed.

'It's our school library,' I explained.

She noticed a copy of *The Lion Children* on the desk, and leafing through it she smiled. Lying next to it was a well-thumbed copy of *The Complete Guide to Colleges*.

'Which colleges are you applying to?' she inquired.

'We're working on that... it's all pretty bewildering,' I said, 'frankly it's terrifying.'

'Well if I can help... I've just retired. I was the Dean of Admissions at Cornell.'

Of all the gin joints, in all of the towns... a primeval awping arose from my depths, and I believe I clutched her to my bosom.

'You're staying for lunch... all of you... oh my giddy aunt... children – gather... set the table we must feast.'

Sitting at the kitchen table in Comeragh Road, Travers and I giggled, remembering how he had used up a week's food supplies creating a sumptuous spread for the merry academics, while the ex-Dean and I exchanged information.

'Well, your address is working for you,' she had laughed, 'Lion Research, Box 66, Maun, will capture their attention. And take no notice of instructions – *do* send accompanying documents: he's been homeschooled so offer a couple of examples of marked essays so they can assess how you guys work, and without fail send a copy of The Lion Children. Colleges don't get many applications from published authors raised in the Okavango. This is not a disadvantage,' she had teased.

'You were so right Mum,' said Travers, 'the book opened doors for all of us.'

He'd been home for a while and was looking rested and less anxious. Though there was still an involuntary catch of breath in his throat from time to time. On reflection, it wasn't surprising that he had released the pain: everyone in the family was in a good place. The young brother he had helped raise was happy and strong in Santa Barbara just down the coast; Angus was editing the *Santiago Times* in Chile; Maisie was winning prizes for her work in Dublin, and loving her Irish life; Emily was snuggled in, like a bear, with her family and teaching in a school she liked. And I was Mum again. Travers could let go now.

As predicted he did protect me: he talked about the dark days but he didn't release his anger. We had quiet private time together and during those weeks he reconnected to an umbilical trust. No bells and whistles; no pretence that harm had not been done, no fake forgiveness: forgiveness has its place, but I'm not convinced by its curative powers. It is healing when it arises instinctively, but the notion that forgiving is a required aspect of healing is brutal. I don't forgive the men who raped me nor do I expend any energy thinking about them. They were never caught. I don't ask the children to forgive me for the hurt I have inflicted. I forgive me but that's a private thing and it doesn't nullify regret. I like regret – it's part of learning – it keeps you on your toes as you move forward.

When Travers was ready he went home to Jenny and to the life they had made together. Was he resolved? No. But he had rediscovered the pathway to trust, and he was no longer afraid of walking towards me. I don't drink now because not drinking is a symbol of trust reclaimed: a symbol I guard with pride.

Each child is different: my unravelling with Angus happened unexpectedly. We'd had a happy evening cooking upside-down apple cake. I don't know what caused the plug to be released, but suddenly his story gushed into my ears: some of it new to me, some unbearably familiar. He drank red wine and did not get drunk – I drank Diet Coke and did not falter. Angus and I rummaged in the family Gordian knot for hours and finding his thread we followed it as far as he needed to. We used words carefully and we used many. We talked until dawn and rested in the day. The following night we dug deeper and we cried. That was the night he said: 'Mum, I wish it hadn't happened to you. I wish it hadn't happened to us. But getting through it made me who I am today: and I like who I am.'

When he graduated from the London School of Journalism Angus wanted to carve out a new life, and he decided to do his required stint as a regional journalist in the New World. Typically relaxed, he set off for Chile with no more than a large backpack, a stout pair of hiking boots, a sleeping bag, a pup tent, £200 sterling, and not a word of Spanish. His plans were fluid. Basically, they amounted to arriving in Santiago and taking it from there.

While his father squeezed the luggage into the back of his mini, ready to drive him to the airport, I kissed Gus goodbye on the doorstep. Looking into my son's kind eyes, my heart welled. Was it possible

I had once looked into those eyes and said, 'I don't love you'? Who was that person?

'Bye Mum, I'll let you know where I am when I find a place to stay. I love you Mum, it's been such a great year... so happy.'

Suddenly he looked vulnerable.

'It's been the best, my Gussock, I love you to bits and back... blimey this must feel scary.'

'Just a tad.'

'You'll be fine, I'm not worried, Gussie.' It was true. I knew he had the skills he needed to make a new life. I was going to miss him but not fear for him.

'I'll do my best to come out to you... I've always ached to see the Andes... and the jungle... I'll bring Maisie too... and Gus... if it all goes tits up... you'll make a plan.'

He grinned.

'We always make a plan don't we Mum?'

Standing on the top of the steps, I waved to him until the car disappeared around the corner, and with a light heart I turned back into the house.

He was walking towards something, not walking away – and that makes all the difference.

51

Gomoti Camp, 2003

Travers took me aside before he left for college and begged me to keep steady.

'Mum, for the others. You don't know how frightening it gets when you and Pieter are fighting. It's not fair Mum. It's not fair on any of us. Please... I can't go to college feeling so scared... please Mum, for me.'

It had been easy to reassure Travers. The mycelium threads that linked me to my family were growing back and stretching outwards again. I had meant it when I promised I would stop. I might have stayed strong... I might have been able to keep going if I had just been given time... but life doesn't care... it keeps on rolling... pressing down... chopping... crushing fresh shoots. But for a while I was steady... I can do this... I can be a mother. The children began to test the water to see if I was safe again.

It was surprising when, one evening, Oakley announced he wanted to stay in camp instead of going on the game count.

'Are you feeling sick, boy?' asked Angus.

'No... I just don't want to go tonight.'

He was usually the first to clamber up onto the mattress on the roof of the Land Rover and take hold of the million-candle spotlight from Pieter – who always gave the same instruction: 'Shine slow and steady... no waving around.'

The monthly game count was part of the fabric of our lives.

Pieter would drive slowly along the same route, Steenbok Loop, while the children sat on the roof taking it in turns to shine the light into the darkness picking up reflections from animals' eyes. Sitting beside Pieter I would record the data called down to me.

'Six wildebeest Mum... no – hang on – make that seven. Did you get that?'

'Oh, and another spring hare.'

The gentle companionship of shared purpose was peaceful, and although some counts were more exciting than others we always enjoyed them. Monitoring seasonal fluctuations in prey species over the years enriched the mosaic of data.

That night, Oakley handed a packet of sustaining gingernut biscuits up to his siblings sitting on the roof, then he and I watched the Land Rover trundle out of camp. We waited until all was still and quiet.

We had already cleared supper away and the night-time chores were done.

'Do you want to play a game, Oaks?'

'No, not really... story?'

'Brill. Let's snuggle in.'

I chose a Sherlock Holmes story that was unlikely to ignite powerful emotions: earlier in the day Oakley had been heartbroken by the death of Reepicheep in *The Voyage of the Dawn Treader*. The noble sword-wielding mouse had captured Oakley's heart, and burying his face in his favourite soft-toy lion he had wept a storm of furious tears.

'Why? Why did he do that? Mum... does he come back?'

'No, my darling I'm so sorry he doesn't.'

It wasn't just the mouse he was grieving for – he was missing Travers. We all were.

We parked the car outside my tent and Oakley and I settled in for the night tucked up with Watson and Sherlock. We both wanted to snack on a biscuit but the no-food-in-the-tents rule was written in stone, so we made do with a warm glass of orange squash. Lying beside me, Oakley's usually snapping blue eyes were thoughtful: hooded. While I read 'The Speckled Band' he leaned against me, nonchalantly squeezing sand worms out of his arm: he called them his 'pets'.

'When will we see Travi, Mum?' he asked when I had finished the story.

'Christmas, Oaks... in Hollybush. All of us together again, Ems, Jack, Jimmy, Neecie... everyone.'

'When?'

'I'm trying to sort out tickets... they're mega-expensive at Christmas... but I'll make a plan. The tenants have said we can have the house from December the twentieth for a few weeks while they are away... how cool is that?'

'Very.'

We lay together quietly listening to the crickets. The lions were silent.

'Mum?' his voice was small.

'That's me.'

'Are you happy now?'

My bones ached with regret.

'Yes, my darling one, I'm happy now. I'm so sorry I have been so horrid.'

'No Mum... you're not horrid.'

Presently, Oakley's nostrils flared and his lips tightened.

'I hate red,' he growled.

'Why?'

'You know, Mum,' he snapped.

'I don't... truly.'

His words came out pinched.

'One of the men who r—ed you. He was wearing a red T-shirt.'

How did he know that? Had I said?

'I hate red so much.'

He leaned his head into my shoulder for a moment before looking me straight in the face.

'You're happy Mum... are you sure?'

I was sure of nothing. The reconnections were so new... I was learning to be me again.

'I'm sure Oaks.'

He slumped back onto his pillow. He was so weary.

The crickets fell silent. Something must have happened out there in the darkness.

I could hear Oakley's heart beating. Presently he chirruped: 'Mr and Mrs Thene and their daughter Polly.'

'Mr and Mrs Athema and their daughter Anne,' I rejoined.

'Mr and Mrs Key and their son Allen.'

'Mr and Mrs Tation and their son Dick.'

'Mr and Mrs Pede and their daughter Millie.'

We played the familiar game, until we were rudely interrupted by a hyena rummaging around in the kitchen.

Oakley sat bolt upright.

'Do you think it's the same hyena as last night Mum?'

I sincerely hoped not: over the last week we had been troubled by a fearless loco hyena, and it was quite disquieting.

'No idea but let's drive it off... now.'

Oakley's eyes sparkled: hyenas in the kitchen were something he understood... he could do something about that. Bouncing out of bed, he was in the driving seat in a matter of seconds.

'Come on Mum hurry,' he urged excitedly, 'it sounds like it's trying to get into the pantry.'

It *was* the same troublesome animal we had seen the night before.

It had been a revealing night. Pieter had gone to bed early, and the children and I had stayed up watching *Lord of the Rings*. Oakley had been Legolas all week, and was inseparable from the bow and arrow Stephen had made for him. The sound of a dish crashing to the ground in the kitchen had startled us, and the sight of an adult hyena with a ragged ear helping itself to the remnants of our vegetarian lasagne had us on our feet and yelling at the top of our lungs. It was unusual for an animal to be so fearless around people, and my full-throated Anglo-Saxon language did nothing to deter it. Yelling for Pieter, I watched the hyena lollop past the kitchen table towards us.

Despite being told to go to the back of the tent, the children formed a phalanx beside me, and Oakley had an arrow set in his bow ready to shoot. The hyena kept on coming, and crossed the shade-cloth threshold between the kitchen and the mess tent. The only thing between it and us was a low sofa. The intrepid animal paused briefly and looked me in the eye. I screamed for Pieter. The creature took no notice and, leaning against the back of the sofa, it stretched its great sloping neck towards us; in desperation, I picked up a pillow and hit it repeatedly over the head as hard as I could. Through my arms I could feel the useless softness absorb the hardness of the animal's skull, but though it was unharmed by my futile attack it was puzzled, and wheeled away into the darkness yelping. At that moment Pieter sauntered up the path – fully clothed – shoes laced up – belt buckled. That was when I knew for sure he had fallen out of love. A fact I filed away for later: grown-up hearts were too complicated.

Dealing with the hyena, from the safety of the car, was straightforward. Oakley drove up to the kitchen tent and waited for the animal to emerge. Then he drove up behind it and guided it out of camp towards the river. Easy. Oakley's needs were simple. I could manage them. I could hold on.

I've got this under control.

I believed that. I really did.

52

Comeragh Road, London 2015

'Kaaaait,' a small Russian person whispered, popping his ash-blond head around my bedroom door. It was eleven-thirty at night and I was propped up in bed preparing classes for the next day.

'Boris my darling, what's up?'

'Kaaait, I am sick . . . werrry sick . . . in my stomach.' Boris was six, and as his older brother had before him, he was staying with me as a residential student while his parents were away.

'Come in, come in,' I cried, hauling myself out of bed. He looked pink-cheeked and perfectly healthy, standing staunchly in his racing-car pyjamas, tears glistening in bright-blue eyes.

'It's horrid feeling sick, would you like to sleep there in my grand-children's bed just in case you are sick?' I said, pointing to the daybed in my bedroom, covered in a patchwork quilt and Oakley's tatty old stuffed lion, used as a cushion in the mess tent for so many years. Boris clambered into bed in a heartbeat, and I gathered vomit paraphernalia.

'Just in case you can't make it to the bathroom,' I said, setting a bowl, a towel and some wet wipes beside his bed – knowing full well it wasn't his stomach that was aching. 'Would you like me to read you a story, then I'll get your iPad, and you can play something while I finish my school work.'

'*Frog and Toad*?' he asked brightly.

'*Frog and Toad* it is,' I said, reaching into the bookshelf by his bed, and pulling out the well-worn volume of *Frog and Toad Are Friends*, 'just two chapters, Spring and Summer – okay?' I added, lying down beside him.

'Kaaait?'

'That's me,' I said.

'Can I have pancakes for breakfast?'

'Indeed you can my angel, with maple syrup... now... Chapter One... Spring. "Frog ran up the path to Toad's house. He knocked on the front door..."'

Boris was sound asleep before Summer.

53

Gomoti Camp, 2003

While romance faded, school blossomed. After Travers had left for college two of the children's friends joined Lion School. Welcoming Matthew and Pam to camp was a joy: my children needed fresh minds around the table, and teaching children who had chosen to come to school under a tree was a privilege.

Pamela was fair-haired, wire-thin and bold. She had dropped out of school some time ago, but she liked the way Lion School was run, and wanted to give learning another try. Matthew was a gentle, calm-spirited boy with a headful of wild dark curls that danced like unruly springs. His mother lived in America and he and Angus were preparing for their college applications.

'Oaks, come upstairs – breakfast's ready, we've started without you,' Angus called: for reasons passing all understanding the children referred to the kitchen as 'upstairs'. It was 6 a.m., school started early in the heat of the rainy season. My youngest appeared wearing a floor-length black plastic coat, thigh-high boots (constructed from an inner tube), the tyre iron slipped casually inside his belt, and a pair of dark glasses. Pausing briefly in the entrance for full effect, he sat down and poured himself a bowl of Honey Nut Loops.

'And who are we today?' asked Pieter, looking over his glasses with a twinkle in his eye.

'The Matrix.'

'Of course you are,' said Pieter, rocking back in his chair and lighting a cigarette, 'you do realize that in this heat you will have formed a puddle of melted matter by lunchtime?'

Oakley shrugged and chomped on his cereal.

Breakfast was peaceful.

'Right,' said Pieter, putting his plate and mug in the sink, 'I'm off to Abaquo this morning... it's never easy out there... I may or may not be back at lunchtime. Oaks... that tyre lever... off your belt and back into the workshop... now.'

Pieter put some water and beer into a cooler box and drove off without saying goodbye.

I wanted to mind but I didn't care. For every action there is an equal and opposite reaction: when those men pumped their semen into me, my caring was sucked out. It returned sluggishly in dribs and drabs. By then I had stopped seeking isolation. Instead, I hungered for the children's clean company. When I was numb, Maisie was sensitive. When I was cruel, Angus was kind. When I was sad, Oakley was funny. They were stuck on my treadmill. Healing is a selfish process.

While breakfast was being cleared away, I set out some objects on the kitchen table. I did this most mornings, just odd items to trigger ideas for poems – I still have the poems written by the children in early-morning companionship. That morning I put out a book, a map, an egg timer, a candle and a spoon, and Oakley's simple Dickinsonian lines were deemed the best:

> A book is not a book –
> A book is a world on a page.

Pam was a sponge and, much to Maisie's dismay, a fast learner. Poor Maisie, she had hoped studying with a peer would make life easier, but Pam's determined curiosity was insatiable; and Maisie's competitive spirit was stirred into a frenzy, resulting in glowing work and glowering eyes. Pamela was rarely seen without a book in her hand. When we were with the lions she was reading, while we were eating she was reading, and while I was cooking supper Pamela would sit at the table showering me with questions; Maisie sat at the table reading *You* magazine in determined silence.

Maisie was whip-smart, and a good writer, but her thoughts were translated through her hands, not her mouth. She drew all day long: in class, while being read to, while eating, in the back of the car, in her tent. I cannot draw a pin man and had nothing to offer Maisie but admiration: flattery she rejected with an irritated shrug.

A few years earlier I had had a Eureka moment. I called the Royal College of Art in London and asked if they could find a graduate student who would like to come out to lion camp to teach Maisie in return for spending time with the lions in the afternoon. A six-foot-six Cornish ex-fisherman called Duncan rallied to the call. I cancelled all Maisie's classes for a term and she and Duncan worked alone together. He was an inspired teacher and her talent was enriched under his care. But now, two years later, Maisie was hungering for more. I knew all this... I was connected... I was nearly there... but sometimes the pictures in my head faded into blackness. Maisie needed the mother she used to have.

She and Pamela decorated their tent with silk scarves and home-made dream catchers, and spent hours together chatting and listening to music. In the late afternoon they would drift off alone on a sunset game drive and I beamed with pleasure.

'Bless them,' I thought, 'so precious... time together in Nature. What a gift.'

It would be a few years before I learned from Maisie that the girls had actually driven to the river for a smoke. Apparently, Pieter had noticed his tobacco supply being slowly depleted, but had wisely kept quiet about it. Teenagers need rebellion, and an illicit ciggie by the river was a misdemeanour not worthy of awakening my beast.

In November, Matthew and Gus sat their SAT exams. We gathered at the bus stop in Maun and watched the boys clamber aboard a ramshackle bus along with a throng of people, some clucking chickens and a goat. My heart welled with love at the sight of the boys setting off for the twelve-hour drive to Gaborone, squeezed between two large mammas and their babies.

Angus and Mattie sat their exams in a broom cupboard. The people at the testing centre had forgotten they were coming, and it was the only space available. For a goodly part of the time two janitors were engaged in an animated exchange outside the door, from time to time striking each other and beating various body parts against the door. Unperturbed, and sweating profusely, the boys underwent two days of examination in their allotted space and trundled back to Maun on the next bus out.

Funds were limited, and they could only apply to a few colleges. Matthew applied to the University of Austin, Texas; Gus applied to Stanford, Duke and CCS Santa Barbara. They worked tirelessly on their applications and were accepted by all colleges. Gus was offered the Melinda Gates scholarship at Duke, and a full academic scholarship to Stanford: he chose the latter.

Good times – they didn't last.

I slipped into the slime. My self-loathing was all-obliterating. I moved back to Maun for more futile counselling.

Maisie was fifteen when she wrenched a bottle of rose-scented lavatory fluid from my hands: to stop me from drinking its contents. The guilt was overwhelming: my filth festered.

I had been getting better: how long was this nonsense going to take? I hated the rot inside me... I hated me so much I punched my own face...

> Oh, the grand old Duke of York,
> He had ten thousand men;
> He marched them up to the top of the hill,
> And he marched them down again.

And when they were up, they were up,
And when they were down, they were down,
And when they were only half-way up,
They were neither up nor down.

I marched up and down the frigging hill trailing my children with me...

And Pieter? He stayed with the lions and came to town at the weekends. There were good days: we did try to create something from the detritus of our broken relationship, but nothing stuck.

School spluttered on... months dragged by.

Maisie's work floundered and her dogged energy was focused on what she was not going to do. She was marooned. Stuck with me. Wanting to help her little brother, but needing to save herself. She spent most of her time living with her friend Melissa and her father Brian Schreiber. He ran the workshop in one of Maun's many busy garages. He knew I was battling, and he knew what it was to love a child. He opened his doors to my girl and gave her peace. I will never forget his non-judgemental kindness.

Oakley ran wild after school, riding donkeys with his gang of river kids. From time to time I would catch sight of him on his way back from the village well, his legs dangling from a bedraggled animal loaded down with slopping water containers to be delivered to some mamma in the village. He was a resourceful little soul and started the Stonebreakers' under-ten football team: he had a meeting with the chief and asked permission to use the full-sized football pitch for practice. At the agreed hour, the barefoot team gathered and practised their ferocious lawless skills on the pitch with broken poles for goalposts. Oaks took his task seriously and arranged matches with neighbouring wards. I ferried the lads to matches and tried to keep them hydrated while they played speedy, competitive games. I bought the Junior Stonebreakers' kits from the PEP store in Maun, only matching shorts and T-shirts, but they were worn with pride. I could manage Oakley's practical needs: they were uncomplicated.

But my girl... her needs... so female... I can't be a mother... I don't know how to be a woman. Don't let her down... school... don't mess with her future... fight for her... Plumfield may have gone up in a puff of smoke... Lion School hasn't... fight... education is power... those men have shattered me... maybe I'll never be me again... so what... so fucking what... I'm shit anyway... they can't stop the learning... that's the only bit that's clean... I remember the fucking emission spectrum of helium now... you bastards... I remember everything.

Why did I keep shattering? Was it the alcohol? Was that to blame for everything? Or was it the fear... worming its way up through my soil... screaming like a mandrake when I pulled it up by its roots to look it in the face? Digging... so much digging.

Maisie did lessons in the morning with her brother. They held on. But the joy had gone. Trust had faded.

'I'm not doing it.'

'You are. There's no choice here Maisie.'

'I hate you.'

'Well frankly I'm not that keen on you either.'

The row was about community work. All the children had to do it as part of the Lion School curriculum. Travers and Angus had helped build a classroom in Bana Ba Metzi, a bush school for misfit boys near the Delta Panhandle. For her community work Maisie was going to give art classes to adults at the HIV/AIDS counselling centre in Maun.

The counselling centre offered a safe space for HIV-positive people to gather. In those days, infected people were shunned in their villages. Women who bottle-fed their babies, to avoid passing on the virus, were often ostracized. It was hardly surprising that so many preferred not to be tested for fear of the harsh social consequences. But in the Maun centre they could relax and talk openly, or just rest in quiet companionship. Many travelled miles to get there, and I had bought mattresses for them to lie on while they recovered from the rigours of their journey, and paid for a weekly supply of fresh vegetables and rice.

'I'm not going to college so I don't need to do community bloody work.'

'Marvellous attitude Mais.'

She was adamant that she was not going to college in America, and I had no issue with that. She was free to choose where she wanted to go to university, but she was not free to opt out of her education.

Despite her desolation Maisie did her community service, and she was magnificent. I took her to her first class, and in preparation we picked through the flotsam and jetsam in the grey sand of the compound looking for items that could be glued or sewn onto greetings cards: twisted wire, a discarded mielie sack, a filament from a plastic bag, seedpods, dried grasses, leaves, snail shells, snake skin, termite wings. Maisie's eyes didn't miss a detail: she found beauty hidden in the dirt. She had made some elephant-shit paper, and had asked friends to donate some recycled paper.

As she walked into a room filled with twenty eager adults, her rage evaporated and her gentleness returned. I left her to it. By the end of the week, encouraged and supported by Maisie, the group had produced enough cards to sell at a local art and craft centre. By the end of the month Maisie and her group had generated a small business that the counselling centre continued for a while.

I was so proud of her, but at that time my pride had little value.

54

The Amazon Jungle, Bolivia 2014

Angus watched in awe as Maisie moved deftly across the forest floor: her eyes refreshed by a new environment. An hour ago we had stepped off a weather-beaten boat that had chugged for eight hours up a Bolivian tributary of the Amazon, and delivered us onto a rickety wooden dock hewn into a high riverbank. As Maisie climbed towards our destination, the back of her T-shirt became stained with sweat, and when her hair fell damp across her face she tied it back in a hurried knot. The Amazon heat energized her – her nimble steps transferring the spring of the rich, dark topsoil into light energy. It seemed she could see through leaves: she found a tiny frog, no bigger than a man's thumb, nestled under the shade of a variegated emerald and grey leaflet. As once she had seen the shadow of a leopard in a tree, now she caught the glint of a jewelled beetle resting on a swaying stem, or the image of a rose drawn in mould on a leaf fluttering above her in the understorey. She found clarity in the biochaotic abundance of the rainforest: the smell of rain carried new olfactory messages for her to learn. She was at home in the wilderness.

Months later she moved to Peru, as artist in residence for three biological research stations in the rainforest.

55

Comeragh Road, London 2015

Early in December, I was sitting on my bed filling a Christmas stocking to send to Maisie, and I was feeling restless. When problems sap rather than invigorate it's time to make a change. College fees were paid. Oaks had graduated, and had an interesting job in the States: he was building his own life. My small homeschool was flourishing, but London rent was thwarting: the house in Comeragh Road had done its job.

I wondered, what would have happened if Oakley hadn't sighed on top of a London bus? I wondered what would have happened if I hadn't heard the message in a catch of breath? There had been so much growth in Comeragh Road. Oaks had chosen the house from several we had viewed. He had been certain.

'This is the one Mum, this'll be a great Christmas house.'

He was right. Our Christmases had been magnificent: a familiar riot of jostling and feasting. The whole family squeezed around an uneven selection of tables cobbled together: Neecie and Cindy; Travers and Jenny; Emily, Jimmy, Jack, Eliza and Bella; Oaks, Gus, Maisie and me. Home-made food and decorations: dried sliced oranges hung on ribbons, trails of glossy ivy, cut free from the patio walls and draped over doorframes, and familiar felt figures standing on cotton-wool snow.

Glistening with Pound Shop Christmas lights and tinsel, the house stretched out its arms and settled the family in beds, on mattresses on floors or snuggled on sofas. And each year, in pride of place, the

Christmas tree stood naked – waiting for my grandchildren to decorate it on Christmas Eve. This would be the last time I walked down the North End Road to buy our tree from 'the Christmas tree man'. I never knew his name and he never knew mine, but our cheerful annual meetings were part of the ritual of London Christmas.

My bed was littered with snippets of misjudged wrapping paper cut too small, and bits of discarded sellotape had stuck to the duvet. Stuffing a parcel deep into the long woollen sock, I wondered where the stockings would hang next year. It wasn't bleak, not knowing; nor was it bleak realizing that my time as the Christmas matriarch was waning. But it was surprising.

The past can't be relived and families change shape – that is the natural order of things. The family had healed in Comeragh Road and healing leaves scars – marks on our skin and on our souls that remind us we have lived. I like my scars. But healing doesn't mean going backwards. The children were cooked and my role had changed. It was time to move forward into a new unknown.

The notion of home had been reconstructed. There would always be a wrenching hurt that Hollybush and camp were lost: the stories in the stone and in the trees could not be reread, only remembered in our collective memories. From now on where I lived would be a place my children visited, and that was a challenging realization.

But when it's time to go – it's time to go. But where? That was exciting. For a long time I had felt that Italy would be part of my life. The shadow of so many ideas had quivered when I first read *Franky Furbo*. Perhaps now was the time. No rush... I ambled down the North End Road to the DHL office, where I squeezed the bulging woollen stocking into a yellow box addressed to an office in Cusco, Peru.

'Is that where your daughter lives?' asked the man behind the counter.

'No, she's living somewhere in the jungle,' I replied, 'not exactly sure where.'

He looked surprised.

'No worries,' I beamed, 'someone in this office will make a plan.'

They did. Along with camp supplies, the DHL box was loaded onto a boat, puttered up the Amazon, and deposited on a jetty somewhere below the Cloud Forest. The howler monkeys were calling when barefoot Maisie meandered down to the river to pick up her Christmas care package, and bring it back to the hut she was sharing with new friends: in her new world.

She had built a wooden Christmas tree, and decorated it with jungle ornaments.

56

Mill Park Hospital ICU, Johannesburg 2004

Stretched functionless across his bones, Pieter's skin was the colour of husked rice. He looked empty. There was a faint smell of lemons. While I was in the loo the nurse must have refreshed his mouth with a cotton bud soaked in mouthwash; his hair had been smoothed – little crusts of dried blood flecked his scalp. My hands were still sticky from the antiseptic sanitizer I used going in and out of the Intensive Care Unit, and I rubbed my palms until the last of the alcohol had evaporated. The only sounds were the steady pulse of unsyncopated ventilators and the soft buff of white lace-up pumps as nurses moved across the gleaming floor.

His wounds were covered in thin dressings – the crushed hairs on his arms and chest visible through the transparent adhesive borders. Metal rods rising up through the bones in his legs were held in place by a brutal medieval apparatus on which my eyes refused to focus. Only a few bones were left intact. If he had been allowed to feel the pain it would have killed him, so they held him in a medicated coma.

My body beside his bed: floating, somewhere. I took his hand, antiseptic-clean – white nailbeds – no thread of oil. Kissing the blue-veined ridges on the back of his hand I caught the distant smell of death and Betadine. One of the surgeons who had worked on him came to check the charts. He spoke quietly with the nurse before turning to me.

'He's stable. We did what we could when he came in, but now he needs to rest.'

'Thank you.'

'I know this must be overwhelming – do you want me to go over it again?'

'No, thank you, not just now. I know where we stand.'

'Have you got somewhere to stay?'

'Yes, I'm with friends. I'll rent somewhere later.'

The doctor looked me in the eye.

'Don't make any long-term plans... not just yet.'

I tried to understand what he was trying to say... I looked past the doctor at Pieter... he was somewhere... but not with me... this wasn't real... this couldn't be real... we had loved each other once... that was real... we had been so happy once... when everything was tangible...

57

Gomoti Camp, 2000

Pieter arrived back in camp after a day in Maun and handed me a bunch of long-stemmed red roses.

'They're a bit sad,' he grinned, 'I had to dunk them in puddles on the way home to perk them up.'

Picturing him thoughtfully refreshing the heat-wilted blooms made me laugh. I hugged him.

'No rose will ever top these.'

I opened his shirt so I could kiss the hairs on his chest and breathe him in.

'Mu-u-u-um,' groaned Maisie.

'Deal with it,' I cried, 'I am a woman in love.'

When the last boxes were unpacked Pieter made an announcement.

'I've got some bad news, guys. Armagnac's been shot.'

'No,' cried Maisie.

'Trophy?' asked Travers.

'Indeed, one of the hunters told me. Asked me if I thought it would have an impact.'

'Well, we can kiss goodbye to his cubs with Clairette and Chinon, whoever takes over the South Pan pride will kill 'em,' Travers commented grimly.

'What about poor Courvoisier? Those boys were joined at the

hip,' Maisie was furious, and the brown flecks in her amber eyes had darkened.

'Life's tough for lions, Mais,' replied Pieter calmly, 'you know that, he'll have to make a plan, but we'll have to prioritize finding Clairette and Chinon.' He nodded a warning in my direction – his subtext was clear. Sampling the Santawani females was taking up a disproportionate number of project hours, and it had become a bone of contention between us.

I called to Angus to come upstairs before the light faded. He had been struggling with a chapter in *The Lion Children*, and had holed up in his tent to ponder. Oakley was out fishing for barbel with Lettie, and I called him from the camp radio to come back to camp now – now.

I was miserable about Armagnac. We were not sentimental about the lions, they were wild animals and our task was to monitor them, as non-invasively as possible, but recently there had been an upward spike in mortality. Several young males we had known since they were cubs had killed cattle, and as a result the lions had officially become Problem Animals, and had been shot.

The mood in camp was subdued. Pieter wandered into the mess tent and glumly recorded Armagnac's death before pouring himself a large whisky. Gus was coming up the path to the kitchen looking disconsolate.

'Don't worry Mum – it's not dusk yet.'

'Good boy,' I said, giving him a kiss, 'any luck?'

'Not really, everything I write feels flat and fake.'

'Do you want to talk about it?'

'Yes, but not now, I need to clear my head... can we have a thinking walk tomorrow?'

'Course, can you give me a clue?'

'I'm writing about changes in perspective and I'm so stuck... trying to remember the boy I was in England... before all this...' – his open face looked ruffled. He calmed himself by chopping tomatoes and onions for a salad. Maisie broke the bad news while she and her brother cooked supper and I marked maths tests.

I had nearly finished when I noticed the light changing: the bush was preparing for the night shift.

'Has anyone seen Oakley?' I asked.

'No, wasn't he fishing?' Gus replied.

'Yes, but not in the bloody dark... right!' I stormed, banging down my pen, 'no video for that bad boy tonight... he knows the rules... he is so naughty.'

I was livid, and feeling guilty because I hadn't paid enough attention to the fact that he hadn't replied to my radio message.

'Just radio him again,' called Pieter, 'no need to get your knickers in a twist.'

But I knew something was up, and clambering into the car I set off to find him. I had not gone far before I came upon my child driving back from the river with no Lettie in the passenger seat.

I waited for Oakley to pass me, and, controlling my mounting rage, I turned back to camp, where my seven-year-old stood waiting: flanked by siblings. Slamming the car door shut, in the hope that some of my fury would be transformed into kinetic energy, I demanded an explanation.

'What happened and why is Lettie not with you?'

'It's not Lettie's fault,' Oaks replied hurriedly.

'Never said it was... I asked what happened and I'm waiting.'

He was ashen, he had clearly had the bejeezus scared out of him, and now the poor little soul was confronted by maternal wrath.

He took a deep breath, and trying to keep his voice steady he told me his tale.

'We were by the hippo pool...'

'Oaks that's much too far away to go by yourself... you know you're not allowed...'

'Let him finish, Mum,' Travers interrupted, and Oakley tried again.

'We were at the pool and Lettie'd got enough barbel for her supper, so I drove her back... she took the shortcut...'

Silence.

'Yes?'

'And then I went back to the river... close... not to the hippo poo—' he stopped, and his feet became objects of fascination.

'You went back to the river... by yourself?' My voice was icy.

'Yes.'

Silence, foot-shuffling.

'And then what?'

'I went fishing, I caught one... a really nice one,' he chirruped.

'I don't give a crap about the fish, Oaks. Why didn't you radio to let me know where you were?'

'There was an elephant...'

'An elephant... where you were fishing?'

'Yes, but I didn't see it and then I looked round and there it was... between me and the car.'

I pictured the scene and felt sick.

'Close?'

'Yes,' his mouth began to quiver, 'it started waving its ears and shaking its head... I made a plan... Mum... I was going to jump into the river if he came for me.'

'Marvellous!'

'It kept looking at me and then it came towards me, not running... just shaking his head,' he caught his breath, 'I stood still... so still.'

'Good boy,' said Gus, and I glared at him.

'Then it turned around and walked to the car,' Oakley was breathing short, shallow breaths, 'it was on my side of the car, so I still couldn't move. Then it walked around and stood on the other side. But I couldn't risk getting closer... in case...'

Silence.

'So, you waited for it to move off? Sensible boy,' I said, more kindly now, 'did it take ages?'

'Yes... I waited... and waited... I was so scared he was going to come towards me again... he wasn't cross or anything... but...'

'But he was big.'

Oakley nodded.

'And could have flattened you like a bug. Well, we can all assume he buggered off.'

'Yes, and I ran to the car...'

'And came home. Good boy,' said Travers with a warning look at me, 'you won't be doing that again in a hurry.'

Oaks was a mighty force, but all of a sudden he looked very small, and then the tears came.

'I'm so sorry Mummy,' he sobbed.

We had a subdued supper that night. We lived in a dangerous space and the more I learned about the bush the deeper my fear grew.

It wasn't a breathy anxiety. No animals were out to get us – they were just living their lives as we were living ours. I wasn't afraid of rats or creepy-crawlies, I wasn't afraid of snakes or lions. We had all learned to 'read' the bush. We used our noses and our ears long before we used our eyes. We read the wind as fluently as we read the faintest twitch in a lion's tail, or the bluff of a mock charge by a naughty elephant; we heeded the birds calling to each other when there was a snake nearby. We weathered storms that wrecked camp, and fought bush fires burning their way towards our home. I was not afraid of what I understood. I was afraid of the nanosecond of unpredictability that could change everything.

I lost my appetite. While the children ate in silence I poured myself another brandy and Source sparkling water. Pieter sighed and stroked my hair. The children looked grave. We had a state-of-the-art medical kit and Angus, Maisie and I had completed Alison Brown's intensive primary care first-aid course, but the kind of injuries wild animals can inflict are so serious that I hoped with all my heart I would never have to manage an open-book pelvis fracture, or use the artery clamps, pressure pads, Ringer's lactate solution or antibiotics against infection from large animal bites.

Pieter lit a cigarette and spoke quietly.

'Our rules are simple and inviolate,' he paused and the children waited. 'I won't bore you by repeating them but I have noticed too many minor infractions creeping in... I will not tolerate any further violations. And under no circumstances do I want any one of you to scare the living daylights out of your mother again. Is that understood?'

Silence.

'Good,' he said. 'Under the circumstances, I shall be choosing the film tonight... so someone fire up the equipment and hook out *O Brother, Where Art Thou?* and let's settle down shall we.'

Soon, I was curled up on the sofa with my litter of young watching George Clooney singing in dungarees.

58

ICU Mill Park Hospital, Johannesburg 2004

By the fourth day in ICU I was tuned to the rhythm of the ward. All was steady. Cool air, soft light, and quiet. Stats checked like clockwork, seamless changes of shift, silent women cleaning around unconscious patients: respectful, efficient. Sudden empty beds told sad tales of loss.

The shock of seeing Pieter broken had worn off and reality was slowly rising to the surface: if he lived, would he walk again? I didn't ask. It wasn't the time.

His body had shrunk into a shape I didn't recognize: his energy was in the ether now. I sat beside him remembering the body I knew so well, the hairs on his chest that I had lain my head on so many times, his fine-boned square wrists, his hands resting easily on the steering wheel, thumbs turned out, the hairs on his forearms shining in the sun. Laying my head on the sheet beside his arm, I breathed him in. Something. Turning my head, I rested my face on his arm and sniffed. I took his hand and put his palm to my face. Yes. There. Just. A whisper of him – no musk but his secret scent – the one I could never understand.

'He smells like him,' I cried.

The nurse looked at me and smiled. She wrote something in his notes.

'What did you just write?'

'His smell is coming back. That's something only you would

know. It's important for us ... it means his organs are beginning to work again.'

Give him time. Let him rest. But they didn't. He was too broken to remain unrepaired. They operated on him again and I watched them wheel him away before going back to Oakley, who was waiting for me at a friend's house up the road from the hospital.

We had been in South Africa for ten days; life in camp had become a mirage. Oakley was the last child standing: he loved me with a heat that held my glue in place. The others were studying abroad – they came home for the holidays but family life had moved on into a new era. Pieter and I were living in patches – good days – bad days – bound by the lions – caught in the vice of the bush – needing the sweet smell of a fresh kill – no longer attracted by each other's sweat – locked in our loveless bed – breathing in woodsmoke under a starry sky and wondering why it didn't matter any more. However hard we worked after 2001, nothing went our way.

In 2001 there had been a moratorium on all lion-hunting – it was intended to stop illegal shooting of problem lions. The consequences were swift and devastating. Cows were baited with poison – indiscriminately taking out anything that nibbled on the deadly flesh: lions, hyenas, jackals, vultures, bone beetles... Oakley shared the darks days with the lions. Oaks was with us when we collared the sub-adult males he had known since they had emerged from their den as cubs, and he followed their meanderings in a wilderness he knew with an intimacy only a child can feel. Oakley was with us when, one by one, we found the lions' corpses. Despite our reports and recommendations, the poisoning continued unabated: a brutal, unsustainable level of attrition. Then another violence disrupted his childhood.

Driving through the leafy streets of northern Johannesburg, I remembered the day of Pieter's car accident: Botswana's Independence Day, 30 September. Punctures and bad temper had punctuated a miserable town day. Pieter had invited people I didn't know to camp for the weekend and I felt unusually unwelcoming. Oakley and I set off for home late in the afternoon with a full load, and Pieter was going to follow after he'd picked up fuel and Oakley's quad bike.

Arriving in camp, Oakley and I unloaded the car while Pieter's guests sat silent and unhelpful. They were waiting for the Lion Man. Their children played with Oakley while I cooked supper. Pieter had not responded to the radio all evening and I assumed he'd had a breakdown and the battery had gone flat. But by ten o'clock I was worried.

'Oaks, I'm knackered. Drive us as far as the vet fence... if he's broken down on this side I don't want to leave him stuck all night... if he's on the other side he'll be okay... he'll make a plan.'

The adults stayed with the beer, and their boys came along for a night drive. I wasn't overly concerned about Pieter, I was just being cautious. He was nowhere to be seen, so we turned back at the vet fence. Oaks drove steadily and took his time. It was an uneventful drive until we turned towards home along our track by the edge of the forest. Suddenly, out of the darkness, a kerfuffle of elephant appeared and charged the car. There was no escape route – one animal pushed against my side of the car. All I could see was a mosaic of cracked grey hide spiked with brown hair: the smell of elephant was overwhelming. Oakley stayed steady. I trusted him. He saw a gap and made his choice. Driving cleanly between two elephants, he sped away leaving them bewildered and wheeling in circles behind us.

He kept going until we turned a corner and they were out of sight.

'You okay Mum?'

'Holy crap... nice work Oaks... that was nasty.'

'Poor ellies... I think they were as scared as we were,' his voice was young and reedy but his eyes were older. Back in camp I made the kids hot Milo and the family went to bed leaving Oakley and me by the fire: just us quietly under the stars.

We both heard the distant revving of a car flying over deep sand. Oakley looked at me. We heard controlled gear changes between acceleration: a good driver was shunting it. No one with good news drove like that at night. We knew the car wasn't going to carry on towards the river, we knew it would turn onto the track that led along the forest where we had just encountered the elephant. We stood up and waited.

Nigel Cantle got out of the car, his face was grey with fatigue and grief. His wife Stephanie stood beside him; she had been crying.

'He's dead isn't he?' I said.

'No, Kate... but it's bad.' My legs lost their power and Nigel held me in his arms to keep me steady.

'He's had a car crash... it's very bad, Kate. Alison Brown wants you to radio her.'

Oakley sat beside me at the desk while I radioed through to Maun. He was shaking. I picked up the mike – it seemed heavy.

'Alison it's Kate come in please.'

'Hello Kate,' her concern carried over the airways. I had never heard her use that tone before.

'Alison just to let you know Oaks is sitting here beside me,' I warned her.

'Copy that Kate,' her Scottish accent rang clear over the crackling airwaves.

'Nigel tells me it's bad.'

'Yes, it's very serious Kate, you'd best come into town now.'

She never used the phrase 'very serious' – not even when we had malaria or Trav had suspected appendicitis, and Maun airport had been opened in the middle of the night for a medical evacuation.

'Is he there?'

'No – he's on his way to the Millpark now. We've just flown him out. Best pack something, Kate.'

'Thanks Alison. Over and out.'

We left camp ten minutes later with one pair of knickers and our passports; it was nearly a year before we saw camp again.

59

Parkview, Johannesburg 2004

Tim Butcher lay stretched out on his sofa with Otto, an Alsatian who thought he was a chihuahua and lived in a permanent state of surprise that he couldn't fit onto a human lap.

'Lioness, you need to have a talk with your boy,' he said, 'Oaks thinks the accident was his fault. I've tried to put him straight but I think he needs a dose of your infinite wisdom.'

I had met Tim in October 2003 when he came to camp for five days to write an article about the impact of FIV on lions for the *Sunday Telegraph*. He had fitted into family life like a pair of familiar woolly socks you've just found in the back of a drawer.

I had only met him once, but on the night of the accident it seemed perfectly natural to call him at two in the morning.

'Hello,' he said sleepily.

'Tim, sorry to wake you... it's Kate, with the lions... do you remember you came to stay with us in Botswana a year ago?'

'Indeed I do... what's up?'

'Pieter's had a car crash... on his way to the Millpark now. Oaks and I will be in Jo'burg at 10.45 in the morning, I was wondering...'

'I'll be at the airport,' he interrupted, 'Jane and I live up the road from the hospital, come and stay with us for as long as you like.'

That was that. Safety offered with simplicity: I will never forget it.

As promised he was at the airport, and on seeing Oakley's shattered face Tim made an executive decision.

'I'm going to drop Oaks back home to be with Otto. Jane's there... she's looking forward to seeing you... not under these circs of course. I'll take you to the hospital when we've got your boy settled.'

'Otto?'

'Our Alsatian.'

'Oh ah,' I said, thinking Tim must be soft in the head. He wasn't. Otto stuck to Oaks like glue, and slept at the end of his bed for weeks.

Tim came up to ICU with me. I don't remember what I felt when I saw Pieter: I remember Tim's catch of breath, his involuntary step backwards. That's how bad it was.

Now, unravelling himself from Otto, Tim got up to pour a glass of wine.

'Oaks told me someone died in the crash,' he said.

'Yes, a woman, she was a passenger in the other car... the driver lost most of his face... head-on collision on an open road. Why on earth does Oaks think it was his fault? He wasn't even there,' I replied.

'No idea, but he does. He mentioned it in passing and it worried me... thought I'd better pass it on.'

'It worries the crap out of me too. Thanks for letting me know.'

I had spoken to Oakley about the crash and he was guarded, but I had no idea he felt responsible. The next day I made an appointment to see the counsellor the hospital provided for family members, or partners, of patients in ICU. The Millpark's provision of professional support was based on an eminently practical principle: looking after the carers promotes the patient's healing.

'Oaks won't come to see you by himself,' I explained to her, 'he has an aversion to therapists, but I think I can persuade him to come to a session with me if I tell him I need his support.'

'I can talk to him then,' she replied.

'Best not directly, I think it might be better if I mention to you that I think the crash was my fault, and you offer me the response you would give to a ten-year-old – does that sound like a plan?'

She rose to the occasion magnificently and Oakley left the session with wide, clear eyes.

'Mum, it's so strange, you and I had exactly the same feeling. I felt so bad because if I hadn't asked Pieter to pick up my quad bike maybe he wouldn't have crashed. But that lady explained it so well didn't she? I'd never heard of the butterfly effect had you? Do you feel better now Mum?... you know it wasn't your fault now... don't you Mum?'

'I do Oaks. I feel much better now... do you?'

'Oh yes, heaps,' he said, and his open face told me the box had been ticked.

In time Pieter was taken off the critical list, but remained in a medicated coma. His skin was pink and he looked alive but that was all. The broken body he inhabited could no longer support his spirit. When they brought him round, how would he face the reality of his injuries? The physical life he led in the wild expressed the essence of him, and I was afraid for him. But there was no time for heartbreak: it was time to make a plan. Pieter's doctors had informed me that recovery would take at least a year. We needed a home.

Recently, Neecie and I had sold Hollybush Cottage: an ending I found unbearable but the practicalities of living separate lives required some finite action. We split the proceeds and for the first time in my life I had money in the bank, so I decided to buy a house in Parkview. It would offer a base during Pieter's recovery and then fund the project when I rented it out on our return to Botswana. I bought the first house I saw because it was a treasure.

It looked like a child's drawing. It was white, single-storey, with a green metal roof, a racing-green double front door and generous square-paned windows on either side. The front opened into a large double sitting room with open fireplaces at either end, traditional beaten-copper ceilings and yellowwood floors. Two walls were painted a warm red. This worried me.

'Oaks,' I said when we first looked around the house, 'we can change the colour: I know you don't like the feeling of red.'

He looked at me and smiled. I had remembered.

'It's only a colour Mum and it looks good in here... keep it, it's jolly. I love this house don't you?'

I did: it wrapped its arms around us and gave us sanctuary, but most importantly it had no stairs and there was a long corridor along which Pieter would later learn to walk again.

While the house was being renovated Oaks and I stayed with Tim and Jane, and their friendship and kindness energized our days. We were a productive household. When I wasn't with Pieter I was busy with the builders or buying furniture: we had nothing, not even a loo brush. Jane was monitoring a female-empowerment business in Soweto, and she spent her days tearing around Jo'burg in her car, with the ever-vigilant Jack Russell, Betty, sitting up beside her. Tim had just got back from following Stanley's journey along the Congo, and was working on the first draft of *Blood River: A Journey to Africa's Broken Heart*.

Tim losing heart was a daily event.

'Why would anyone want to hear about some hack's ineffective meandering?'

'Bollocks and double bollocks... Timbo... everyone wants to hear... it's an amazing story... get back to your computer this instant.'

Oaks and I read Tim's bestseller in Comeragh Road – and remembered hearing his adventures first-hand curled up by the fire with the dogs.

While the grown-ups bustled, Oakley went to regular school for the first time in his life; my feral boy eased into the local government school like an old-timer. He made friends, learned to play cricket, enrolled in beginners' Zulu classes and joined the debate club. He spent happy afternoons boating on Zoo Lake or taking scuba-diving lessons. My landlocked child hungered for water, and earned his open-water PADI licence in the Indian Ocean. His tensions eased.

So I was surprised to be called aside by his teacher one afternoon: she had tears in her eyes.

'Is there a problem?' I asked.

'No, but I wanted to talk with you. Oakley is a remarkable boy,' she said.

I beamed politely.

'I'm sorry for your troubles,' she said.

Assuming she was talking about the crash, I thanked her and told her Pieter was still immobile, but mending and out of ICU.

'I'm happy to hear it but I was talking about you. Oakley gave a talk to his class today,' she continued, 'the children were asked to talk about something that mattered to them. Something they felt was important. He spoke about rape.'

I felt a chill in my stomach.

'What he said was very mature,' she continued, 'he's a kind boy. The children listened to him, Mrs Kate. It's common here in South Africa, but people don't talk about it you see... he was very brave.'

I was floored. The small person who had been trundled sweaty miles across Botswana for Women Against Rape, and had played in the sand with dusty children while I sat under a tree listening to their mothers' stories, had shared his story in class. I had no romantic notion that his openness was 'closure', nor that the child who loved nothing more than chasing a ball across a pitch had suddenly become an activist in gender politics. But I was proud of my boy.

I wish I could tell you what he said, but when I asked the standard question, 'What did you do in school today?' I got the universal response.

'Oh nothing.'

60

ICU Mill Park Hospital, Johannesburg 2004

I was holding his hand when they brought him round. He looked straight at me... he smiled and with a shaking finger he made a circle round my ring finger. He pointed to his heart. Somewhere in the place he had been, maybe he had found his love for me. I waited. He had no voice because of the tracheotomy. I had to be clear. I told him what had happened. I was honest. I named each injury. I told him he would walk again – in time. I told him he would have more surgeries. I knew not to leave anything out. He would know. His eyes filled with tears. I asked him if he understood and he nodded. I held his hand. He mimed writing. I got him some paper and he wrote slowly and carefully on a Post-it note. Long squiggly lines... no letters. I pretended I understood. I kept the paper. It was data. He fell asleep. I waited. When he woke I told him again. It was a lot for him to process through a haze of morphine.

In time Pieter's writing became more legible – thin, spidery shapes spilled down the page like liquid. One afternoon I turned the yellow Post-it note sideways and deciphered the word 'bush'.

I told him camp was safe, Steve and Lettie were still there; I assured him I had arranged for someone to go out to camp with supplies and wages once a month. Friends were popping in at the weekends to keep an eye on things. There was nothing to worry about. Just as we had rented Hollybush we would rent out the house in Carlow Road, to help fund the project. Pieter shook his head and with a trembling hand he scrawled more wriggling shapes down the page. I shook my head... they made no sense. He pointed to the word 'bush' again.

'The lions will be fine... the batteries are still good... no collars need to be replaced... the next FIV blood-testing isn't due for another six months... Rodrigo and I can do that, Pete... it's all going to be okay... just get better.'

He threw his head back on the pillow and turned his face away from me.

His thin fingers fumbled at the tube in his throat, and, turning back towards me, his exhausted eyes bored into me like steel, willing me to understand.

'Bush,' I repeated, 'bush...'

He nodded.

'Oh you mean George Bush,' I laughed, 'you want to know what's going on with the election?'

Pieter heaved a sigh and smiled.

He was on the mend.

A few days later they removed the tracheotomy tube and he whispered morphine-distorted tales about his life on a boat with the Dutch royal family.

A month after he had been admitted they moved him downstairs to the recuperation ward. It seemed a huge move. It was scary leaving behind the routine that was as regular as a heartbeat: the billow of cool, conditioned air on soft curtains, the familiar faces of the nurses by whose clockwork schedules I timed my day.

It was downstairs that Pieter's hard work began. The pain was drip-fed back into his system as they reduced his medication. After eleven operations he was grey with tiredness and skeletally thin. His days were scratched off by small triumphs.

One afternoon I brought in a cool can of Coke and he took it in his hands. The weight of the can made them shake, but he held on and, putting his thumb under the tab, he tried to flick it open. It didn't budge. I pictured him high up in our tree at camp repairing the radio receiver with the boys: powerful, confident, in control, as agile as a vervet monkey – and here I was, watching him struggling with a Coke can. I didn't help. Finally, he let the can slip onto the sheet and breathed deep breaths before picking it up again. His hands were bones. There was no power in his tendons or in his atrophied muscles. The thumb he used countless times a day to effortlessly flick a flame from his lighter was now the centre of his universe. He wrenched effort from the bowels of his spirit, and, sucking air into his lungs through dry lips, he willed his strength into his thumb; with one last push a hiss of carbon dioxide proclaimed his victory. He took two sips without a straw, and the sticky brown liquid spilled down his nightshirt. I put a straw into the can and puffed up his pillows. He sat back and drank as tears rolled down his cheeks.

We didn't speak.

It was going to be a long journey.

61

Johannesburg 2005

One of the bleaker aspects of smart Jo'burg houses was the staff quarters. Across the city grim remnants of apartheid South Africa were hastily renovated and turned into guest houses or pool houses in an attempt to wipe the slate clean. I renovated the recently inhabited staff quarters in Carlow Road, and turned them into a pretty garden cottage for Maisie. She had finished her foundation course in Edinburgh and had decided to go to Dublin for her degree. Because Pieter still required twenty-four-hour nursing, I was unable to continue homeschool so Maisie did her A Levels at the International College. The practical aspects of building a new life quickly and efficiently were easy: head down, keep focused; shut out all peripheral vision. But settling into city life was a form of sensory deprivation and I was unaware of how blinkered I had become until one afternoon a stranger at a set of traffic lights opened my eyes.

The traffic lights in Jo'burg go from red to green then green to red rapidly. Like everything in a city, reaction is what counts. Some intersections offer mildewed amber – half-hearted arrows flashing a brief possibility of passage across paths driven by mothers on their way to school in 4×4 cars with burnished hubcaps, the mud of days splashing silently against the immutable needs of offspring.

After catching red more than a few times I learned to wind

up my window: I dreaded the hands reaching into my moment, tugging at my conscience, offering inflatable dolphins for my non-existent pool or scratching through bundles of cellphone charger cables seeking an eager sale before the lights change and I speed away.

Overwhelmed by the magnitude of need in this smart African city of lights, I longed for a patch of green and a place where sunlight hit a clean horizon. Unconsciously my mind had adjusted to a new speed and was no longer open to the sound of birds. Days that were once photon-sensitive, bright, shadowy days spent looking for the pinprick outline of lions' ears deep in the grass, were lost in the strobe of a city that never rests.

After school one afternoon Oakley and I went to 'Italy' for a few hours, where the sky was painted. Turn right off the William Nicol Drive past the orange plastic beanbag chairs on offer for thirty rand, and there lies a faux Tuscan town, Montecasino, a magnificent erection in concrete. Leaving the day outside, Oaks and I walked up the faux classic staircase and wandered through a fantasia. Our senses were controlled by a panel of computers that cooled the air and cast shafts of yellow light on walls that had no algae growing between their plastic bricks. Fountains tinkled in piazzas with tables set under a cerulean sky that had worn patches round the edges. I hired Oaks a helmet and a ticket for two hours on a skateboard half-pipe. I bought sour plums from a Chinese street vendor and tickets for the Moscow State Circus: very cosmopolitan.

I passed fat men and brightly painted women, lulled into a false sense of security, gambling in the soft light of the casino. 'What would you do for love? Win 50,000 rand TODAY.'

I wandered into Exclusive Books to breathe in the smell of hope that fresh books offer. Clean, un-dog-eared pages – perhaps they would teach me something new. A kind woman searched for a book that I needed to hold in my hand to stabilize my senses. The book written by my children, when I had the smell of elephant dung in my nostrils and the sound of laughter in my ears. When my eyes were not blinkered and I had owl vision. Botswana where the smell of black skin smoked by night fire made me feel safe.

I needed air. Wandering onto the steps outside, I watched the traffic weaving its way across the cityscape that had once been wilderness. The patchwork pigmentation of the Rainbow Nation lay unsettled – ruckled in hope – waiting for better times to smooth away the creases. Beneath the concrete, leopards had once imprinted their journeys on soil. But their unburnished gold had made way for mined metal glinting on the arms of the chosen few: Jo'burg, the Dutch Eldorado. Trees lined every street: the city is a planted forest so huge, some say, it can be seen from the moon. In time, gnarled, nitrogen-fixing acacia made way for more flamboyant things, and in the spring Jo'burg pulses purple with jacaranda blossom.

Driving home I saw a man in the middle of the highway. The lights were green and he was in my way. I slowed down and automatically wound up my window, and then I saw his smile. It was wrinkled by love. His kindness had not been leached, and as he had once owned his fireside in the veldt, now he owned this concrete space: his patch of Africa on which he had to trust in strangers not to mow him down. But someone must have loved him, for he had no fear.

I gave him my loose change: in exchange he gave me back my acuity.

A gift I do not squander.

62

Hammersmith Embankment, London 2016

Pounding along the Embankment, towards Dukes Meadows where the elderflowers bloom, I was missing Botswana with an ache that consumed me. My stride lengthened walking under Hammersmith Bridge, past the rowing club, past the pretty rose-adorned houses in Chiswick Mall. I tried but I couldn't remember the last time I saw Pieter. Odd that such an intimate piece of history had gone into hiding. I think by then I was just too weary to record the fading pictures.

My pace decreased as I recalled life when he was released from hospital still bedridden. Pieter propped up on an electric bed with a pressure-relief mattress so he didn't get bedsores; the daily fresh flowers and candles in his room; twice-daily bed-baths, clean sheets, nourishing meals. He hungered for isolation but, utterly dependent, he was shackled by the repetition of daily tasks. His faded essence was measured by fluctuating levels of endurance. Pain defined him. Seeping wounds had to be cleaned. I took his temperature four times a day. One afternoon he spiked a minor fever. Furious, he was readmitted. By the time he got onto the ward the fever was raging. They put him on a drip of antibiotics for three days and sent him home. Even sounds hurt. When Oakley and I watched *Friends*, the muffled canned laughter through the walls was unendurable. The man who fearlessly battled bush fires became flustered if his morning yogurt was sprinkled with fresh raspberries instead of fresh blueberries: the loss of small controls was overwhelming.

In time, he shifted his broken body into a wheelchair for a few agonizing minutes a day – each day just one more minute. Angry with pain – begging me to stop – hating me for pushing him. Gradually building to the day he could sit on the balcony and look out onto the newly planted garden. We were both so weary, and the lions were still dying, and the children were learning a new home, and Emily had another baby without me to look after her. Guilt.

Eliza, my Eliza. Ems brought her to Jo'burg the day after her six-week check-up. Jack was three by then. Such happy days. Baby days. Carlow Road was so pretty, so warm, logs in baskets, a cot for Eliza, an old farmhouse dresser in the kitchen, huge white sofas with sackcloth cushions, and vases full of flowers. I had planted the garden with a tumble of wild flowers and vegetables; a sound came out of my throat as I remembered. I stopped, and watched some boys sculling towards Barnes. A pair of desultory London ducks bobbed for weed in the olive water. I had done well in Carlow Road: I had so nearly made it.

The joy when Pieter managed to walk the length of the corridor without his Zimmer frame. The tenderness of the night we became lovers once again, crying, kissing: if we can get through this we can get through anything. In the movies, we would have held hands and, looking fetching in khaki, we would have saved Africa's lions under a setting sun. We didn't.

We were two broken adults. Hungry for the past. Frightened of the future. He was cruel: healing is a messy business. I slipped again. I wanted to die. To stop. Just for a bit. There was nowhere to hide. Every infraction – every mistake – every drink – every hurt – every betrayal – every moment of primal rage – every step towards the temporary death I hungered for witnessed: by children.

No one warns you when you have babies. No one tells you that there may be days when you swim in a deoxygenating goldfish bowl drowning in front of their eyes. The sweat of guilt leaked out of my skin. I wanted to be someone else – someone who hadn't hurt her children. Who is that Madonna, that haunting perfection? She's no one I know. I breathed in river air and laughed. Fuck it – sometimes being sorry is as good as it gets.

I walked on. Remembering. Filtering. I don't remember the last time I saw Pieter. Have I just thought that? In time he got well enough for me to leave him alone in Carlow Road. I sold my stick-shift car and bought an automatic that he could use to pop down to the shops. He was afraid to be left alone, but part of his rehabilitation was to learn to function by himself. During the August school holidays I went back to camp with all the children.

Our return to camp was desolate. As we drove closer to home, no welcoming lights twinkled in between the trees and on arrival we found rat shit on the pillows, rat piss on the sheets, a dead bird on the kitchen floor, wasp nests in neglected bookshelves and a fine film of sand on every surface. The ladies were in town and Stephen was asleep. So, we cleaned and I shouted like a sea captain on shore leave. It was all hands on deck because the next day one of Angus's professors from Stanford, his family and the project vet Rodrigo Serra were arriving on the afternoon flight. Rod was part of the rhythm of our life: he was like a son to me.

For the next few weeks Rod and I checked the lions' collars, put a new collar on a sub-adult male we were concerned about, and did the annual blood-sampling. With the children's help it was the ideal time to train up the postgrad research assistant I had invited to assist Pieter when he went back to live among the lions again. The treacherous little soul had a natural aptitude for fieldwork, and she was a fast learner. She did excellent work: a few months later when Pieter went back to camp she supported him well. I remembered the last time I saw her.

The air cooled, and a breeze blew in from the river as I walked along a narrow path leading through a thicket that wound up onto the open grassland of Dukes Meadows. Sitting on the grass I watched a boy throw a Frisbee for his dog to collect. A bunch of kids were kicking a football around and a pair of teenage lovers were locked in a munching embrace of such ardent length I feared they might require oxygen. It had been so long since I'd had sex: if I saw a naked man again I'd need a map.

Lying on my back, I let the English sun burn down onto my skin, while picturing family days in camp before another female sprayed on my territory. When Pieter went back to camp I had stayed in Carlow Road. How diligently his assistant had obeyed my instructions. Without fail once a week she emailed me spreadsheets on the lions and updates on Pieter's health. I remembered sobbing over my computer, hating the girl who was living in my home, working with the lions I hungered for. One week she told me she and Pieter had found Vouvray dead under a tree on the Mogogelo: her tiny cubs had died of starvation. I noted Pieter had allowed her to name the cubs before they were a year old: the female cub had her name. I could picture her in the evenings, her elbows on my table, her chin cupped in her hands; gazing adoringly into Pieter's eyes. I pictured him rocking back on his chair and lighting a cigarette and teaching her all he knew about the wild, while the acacia rat ran along the rafters and nibbled on boxes in the pantry.

I was unpractised in the art of jealousy: it makes fools of us all; but I wasn't wrong. When I moved to London and unpacked my books from Africa I found a letter she had written to Pieter – not a sexual love letter, but a brutal appraisal of how bad I was for him: how he would be better off without me. Perhaps she was right after all. Anyway, she was no more than a hiccup in our story: she couldn't hurt us; we were already broken.

A tremor of air stirred upwards in the heat and I began to sun-sneeze.

All the lions my children had grown up with were dead by now. That was natural. But the decline in overall numbers was not. In 2006, when I presented at a lion conference in Jo'burg, there were only ten cubs in our study area and one pair of males had dominated three prides for three years. The days of tracking for nomads were over. Poison had ensured there were no new adult males roaming the territories. I hoped things had changed.

My sneezing turned to sobs and an aching grief for something that was never mine to grieve: the lions belonged to no one but I had loved them. Africa was losing them – numbers were plummeting across the continent. Already some populations had gone extinct. Botswana spat us out: why? What a pointless thing to do. Our work on FIV was deemed unnecessary for long-term lion conservation.

I pulled out tufts of grass by the roots and shredded the narrow leaves with angry fingers. Choose your battles. Hold steady. Choose battles that can be won. Prioritize. The children are grown up now, they are happy, invigorating, kind people doing good things in the world, but somewhere they will still remember the cruelty of drunkenness.

'But the words we hear, Mum the words we hear, they mean something to us.'

Look at the grass, Kate. The rooted clumps are all connected by stolons running along the surface, or rhizomes running underground passing nutrients back and forth feeding each plant. Above ground or under we are all connected. But we can choose to what and to whom we remain connected. Freedom is found in the choices we make. I choose to be uncluttered. I choose to live days with the space to learn and to revel in the wonders of the twenty-first century.

The darkness comes rarely and fleetingly these days; when the feeling comes it flares up from a black pip into full-blown filth: I want to take a scouring brush to my vagina; but I don't. I want to be sick; but I'm not. When my limbs stop working I can control them and make them move. When self-loathing burns my insides I can redirect it: I'm no longer a wildfire. Maya Angelou was right: 'Bitterness is like cancer. It eats upon the host. But anger is like fire. It burns it all clean.' A controlled burn is cleansing. These days I burn alone: briefly, proudly and harmlessly. Fresh shoots rise up through my scorched earth.

An ant walked across my skirt and I smiled. It reminded me of Travers. When he was doing his MSc, he asked me to come to Oxford for a few days to read through papers with him. His study area had been in Greece, where he had been looking at the role ant species play as bio-indicators of land recovery after wildfire. The earth heals in ebbs and flows, and as niches arise and fall so different ant species come and go in direct response to available resources. I had felt so proud Travers had asked for my support. We worked hard: ordering papers, ordering thoughts, highlighting citations, reading carefully, seeking the big picture hidden among the fragments: it was peaceful companionable learning. The ants led us back onto a familiar path.

Lying on the grass I flung my arms open wide: my freedom stretched before me. For sure, freedom constrained by meagre funds, but constraint inspires creativity. I was proud of how I had earned the money to pay for Oakley's college – teaching brave Russian children I had grown to love. It was time for my homeschool to put down new roots.

The Internet opened out infinite vistas of learning, and, supported by books that were old friends and by the generosity of teachers who shared their skills over cyberspace, I could learn every day, and teach anywhere using Skype.

Time to get up off the grass and take action. I walked home briskly, and scrolling through the Internet I searched for houses for ten thousand euros and under. I found a small stone house in Palmoli, an Apennine mountain village in Abruzzo, Italy. I told the children, who were excited, supportive and amused (envisaging the house as habitable required a leap of imagination), I emptied my bank account and I put down a deposit.

Italy is a new adventure: I have no definite plans; something will turn up: it always does, and when you least expect it.

63

Gomoti Camp, 2007

It was the last time we were all in camp together. Pieter was well again, and the older children were home for the holidays. It had been a busy morning – Travers, Angus, Oakley and Stephen had dug trenches around the tents to prevent flooding when the rains came. Pieter was still tinkering with the generator, which was on its last legs, and Maisie and I were loading the car with the darting equipment. We were all going to track for Cristal, to take off her collar: the project was over.

The wildlife department had rescinded our research permit. Apparently, we had had long enough to study the impact of FIV, and we had produced no evidence that the disease was having an effect. This showed a sorrowful disregard for the results we had given the government, and a disregard of the time frame required for serious work. We needed data from at least another two generations of known lions. By non-invasively accessing molecular evidence, we were asking dynamic questions in collaboration with scientists from highly respected institutions who were keen to help conserve Botswana's lion population. Telling our collaborators that the project was over had been embarrassing, as well as heartbreaking – it seemed unimaginable Botswana was turning its back on information that might improve the management of one of Africa's few viable populations. I loved Botswana and had, and have, the greatest respect for its government, but all too often field researchers are at the bottom of the food chain when it comes to making political decisions that concern wildlife. We were not the first or the last project to be shut down.

As we had done so many times before, we loaded the dart gun, the foot pump, the medical kit, the veterinary box, a cloth to cover the lion's eyes, a jerrycan of water to keep the lion cool, water and snacks for the family, and books to while away the time while we waited for the lion to come round from the drugs.

'Do you remember the first time we saw her, Mum?' said Maisie, 'just a little dot tottering along behind Sauvignon.'

'Fuck and fuck and double fuck,' I growled, throwing a roll of loo paper into the back of the car: the boys always forgot the loo paper.

'You all right Mum?' said Maisie.

'No, so not actually.'

Maisie laughed.

'Too sodding esoteric?' I mumbled.

'What?'

'That's what I was told once at a workshop in Maun. My hormone work was too esoteric. Tell me what's eso-frigging-teric about having a better understanding of a species' reproductive system.'

'But you didn't publish, Mum.'

'No, because I'm an idiot perfectionist and wanted to repeat the work with another pride. And now I can't. I thought I had time...'

I took some deep breaths and looked around camp. The mess tent had worn well and so had the old sofas. Oakley's stuffed lions were still the favoured pillows to lie against in the evenings when we settled in for the night to watch a movie. While we were in Jo'burg, potter wasps had built nests on some of the books, and other tomes had been partially devoured by boring creatures tunnelling through the pages: it was a nourishing library.

Before the bad news from the Department of Wildlife and National Parks we had spent a happy day with Lettie replacing the termite-chewed reeds, and the fresh reed walls were looking good. The machete was in its place, propped up with the brooms, in case of emergency. And the rugs had just been washed and were looking very smart despite some rat nibbles around the edges. The old oven the children and I had bought in our first week in Botswana was still going strong. Earlier I had cooked vegetable lasagne and left it in the oven ready to warm up quickly for supper – we would probably be home late and hungry – immobilizations took time.

I wandered over to the camelthorn that had protected us for so many years. The metal label with our census number embossed upon it was still held in place by tintacks. Home. I put my arms around the trunk and thanked it.

'Look at Mum, she's a bloody tree hugger' Travers yelled across camp to his siblings, who mocked me mercilessly.

'You can all sod off,' I laughed, 'now to work. Pete saw the girls moving towards Steenbok Loop yesterday so might as well start there.'

We set off in two cars. The first rains had yet to fall and the wheels of the car Travers was driving sent out clouds of dust, so Pieter fell back as we trundled from tracking mound to tracking mound along Steenbok Loop. It was still hard for Pieter to clamber up onto the roof so Gus did the tracking.

In the old days I would have rested my hand on Pieter's thigh, but those little intimacies were no longer part of our language. He was going to stay in camp until the end. I was going back to South Africa. I had sold the house in Johannesburg, and had bought a farm in the Eastern Cape. I had big plans. But my plans changed the day Oakley sighed on the top of a London bus.

In time, Gus picked up a signal, and we found Cristal lying with Freixenet in an open area, perfect for darting. She had always been an easy lion to work with and she only needed a light dose of the combined dissociative and sedative drugs we used.

'Trav, stay back,' Pieter ordered over the car radio, 'wait until I tell you.'

'Will do,' replied Travers, and I saw the boys settle in – feet up on the dashboard.

Oakley passed Pieter the vet box and I smiled watching Pieter tuck his thumbs under the stiff hinges and flick them open with ease. Everyone was quiet as he fitted the sterile needle onto the dart and measured out the drugs. Methodically he stroked the red fluffy end of the dart slowly between his thumb and forefinger. I had always loved watching the little ritual: it was calming. The memory of being in love peaked inside my body, and then faded into a lonely weariness.

'Pump, Oaks,' demanded Pieter, and Oakley leaned into the back of the Land Rover for the foot pump and the air rifle. Pieter attached the pump to a nozzle on the gun and, putting the machine on the floor, he pressed down on the metal pedal with his foot. Forcing the energy down his leg, he pumped air into the rifle and grimaced in pain. The strapping round the skin graft on his ankle offered no protection from the pain that infiltrated his life. His lips lost their colour, and he stopped pumping to catch his breath. He looked at the gauge: two, perhaps three, more pumps would be enough. No one dared to breathe. Summoning his strength and clenching his teeth, he pumped until the gauge was set to the pressure he required. He leant back on the headrest for a moment and closed his eyes.

Then he rested the gun out of his window and, driving with one hand on the wheel, he approached Cristal gently: she didn't even raise her head. Angling the car to ensure he got a clear shot of her hindquarters, he turned his body away from me, and resting his arm on the windowsill he brought the air gun up to his shoulder. The silver hair on the back of his neck shone in the sunlight. He looked down the barrel of the gun to get his line of sight, and then – phut – the dart left the barrel and hit Cristal in the muscle of her hindquarters. She jumped up and looked around.

Botswana 2007

Freixenet glanced up, watching her pride mate turn in circles. The dart delivered the drugs and then fell out onto the grass. Cristal walked for a few yards and we waited for her to begin to totter.

'Trav, wait till she goes down then push off Freixenet and come back to form a V around the lion.'

'Will do.' Travers waited until the lion flopped down. Then he drove towards Freixenet and gently urged her onto the edge of a thicket. Looking somewhat affronted, she complied and settled down under a tree, all the while watching the sleeping Cristal.

We drove the cars slowly towards the lion, forming a V shape around her to block her from Freixenet's line of sight. Oakley and Maisie knew their task – they had been doing it for years. I got out of the car to work on Cristal, confident my children would never take their eyes off Freixenet who was relaxed, but alert to the action.

I put ointment on Cristal's eyes to stop them drying up, and covered them with a soft cloth. I poured water from the jerrycan under her armpits and over her body to keep her cool. Pieter found a vein and I pressed my finger down on it until it engorged enough for him to put in a cannula and draw blood for the final time. I removed ticks from around the lion's eyes and a few that were burrowed into her short fur. Then Pieter took the spanner and unscrewed the bolts on her collar and removed it. He stroked her naked throat: his hands were strong again.

'Good luck, girl,' he said.

I soothed her and kissed her behind her ears where her fur was softest. I lay my head on her great body and wrapped my arms around her, before taking the precious vials of blood and putting them in the vet box along with her redundant collar. Travers and Angus watched from their car.

'Mum,' whispered Maisie, 'Freixenet's settled, can we say goodbye?'

'For sure,' I said, 'just take it in turns. I'll watch out for you.'

One by one the children got out of the cars. One by one they kissed goodbye to the lion they had known for eleven years. Then we got back in our cars, and withdrew to give her space while she came round. We waited until she woke, and we watched her wander off into the thicket with her companion.

    She didn't look back: we meant nothing to her.

Acknowledgements

First and foremost, I want to thank Emily, Travers, Angus, Maisie and Oakley: they have read many drafts and have been untiring in their support and encouragement. Maisie was living with me in Rome when I rewrote and restructured the book, and her insight and advice were gratefully received and acted on.

I want to thank my agent Caroline Michel who believed in me enough to reject my first drafts and inspired me to rethink. I value and respect her compassion, keen intelligence and honesty. And many thanks to Peter Florence for reading my book proposal and introducing me to Caroline: what a gift!

Thanks to my editor, the elegantly thoughtful Alan Samson, who has guided me with clarity and sensitivity. His delightful team, in particular Lucinda McNeile, has enriched the journey and made the entire process a joy.

Sarah Standing played a seminal role in getting this book to publication, and a phone call with her, while I was walking down the Via Giulia one balmy evening, gave me the courage to carry on.

Thanks to Richard Dawkins and Lalla Ward Dawkins for their friendship and mentorship over the years: I will always associate Richard with the sound of doors swinging wide open.

Thanks to Steven Pinker for letting me use quotes from *The Language Instinct*, and for his joyful inspiration and humour.

Over several years trusted friends have read various drafts and snippets, and their wisdom and encouragement have been invigorating: Sandra Rothschild, Jillian Edelstein, Bernard Borchardt, Kate Evans, Sinead Cusack, Sophie Dahl, Bryony Longdon; fellow writers and friends at the 'green-table' meetings in Rome: Alex Gregor, Morgan Chiraella, Lauren Mouat, Eric Lyman, Francesca Ruffo, Paola de Santiago Haas, Jordan McCord and Philippa Torlonia.

Thanks to Eleanor David for her friendship, humour and support when I arrived back in London from Africa: many happy evenings spent talking and laughing around her fireplace gave me the confidence to embark on the writing the book. A special thanks to Rosemary Willmott for her joyous friendship and her loyal support during hard times, and for her patience reading various drafts over the years.

My friendship with the Longdon family – Bryony, Tim, Pia, Maxi and Blythe – began on their ostrich farm Maun and continues to this day in the Golden Valley, Herefordshire. While writing the book, and for many years before, Bryony's empathy, humanity and wisdom has guided me, given me strength and enriched me.

My thanks to Cathy Zurbe, who helped me so much with homeschooling in Botswana, and to whom I owe a huge debt of gratitude.

My thanks to the many friends in Maun who helped and supported me and the children: they remain dear to us all. I am sad that it was not possible to fit into the narrative the many adventures, acts of kindness and huge fun we shared over the years.

And finally, many thanks and much love to Ian McNeice and his partner Cindy Franke. They have been generous in their support and love in all matters, as well as with the book. Today I am looking forward to Christmas with Emily in Littlehampton, and to our burgeoning family feasting together again sitting around the old Hollybush table.